THERMOPYLAE
THE BATTLE
FOR THE WEST

THERMOPYLAE
THE BATTLE
FOR THE WEST

by
ERNLE
BRADFORD

DA CAPO PRESS
A Member of the Perseus Books Group

Cataloging-in-Publication data for this book is available from the Library of Congress.

ISBN-13 978-0-306-81360-3; ISBN-10 0-306-81360-2

This Da Capo Press paperback edition of *Thermopylae: The Battle for the West* is an unabridged republication of the edition first published in New York in 1980 under the title *The Battle for the West: Thermopylae*. It is reprinted by arrangement with the estate of Ernle Bradford.

Published by Da Capo Press
A Member of the Perseus Books Group
http://www.dacapopress.com

Da Capo Press books are available at special discounts for bulk purchases in the U.S. by corporations, institutions, and other organizations. For more information, please contact the Special Markets Department at the Perseus Books Group, 11 Cambridge Center, Cambridge, MA 02142, or call (800) 255–1514 or (617) 252–5298, or e-mail special.markets@perseusbooks.com.

EBC   20 19 18 17 16 15 14 13

For friends long dead on the sea-lanes of summer
Crete, Malta, Tobruk

THE worth and value of a man is in his heart and his will; there lies his real honour. Valour is the strength, not of legs and arms, but of heart and soul; it consists not in the worth of our horse or our weapons, but in our own. He who falls obstinate in his courage, *if he has fallen, he fights on his knees* (Seneca). He who relaxes none of his assurance, no matter how great the danger of imminent death; who, giving up his soul, still looks firmly and scornfully at his enemy – he is beaten not by us, but by fortune; he is killed, not conquered.

The most valiant are sometimes the most unfortunate. Thus there are triumphant defeats that rival victories. Nor did those four sister victories, the fairest that the sun ever set eyes on – Salamis, Plataea, Mycale, and Sicily – ever dare match all their combined glory against the glory of the annihilation of King Leonidas and his men at the pass of Thermopylae.

MONTAIGNE, trans. Donald M. Frame

CONTENTS

CONTENTS

LIST OF MAPS

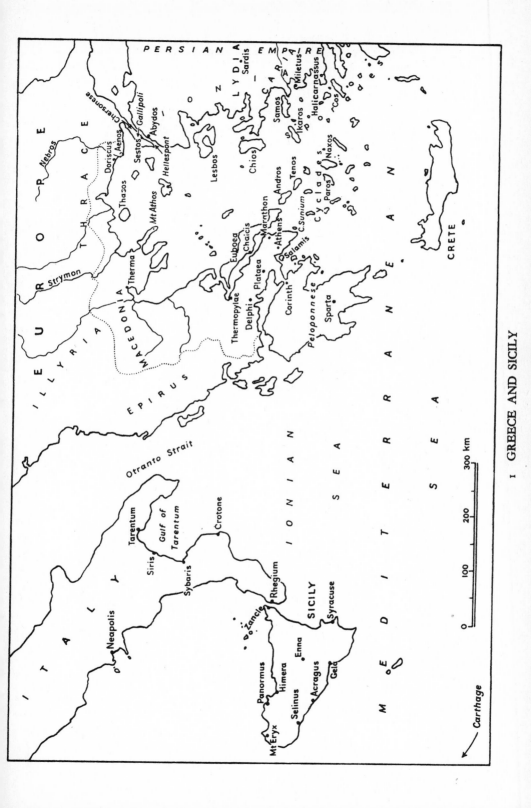

1 GREECE AND SICILY

2 GREECE

PREFACE

A GREAT MANY distinguished scholars have devoted intensive research into all and every aspect of the Greco-Persian wars. Many seem to have been writing for other scholars, or only for those fortunate enough to have enjoyed a classical education. But in twentieth-century Britain when, with a few notable exceptions, a knowledge of Greek is almost totally absent from members of the House of Commons (and where even a simple Latin quotation would fall on stony ground) the memory of the classical world is fading. We do not live in the age of Pitt or of Gladstone. We have progressed in technological terms, but we have forgotten the roots of our culture. Behind the surface appearance of our everyday world there lies always the image of classical Greece; from the seed of whose mathematicians, architects and scientists even our most remote modern machinery and artefacts are ultimately derived. In terms of the arts there has never been any doubt, at least among the practitioners of them, of the contribution that the Greeks made in triggering off Western European culture. 'The Glory that was Greece' would never have come to flower, let alone fruit, but for the astonishing events of 480 B.C., when a handful of men defeated what was then the greatest empire in the known world.

My first acquaintance with Greece, the Aegean, and the Near East was over a period of three and a half years during the Second World War. At a later date I was able to return at leisure several times at the helm of small boats, and come to know intimately these seas and lands once fought over by the warring armies and fleets of the Greeks and the Persians. It may not help to have sailed around Salamis, to have circumnavigated Euboea, or to have felt the lash of an Aegean storm, but it did serve to shed a new light upon the classics, and to make the great struggle between Greece and Persia comprehensible in geographical and nautical terms. It is true that, over two millennia, many geographical features have changed – the Pass of Thermopylae is the most obvious instance – but, by and large, the land, especially when approached in a small boat, remains timeless. The Turkish coast, and even the mainland, has changed least of all, and it is not too difficult to recapture the feel of ancient Ionia.

While researching the history of this momentous year I found that, among the numerous scholars who had published full-length works and many a learned treatise, nearly all seemed to share one thing in common. This was a natural and, to my mind, inevitable pro-Athenian bias. I say 'inevitable' because the great result of the Persian defeat in Europe led to the shining fifty years (or less) in which Athens transfigured the whole of the West through her architecture, her drama, her poetry, her sculpture, philosophy, and her whole attitude towards man's predicament in this temporal world. On the other hand, the Spartans – those strange and remarkable people, whose virtues the West would do well to emulate in our time – are somewhat absent from the records. They are there, certainly enough, but their presence is obscured by the fact that they abstained from literature. The fact that a Spartan admiral, Eurybiades, was in command at the naval battles of Artemisium and Salamis is somewhat glossed over. (He remains, as in some British accounts of the Second World War, a figure rather like General Eisenhower: a man who had never fought a battle, but who could achieve some kind of stability between unstable allies.) 'I fear the Greeks, even when bearing gifts . . .' and the gifts of the great Athenian poets, dramatists, and historians must always be a little suspect in terms of Truth.

The last stand of King Leonidas and the Spartans was told as a golden story in my youth. Since then it would seem to have been downgraded, perhaps because their military outlook and stubborn courage have made them unattractive to a hedonistic society. Without courage, Man is nothing. Without the Battle of Thermopylae, that pass held against all odds, there would never have followed Artemisium, Salamis and Plataea. Distasteful though it may have been to later historians, preoccupied with Athens, it was very largely the generalship of the Spartan Pausanias that made the victory of Plataea possible.

I have ended this brief account with the battle of Plataea itself.

The subsequent Ionian revolt against the Persians was inevitable' The destruction of the Persian fleet at Mycale was, although a story in itself, equally inevitable. Plataea closes the door.

Kalkara, Malta – Fordingbridge, Hants   ERNLE BRADFORD

ACKNOWLEDGEMENTS

I SHOULD LIKE to express my particular thanks to Mr A. R. Burn, whose writings on this subject first aroused my interest and enthusiasm some years ago. While the book was in preparation Mr Burn was good enough to assist me in many ways and to enlighten me in depth on many aspects of even the most recondite of matters relating to Xerxes' invasion of Greece. I would like to stress, however, that all errors remain mine, and I would also like to thank him for permission to quote extracts from *Persia and the Greeks* (1962) published by Edward Arnold (Publishers) Limited.

I am indebted to the Society for the Promotion of Hellenic Studies for permission to make use of their invaluable library. I am, as always, deeply indebted to the London Library, that remarkable institution without which writers like myself, who do not live in London, could never have access to half the authorities required for research work.

I and my publishers also wish to thank the following who have kindly given permission for the use of copyright material: Basil Blackwell Publisher Limited for an extract from *Sparta* by A. H. M. Jones; Edinburgh University Press for an extract from *Arms and Armour of the Greeks* by A. M. Snodgrass; David Higham Associates Limited on behalf of Peter Green for an extract from *The Year of Salamis*, published by Weidenfeld (Publishers) Limited; John Murray (Publishers) Limited for an extract from *The Great Persian War* by G. B. Grundy; Penguin Books Limited for extracts from Plutarch, *The Rise and Fall of Athens* translated by Ian Scott-Kilvert, Penguin Classics 1960, Copyright © Ian Scott-Kilvert; *Herodotus*, translated by Aubrey de Sélincourt, Copyright © The Estate of Aubrey de Sélincourt and A. R. Burn, 1972; and *The Greeks* by H. D. F. Kitto, 1951, Second edition 1957; The Society of Authors on behalf of the Estate of A. E. Housman for an extract from *Collected Poems*, published by Jonathan Cape Limited; Weidenfeld (Publishers) Limited for a quotation by H. Humback from *The Heritage of Persia* by R. N. Frye.

CHRONOLOGY

EARLY HISTORY

B.C.

550 Foundation of the Persian Empire by Cyrus the Elder.

547 Defeat of Croesus, King of Lydia.

539 Cyrus incorporates Babylon and all the lands adjacent to Persia including Syria and Phoenicia.

530 Accession of Cambyses, who incorporates Egypt into the Empire.

522 Accession of Darius.

513–12 Darius extends Persian Empire to Scythia and establishes a bridge-head into Greece by subduing Thrace.

500 Revolt of Ionian Greeks (in Asia Minor) against Persian rule.

494 Final suppression of Ionian revolt.

490 Persian invasion of Greece is defeated at Marathon.

486 Death of Darius and accession of Xerxes.

THE INVASION OF XERXES

481 *Spring*. Xerxes sets out from Susa.

Autumn. Sends demands for submission from Greek states. Spends winter in Sardis.

480 *Spring*. Xerxes crosses the Hellespont.

Greeks withdraw their advance force from the Pass of Tempe.

Late June–early July. While Xerxes and the army move south the Persian fleet heads for the canal cut behind Mount Athos.

Mid-August. Bulk of Greek fleet moves up to Artemisium. Leonidas and his small holding-force march north to Thermopylae.

Leonidas fortifies the pass at Thermopylae and raids the country to the north of it.

The Persian fleet is caught in a storm off the Greek coast north of Cape Sepias and suffers considerable losses.

c. 17 August. Themistocles persuades the other Greek naval commanders to attack the Persian fleet which is regrouping after the storm in the Gulf of Pagasae.

On the same day Xerxes orders his crack troops forward for the first attack on the Spartan position. They are repulsed with heavy losses.

In a further great storm part of the Persian fleet, which had been sent to round Euboea, is wrecked off the southern coast of the island.

Second day of the Battle of Thermopylae. The Persians are again badly defeated. The Greek fleet scores another small victory.

Third day of the Battle of Thermopylae. During the previous night Xerxes' imperial guard, the Immortals, have outflanked Leonidas by following the route over the mountains behind the pass. In the morning Xerxes orders another frontal attack on the Spartan position. Meanwhile the Immortals have come down the mountain and take the Spartans from the rear. Leonidas and a chosen handful die to a man. On the same afternoon the Greek fleet scores an important victory over the Persians at Artemisium. (The day that Thermopylae was overrun was possibly 20 August – the day of the Spartan festival, the Carneia, which had been the cause of the main body of their army being withheld.)
The same night, on hearing the news, the Greek fleet withdraws from Artemisium, southward down the Euboea Channel.

23 August (?) Xerxes' army advances into southern Greece. By the end of the month the main body of the army is into Attica itself.

Late August. Failure of the Persian-inspired Carthaginian attack on Sicily.

First week of September. The fall of the Acropolis of Athens.

c. 20 September. The Battle of Salamis. A few days after this crushing defeat Xerxes and the main body of the army begin their withdrawal from Greece.

480–479 *Winter*. A picked body of the Persian army under General Mardonius remains behind in Thessaly to prepare for an offensive in the spring.

479 *Late spring*. Mardonius and his army march south. Attica is once again overrun and Athens reoccupied. The Athenians once more withdraw to Salamis.

Early summer. The Spartans and their allies march north to join up with the Athenians. Mardonius relinquishes Athens and Attica. He withdraws to Thebes and his Greek allies in that area. The Persians encamp on the north bank of the River Asopus, covering the roads leading to Thebes itself.

479 *Plataea*. The final battle. The Persian invasion is over.

1

THE GREAT KING

THE WHOLE OF THE EAST was on the move. So indeed it must have seemed to some peasant, looking up bewildered from his patch of land, as the army surged past like a river in spate. Day after day, as if driven by the hunger that sometimes forces great masses of the human race to migrate in search of new pastures, thousands upon thousands of men had been passing through the lowlands of Asia Minor. They were men of many races: Persians, Medes, and Bactrians, Arabs on camels, mountain men from Caucasus, Libyans driving chariots, and horsemen from central Iran. There were even primitive Ethiopians painted in savage style, whose Stone Age weapons contrasted strangely with the sophisticated armour and swords of the immaculate Persian royal guard. It was the year 480 B.C. and Xerxes had given the order for the invasion of Europe.

The King's writ had gone forth, and when he himself went to war, every nation, tribe and race within the vast Persian Empire was expected not only to furnish its due contingent of men, but those men must also be led by their own kings, leaders, or princes. All were vassals of the Great King, who had described himself in an inscription at Persepolis: 'I am Xerxes, the King, King of Kings, King of the lands . . . son of Darius the king, the Achaemenian; a Persian, son of a Persian, an Aryan, of Aryan stock.'

The eldest son of Darius by the elder daughter of Cyrus, Xerxes was thirty-eight years old. Although the picture of him that was subsequently drawn by Greek historians and dramatists shows us a traditional Oriental tyrant, it is noticeable that Herodotus himself concedes a number of virtues to this arch-enemy of his people. Xerxes, as he depicts him, is capable of compassion as well as of regal munificence. He had, as was natural for a Persian of his rank and breeding, not only a love of the chase but also a rich appreciation of the natural beauties of the world. A deeply religious man, he was a Zoroastrian. While the great achievements of Greece in philosophy, science, and speculation about the nature of the universe largely lay in the future, the amoral Gods of the Homeric world were still dominant in the religious conceptions of most Greeks. Xerxes, however, believed in the inspired message that Zoroaster, the prophet, had left behind many centuries before. What distinguished the religion of the Persians from that of the contemporary Greeks has been summed up by H. Humbach, the translator of verses which are ascribed to Zoroaster:

> It is really the knowledge of the directly imminent beginning of the last epoch of the world, in which Good and Evil would be separated from one another, which he gave to mankind. It is the knowledge that it lies in every individual's head to participate in the extirpation of Falsehood and in the establishing of the kingdom of God, before whom all men devoted to the pastoral life are equal, and so to re-establish the milk-flowing paradise on earth.

An inscription at Persepolis made early in the reign of Xerxes records the ruler's dedication to his religious faith: 'A great god is Ahuramazda, who created this earth, who created man, who created peace for man; who made Xerxes king, one king of many, one lord of many.'

Xerxes, as his conduct shows, was prepared to concede that other variants of religious belief were recognised in various guises by other nations. In his conquest of 'rebellious lands', primarily Egypt, he had done his best to uproot the polytheism that he had found rampant everywhere. But the one thing that the Greeks, against whom he was now to wage war, could not ever accept was the fact that Xerxes, like all Eastern potentates, claimed for himself the divine right of kings – 'one lord of many'.

The invasion of Greece, which was about to take place, was in no sense a religious war: such a concept had hardly evolved, except, perhaps, among the Jews, who saw themselves as God's chosen people destined to bring the light of their knowledge of God to the heathen by whom they were surrounded. No, what the Greeks resented above all – though almost every small area and city-state was at variance with the other – was the assumption that any man could call himself the God-appointed ruler of all other men. What, on the surface, almost united Greece in the struggle that was to follow was the simple survival instinct. The invasion of Greece made the turbulent, brilliant people of this mountainous and largely inhospitable land aware that they shared one thing in common: a belief in the individual human being's right to dissent, to think his own way, and not to acknowledge any man as a 'monarch of all I survey'. Curiously enough, the state of Sparta, which was to play a large part in the campaign, was the only one where men had evolved a constitution in which the individual was trained and disciplined to be totally subordinate. The difference was that the Spartans were indeed subject, although not to a 'Great King', but to the concept of the State itself. Perhaps Demaratus, the exiled king of Sparta, who actively helped Xerxes in his campaign, put it best: 'Even though the Spartans are free, still they are not wholly free. The law is their master, and they fear this more than thy people fear thee.'

Xerxes in his great proclamation at Persepolis, after recording how he had put down a rebellion in what one presumes was Egypt, had it inscribed that:

Within these lands there were places where formerly the *Daevas* had been worshipped. Then by the will of Ahuramazda I uprooted the cult of the *Daevas*, and made proclamation: The *Daevas* shall not be worshipped. Where formerly the *Daevas* had been worshipped, there did I worship Ahuramazda according to Truth and with the proper rite. Much else that was ill done did I make good. All that I did, I did by the will of Ahuramazda. Ahuramazda brought me aid until I finished my work. Thou who shalt come after me, if thou shalt think, 'May I be happy while alive and blessed when dead,' have respect for the law which Ahuramazda has established, and worship Ahuramazda according to Truth and with the proper rite.

The false gods (*Daevas*) whose worship Xerxes had forbidden were, in this case, the vast pantheon of Egypt. It is significant that there are no statues of Xerxes in Egypt. Where the great Darius had been tolerant in his treatment of foreign religious practices, Xerxes would seem to have taken the commands of Zoroaster more literally. It was not without some crusading zeal that he now set in motion the invasion of Greece. With the aid of Ahuramazda he would avenge his father's defeat at the hands of the Greeks, and bring these dissident worshippers of false gods within the divine rule of Persia and its monarchy.

He had set out from Susa in the spring of 481. On 10 April of that year there had been an eclipse of the sun (Herodotus wrongly assigns this to the year 480). Not unnaturally, in view of the immensity of the preparations, and the fact that Darius himself had suffered defeat on a similar expedition, this eclipse caused considerable concern, if not consternation, in the court and among the people.

However, the Magi (the wise men who watched the stars and attended to religious rituals), primed with knowledge of the Universe that had been largely acquired from the absorption of Babylon into the Persian Empire, hastened to reassure the Great King. It is possible that, from the Babylonian astronomers, they had learned that the moon is the eclipsing body. Their explanation of the event was completely consistent with this. The sun, they said, symbolised the Greeks and the moon the Persians. The eclipse was not an ill omen therefore. It showed that the Greeks were destined to be overshadowed and conquered by the Persian moon.

Having spent the winter in Sardis, while all the contingents of his army assembled ready for their march north in the following spring, Xerxes could certainly reflect that he and his advisers, his ministers and his overseers of the various work-forces had done all that was possible to obviate any obstacles in their path. His invasion of Europe was so well planned that one is astonished at such efficiency and logistical preparation at such an early date. When one compares the inefficiency of the Crusades many centuries later, or even the relatively poor comprehension of the necessity for long-scale planning and forethought in major wars and campaigns right up to the twentieth century, one can only marvel at the organisation and bureaucratic competence of the Persian Empire. While the Greeks were inclined to see in the preparations made by Xerxes no more than that *hubris* or megalomania which they associated with all despots and Oriental monarchs, there is – to modern eyes – nothing to show that Xerxes and his staff were anything other than magnificent planners, on a scale undreamed of at that period in history.

The preparations for this massive expedition against their country had been known to the Greeks for years. It was not possible that they could have been kept secret, for they involved an immense task force, and works of so extravagant a nature that they almost rivalled the building of the Pyramids. First of all, Xerxes had no intention of allowing his fleet to be brought to ruin off the stormy peninsula of Mount Athos – as had happened to the fleet of Darius during his invasion of Greece ten years previously. The expedition of Xerxes was four years in preparation, and one of the main projects was the digging of a canal through the isthmus of Mount Athos. The mountain, as Herodotus writes, 'is very well-known and high and stands out into the sea. It is inhabited, and on the landward side where the heights end there is a kind of isthmus roughly a mile and a half wide. All of this is level land or small hillocks. . . . The inhabitants [of the mountain] Xerxes now intended to turn into islanders.'

He goes on to describe how the canal through the low land was cut. Conscripted Greeks from the neighbouring areas were used for much of the labour, while skilled workmen were also brought over from Asia Minor. Outstanding among them were the Phoenicians (one of the most technologically advanced people of that era, and the nation which also formed the backbone of the Persian fleet). Herodotus makes the comment that, while the other 'nations' engaged on the task of digging the canal had constant trouble with landslips, caused by the fact that they dug their part of the canal like a simple ditch with straight sides, only the Phoenicians realised that the digging must be much wider at the top in order to leave what engineers call an 'angle of rest'. (Centuries later similar difficulties had to be overcome during the digging of the Suez Canal.) 'They proved their remarkable skill,' he writes, 'for, in the section that had been allotted to them, they dug a trench twice the width required for the canal itself when finished. Digging at a slope they narrowed it as they went further down so that at the bottom their section was as wide as the rest.'

Everything was provided for: there was the equivalent of a canteen for the workmen, with grain brought from the homeland, as well as a forum or meeting-place, and an open market – proof in itself that the workmen were paid in coin. Herodotus' conclusion about the gigantic labour of the canal was that the whole thing was no more than yet another example of the ostentation of Xerxes. 'There would not have been any difficulty', he wrote, 'in having the ships dragged across the isthmus on land, yet he gave orders for the canal to be made so wide that two warships could be rowed abreast [down its length].' The historian was thinking, of course, of the practice at Corinth of dragging ships across the isthmus which connects northern Greece with the Peloponnese. His great mistake, however, was to equate the routine passage of merchantmen and warships between the Gulf of Patras and the Aegean Sea with the emergent movement of a large fleet into hostile waters. While waiting to take their turn for haulage overland, they might well have been overwhelmed by one of the sudden and violent storms that quite often afflict the Aegean.

Nothing was left to chance. Dumps of provisions, both for men and for their animals, were sited at regular intervals along the route that the Grand Army was to take. The Persians, unlike the Greeks, were not principally bread- or grain-eaters (as most Mediterranean peoples are to this day). Meat was a staple part of their diet, and 'meat on the hoof' was brought into the principal supply depots long before the army moved. At the same time great quantities of salted-down meat were stockpiled. The army, of course, as it moved across Asia Minor, and later into Greece, was expected to live off the land to a large extent, but Xerxes and his commissariat organisers did not make the great mistake of many later armies in assuming that so large a force could necessarily supply itself in this hand-to-mouth fashion. In *Persia and the Greeks* A. R. Burn quotes the description of Persian preparations for war by Theopompos of Chios. It is true that Theopompos was writing much later about an expedition against Egypt, but there is little reason to believe that Persian thoroughness had changed since the time of Xerxes. He records the

tens of thousands of stand of arms, both Greek and oriental; vast herds of baggage animals and beasts for slaughter; bushels of condiments, and boxes and sacks, and bales of paper and all the other accessories. And there was so much salt meat of every kind, that it made heaps, so large that people approaching from a distance thought they were coming to a range of hills.

The reference to the bales of paper can only bring a wry smile to the face of anyone who has served in modern wars. Persia was nothing if not a bureaucratic state, and they had learned largely from the Egyptians, with their tradition of meticulous public records, that the organisation of a great country, and more especially an empire, required scribes and civil servants and departmental organisers. They were among the forerunners in the large-scale use of paperwork – under which so much of the world groans today. (Byblos, one of the principal Phoenician cities, which came under the sway of Persia, was credited with having been the inventor of paper – made from papyrus. The word Bible ('Book') derives from Byblos.)

Especial provision was made in the way of stores for the army when it should have crossed into Greece. While in Asia Minor they might be expected to feed off the land to a great extent, since all of the area came under Persian rule. Such could not be expected in Greece itself once the army was south of the pro-Persian north. The River Strymon, which empties into the sea to the north of Mount Athos, was bridged for the passage of the army, and in several parts of this region of Thrace great provision dumps were established. The largest of these was at the White Cape on the Thracian coast and another was at the mouth of the Strymon near the new bridge. Yet others were sited to the south, in parts of Macedonia.

So much that Herodotus and later Greek historians considered as evidence of the megalomania of Xerxes and the *hubris* of a typical Oriental tyrant was no more than evidence of forethought, excellent logistics, and planning superiority over the Greeks of the period. The small Greek city-states could not understand what the organisation of a great empire and the movement of many thousands of men entailed: they themselves thought in terms of hundreds or at the most a few thousands. It would be well over a century until a Greece, unified under Alexander the Great, would have to tackle the problems of Empire. The principal source of amazement, not untinged with some reluctant admiration, was the great bridge of boats which Xerxes ordered to be constructed across the Hellespont at the narrows between Abydos on the Asian side to a point near Sestos on the European side: a distance of about seven furlongs or 1400 yards.

There were two bridges supported on 674 biremes and triremes which were used to form the floating platforms upon which the carriageway itself was laid. There were 360 vessels on the side towards the Black Sea and 314 on the southern section. One of these was allocated to the Egyptian workmen and the other to the Phoenicians. One may suspect that the Phoenicians built a better bridge (admirable though the Egyptians were as architects, they were not so distinguished a seafaring people as the masters of Tyre and Sidon). Nevertheless a storm of 'great violence' smashed both bridges shortly after they had been completed. Xerxes' reaction was, in accordance with the Greek view of Herodotus, that of a maddened tyrant who expects that even the winds and the waves will respect his wishes. He gave orders that the Hellespont should be given three hundred lashes, that a pair of fetters be thrown into the sea, and even that it should be branded like a common criminal. Herodotus, like all Greeks (who made their living so largely from the sea and to whom the sea-god Poseidon was a deity always to be placated), regarded this not only as a barbarous, but indeed a maniacal act. 'You salt and bitter current,' Xerxes is said to have ordered the men who wielded the whips to say, 'your master inflicts this punishment upon you for doing harm to him, who never harmed you. Nevertheless Xerxes the King will cross you with or without your permission. No man makes sacrifice to you, and for this neglect you deserve your neglect because of your salty and dirty water.'

Curiously enough, although much of this might be taken as the ravings of a paranoiac oriental monarch (as the Greeks thought), Xerxes' behaviour was not so irrational. To the Zoroastrian, for whom the dream of the pastoral life was – like the Garden of Eden to the Jews – the ultimate aim to which the Good must aspire, their heaven was essentially one conceived by landsmen. Flowing streams of clear water were naturally part of this concept. As a land-bound people, moreover, they had a dislike of the sea and an inability to cope with it (hence their employment of the Egyptians and the Phoenicians to man their fleets). 'The bitter water', the undrinkable water of the sea, was symbolic of Ahriman, the evil power against which the true follower of Ahuramazda was pledged to fight. Xerxes' cursing and lashings of the sea, therefore, was possibly no more than a symbolic act done, as Xerxes might have put it, 'according to Truth and with the proper rite'.

His rage against the designers of the two bridges was, however, entirely in accordance with what the Greeks expected of an Eastern tyrant. They were executed. A Greek engineer, Harpalus, is on record as having been the designer of the final two successful bridges; aided probably by Ionian and Phoenician technicians. They were moored slantwise to the Black Sea and at right angles to the Hellespont. Upstream and downstream specially constructed anchors were laid. Those to the east were to hold the bridging vessels against winds from the Black Sea, as well as against the strong current that flows down permanently as the cold river-fed water of the Black Sea pours in to replenish the Mediterranean. Those laid to the south were to hold the bridges, and especially the southerly bridge, against any gales that might strike from the less expected but still not uncommon quarter of the south-west. Despite their lack of modern scientific instruments the technicians of 2400 years ago were more familiar from centuries of experience with prevailing winds and tides than many a modern mariner who glides through the Hellespont with thousands of horsepower under his feet, assisted by efficient lighthouses, radar, and radio beacons. In three places between the bridges gaps were left so that boats might pass up or down the Hellespont. Since the freeboard, or height of deck above waterline, was little more than eight feet in the average bireme, there would have been little difficulty for such a vessel to pass under the three open sections of the bridges – especially when it is remembered that the sailors were constantly used to lowering masts and yards whenever the weather was foul. (The squaresails on vessels of that period were of little use except with a following wind, or one from slightly abaft of the beam.)

One of the astonishing mechanical triumphs of Xerxes' bridges of boats was the strength and the weight of the cables that held them together. The Phoenicians, we learn, used cables of flax, while the Egyptians had theirs made out of papyrus. These large and heavy lengths of cable were almost certainly brought up the Aegean on barges. 'Each bridge', writes Herodotus, 'had two flax cables and four of papyrus. The flax was the heavier – half a fathom of it weighing 114 lbs.' This may be an exaggeration or a misunderstanding of Eastern weights and measures, for this would have meant that over a distance of 1400 yards the total weight of the flax cables alone would have been nearly 100 tons. In any case, the whole project was of such size and scale that it is doubtful whether anything equivalent could have been achieved to equal it in Europe for many centuries to come. (It is only recently, since the aqualung and many other improvements in diving techniques, that enough has been recovered of the remains of ancient ships to reveal how far from primitive were the seafaring vessels of ancient mariners.)

Manpower had built the Pyramids, and manpower and animal power were to remain the gauge of human mechanical achievement until the Industrial Revolution. 'As soon as the vessels were on station', Herodotus writes, 'the cables were hauled taut by wooden winches on the shore.' The next thing was to cut planks equal to the breadth of the floats. These were then laid edge to edge over the cables and were bound together. Finally, brushwood was laid on top, followed by soil, which the workmen spread evenly and trod down flat. Only one last thing remained to do (evidence again of considerable forethought) and that was to erect palisades on either side of the bridges so that the animals which were to pass over would not take fright at the sight of 'the bitter water'. Nothing in the Crusades centuries later, almost nothing until amphibious operations of the twentieth century, was to equal the skill and technical ability of these engineers and craftsmen of the Persian Empire – working in the fifth century B.C.

2

THE GLORY OF THE HOUR

BY THE SPRING OF 480 Xerxes had received the news that not only was the canal bypassing Mount Athos completed, but that both the bridges across the Hellespont were restored and ready for the army to cross. The time was ripe. The spring months, after the gales of winter, and long before the prevailing northerlies of summer set in, were ideal. True, there can sometimes be storms in this season, but they are rare. Most of the Aegean, from the Hellespont southward to the Sporades, Cape Sunium, and beyond that again to the Cyclades, is usually ruffled by no more than the winds known as *prodroms* – the variable forerunners of early summer.

Long in advance of his move out of Sardis Xerxes had sent messengers to all the Greek states asking for those formal tokens of surrender – the gifts of earth and water from their land. It is hardly surprising that many of them, and especially the vulnerable islands, sent back these necessary tributes. According to Herodotus, it was only to the two major states of Athens and Sparta that no heralds were despatched. On the previous occasion, ten years before, when Darius had sent similar heralds, the Athenians were said to have cast them into 'The Pit' – the place for condemned criminals – and the Spartans to have thrown them down a well. Part of this story is suspect, for Herodotus had a pro-Athenian bias and was inclined to enlarge upon their heroic legend. At the time of Darius it seems somewhat unlikely that the Athenians would have acted in a manner so contrary to the international law accepted by all civilised peoples. (Heralds were regarded as sacred and inviolable.) On the other hand, there is real evidence that the Spartans had indeed thrown the Persian ambassadors down a well, telling them to 'get earth and water for their king from down there'. The drastic nature of the action is Spartan, the quoted remark suitably laconic, and it was a known fact that Sparta regarded herself as superior to the law of other States and nations, especially 'Barbarians': those who were not Greeks.

Xerxes and his advisers knew that, if it was intolerable to send heralds to Sparta, it was equally pointless to send them to Athens. The essential core of Greece which had to be destroyed was composed of these two small, even if so dissimilar, city-states. The one was the military muscle of Greece and the other provided by far the greater part of its naval arm. Many of the other Greeks had already 'medised', as the term was: they had, that is to say, shown their willingness to co-operate with the Persians. This was hardly surprising, since to many an intelligent citizen, whether of an Aegean island, or of a city on the mainland, it must have seemed more than clear that, even if all the Greeks were united (which was far from true), they would stand no chance against the massive army and navy that was coming against them out of the East.

Xerxes had made good use of the propaganda effect of his preparations. He had even deliberately allowed Greek spies to infiltrate and witness the gathering together of the army and the building of the navy. His own men, for their part, in the guise either of sailors or of merchants had long kept the king and his inner circle acquainted with the political groups and motivations within the cities and island-states of the Greeks. In nearly all of these there were power struggles between various rich families, or between ruling families and the *demos* or common people. It was easy to see that in many cases, in return for the plentiful Persian gold, one rich family would be prepared to 'sell out' to the Persians in return for becoming the local rulers in due course. Alternatively, an oligarchy, or aristocratic allied group of families, would do the same in return for the monetary and military help that would enable them to keep the *demos* in their proper place – down. (In so many subsequent wars similar arrangements have always been made between the potentially occupied and the apparently all-powerful invaders.) If the Greeks were – as they were indeed – a brilliant people, they were individualistic to a fault, and concerned with the fate and fortune of themselves first of all and, secondly, of their state. Athens and Sparta, although by the nature of their societies basically hostile to one another, were large and important enough to realise that co-operation between the two of them was the only possible way in which the Greeks as a people could survive the

Juggernaut that had some years ago crushed the freedom of their fellow-Greeks in Asia Minor (Ionia).

Although it is true that Herodotus, who was born some four years after the invasion of Xerxes, had access to all the records available, it is impossible to accept the figures that he gives for the size of the Persian army and of the fleet. If one first of all bears in mind that Herodotus was trying to make his figures square with a famous war memorial that had been set up in the pass of Thermopylae, it is not so difficult to see where his added noughts come from in his computation of the Persian numbers. The memorial in traditional Spartan or laconic style reads:

> Against three million men fought in this place
> Four thousand Peloponnesians, face to face.

The fact is that the Greeks, when it came to numbers beyond their normal usage, tended to use the term 'myriads' (tens of thousands) as we, centuries later, loosely use millions or billions – meaning no more than an almost uncountable amount.

The figures as given by Herodotus show an army totalling 1,700,000 infantrymen, 80,000 horsemen, a camel corps and chariot contingent numbering 20,000, and a mixture of Greeks from Ionia, the islands, and Thrace, to the total of 300,000. Burn adds the dry but apt comment

> . . . finding himself still short of the war-memorial's three million, he cheerfully doubles the whole total to allow for non-combatants (cooks, drivers, women – the Guards are reported to have brought their women along in wagons) and reaches a grand total of 5,283,220. The most remarkable thing, he adds, with a decent descent into realism, is how such a multitude was fed.

Other scholars and military historians have debated the size of the army – and of the navy – but the most realistic viewpoint seems to be that Herodotus confused the Persian term *myriarchs*, which meant the commander of 10,000 men, with the other named commanders who, in their lesser sphere, commanded no more than thousands or hundreds. (The Persians worked on the decimal system.) If one removes a nought from all of Herodotus' figures one comes up with an army of 170,000 infantrymen, 8000 cavalry, 2000 camel corps and charioteers, and 30,000 Greeks and Thracians. This seems a far more likely figure in view of the populations (as far as they can be conjected) at the time. It would still make sense, in that it would nevertheless suggest to a Greek accustomed to battles involving at the most a few thousand men an almost inexhaustible flood of troops.

General Sir Frederick Maurice, who had the opportunity of covering the area of the march of the Great King not long after the First World War, came up with the conclusion that the total of the Persian army was about 210,000. Unlike most desk-bound scholars he had the opportunity to travel the whole area, and had excellent military and logistical knowledge of the terrain. He based his conclusions particularly on his observation of the water-supplies available. Maurice had also had experience of moving British military units together with animal transport, and he reckoned that such a force would probably have needed with them about 75,000 animals. Even at this, he reasons that what has sometimes been taken as an unbelievable comment by Herodotus, 'except for the great rivers, their fighters drank the waters up', was probably correct. A river, of course, unlike a pond or even a lake, cannot be drunk dry in one sense, for it is constantly being reinforced. One may also reasonably assume that the rivers in Asia Minor at that time were somewhat larger than they are today. Centuries of the ubiquitous goat, killing saplings, leading to deforestation, coupled with land changes in the earthquake-prone area of Turkey have certainly depleted the forests as well as interfering with natural water sources.

Nevertheless, working on whatever system one prefers, it seems that there is no possibility of the army of Xerxes having exceeded 250,000 men. Even this number, together with all their animals, baggage train and (possibly) camp followers, would have been sufficient to exhaust the water resources at a number of places along their route.

The figures which Herodotus gives for the invasion fleet of the Great King are again, like those of the army, subject to some doubt, although in this case they do bear more likelihood to reality. The Phoenicians, as was to be expected, provided the largest contingent, and it was almost certainly the most efficient. This is given as 300. The next largest contingent, 200, was that of the Egyptians, who specialised in having heavily armed parties of marines aboard their vessels. Cyprus produced 150 ships, Cilicia and Pamphylia between them 130, and Lycia and Caria 120. The Asian Greeks contributed a fighting force of 290 warships, the islands of the Cyclades 17, and in addition there were an estimated 120 triremes from the Thracian Greeks and the adjacent islands. This gives a grand total of 1327 warships, not counting the transport vessels of all and every size, which Herodotus again 'estimates' at about 3000.

It is quite clear from the later history of the campaign at sea that the Persian fleet, when it came into action, did not have anything like the preponderance over the Greek which these figures would suggest. They are nearer, in fact, to what may have been the total of all the shipping available in the Levant and eastern Mediterranean under Persian control at the time. The fact remains that Herodotus gives his list with some confidence, as if he had access to records – and it would seem that that is exactly what he had. Now, Xerxes had encouraged Greek spies well in advance of the campaign to penetrate the shipyards and to count the forces that were being mustered against them. This was all good propaganda. Anything that made his navy and his army seem larger than it really was suited his design of intimidating as many Greeks as possible from taking up arms against him. One may reasonably surmise that Greek intelligence was bamboozled into thinking that the numbers of ships and of men were vastly in excess of the real figures. Naturally enough, after the campaign was over, no Greek, whether soldier or sailor, was likely to reduce the number of ships and men that had come against him. With the passage of years, of course, especially when oral tradition was still the standard method of transmitting information, the numbers were certain to increase, not diminish. (It is only since the Second World War, when the records of both sides have been published, that the reality of the numbers of aircraft engaged in the Battle of Britain, and the casualties inflicted, have proved how erroneous were the reports issued by both sides at the actual time.) It is a natural instinct of man to exaggerate, especially when comparing his prowess with that of an enemy. Herodotus went to such sources as he could find, when he wrote *The Histories*, and it is hardly surprising that the figures he received were usually inflated.

Another reason why, whether exaggerated or not, the numbers of ships involved on the Persian side have seemed excessive to scholars is that so many of them have overlooked the ships involved in supporting the two floating bridges. Even allowing for the fact that the first of these bridges was smashed up in a storm, Herodotus states with conviction that the number of ships required for the second, successful, bridging of the Hellespont was 674. Deducting this figure from the overall 1327 vessels, one is left with 653 ships before the subsequent engagement at Artemisium. Storm losses (quite apart from those in battle) left the Persians with a fleet that, when it came to the ultimate test at Salamis, was little superior in numbers to that which the Greeks had mustered.

Even after the necessary reductions in the numbers of ships and men in the army and fleet of Xerxes it is still true that to any Greek, whose island or city-state counted its inhabitants in a few thousands, the host of the Great King seemed so prodigious as to invite a terrified response. The Persian army justified the lines written by A. E. Housman:

> The King with half the East at heels
> Is marched from lands of morning.
> His fighters drink the rivers up,
> Their shafts benight the air. . . .

Before the invasion of Europe began and the army started to cross the Hellespont bridges Xerxes decided to hold a review of his forces. Herodotus implies that he reviewed the whole army and navy in a day, but this is clearly impossible. The army itself, when it was on the march, moved in columns, baggage train ahead, with half the infantry as escort; then came two brigades of Xerxes' noble guards, the Immortals; the sacred chariot of Ahuramazda drawn by ten stallions, then the Great King, followed by two further brigades of crack infantry and cavalry; the rest of the Immortals; and finally all the other infantry divisions. The whole array, it has been calculated, would have taken seven days to cross the bridges from Asia Minor into Europe. It is clear that what Xerxes witnessed was a selection of the host, together with a few picked squadrons of ships which put on a display of nautical skills just offshore. The throne of white marble, from which he witnessed this evidence of his power and might, was set up at Abydos on the eastern side of the Dardanelles. Here, on a day early in May, while the main body of the army together with all the animals was assembling for the crossing, Xerxes 'saw the whole Hellespont covered in ships, and all the beaches and plains of Abydos filled with men'.

Xerxes, not unnaturally, was filled with exultation at the sight before him – the strait studded with ships, the great bridges, the dust cloud of the assembling army, the brilliant march past of the Immortals and other selected troops, the gleam of spring sunlight on cavalry and armoured men, and all the panoply of war. He then sent orders for some of the ships in his navy to give an exhibition of their prowess. A race was arranged between picked squadrons, the final heat of which was won by the Phoenicians of Sidon. (Sidon, along with Tyre and Arvad, produced the greatest mariners and pilots of antiquity.) 'Xerxes was as pleased with the race as with the sight of his army . . . He congratulated himself – and the next moment burst into tears.' His uncle Artabanus, who had tried from the very beginning to dissuade him from 'Operation Europe', said to him: 'My lord, there is surely some contradiction between this behaviour and that of a minute ago. Then you called yourself a fortunate man – and yet now you weep.'

Xerxes answered him: 'I paused for thought, and it occurred to me that human life is so sadly short. Out of all these thousands of men, not one will be alive in a hundred years.'

Artabanus was quick to seize the chance, while his monarch was temporarily out of spirits, to point out the dangers of the expedition. He was wise for his time. He realised that logistics very largely governed the success or failure of a campaign such as this. The farther the army advanced, the longer its lines of communications, and the greater the difficulty of food supplies. The land itself and the sea, he warned, were the king's greatest enemies. The land that they were now invading would prove hostile and would not afford enough supplies for an army which, he admitted, was quite large enough for the task of subduing the Greeks. The sea was ever a treacherous element and there was no harbour on the Greek coast large enough to accommodate all the fleet in the event of bad weather. Xerxes, his serenity restored by the glory of the hour, was

not prepared to listen to the older man. He was determined to succeed where the great Darius had failed, and he had every confidence
in the careful preparations that had been made to ensure the Persian
success.

'We are following', he said, 'in the footsteps of our fathers. We
are marching to war at the ideal season of the year. We shall conquer
all Europe and, without either being starved or suffering any other
unpleasant circumstance, we shall return in triumph to our homeland.'

(It is difficult for the twentieth-century reader not to be reminded
of the German Fuehrer in 1940 looking across the narrow seas of
the Channel at the cliffs of Dover.)

Xerxes did not wish to be reminded of the possibility of failure,
and the reward of Artabanus for his counsel was to be sent back
home to the capital Susa. There he might act as Viceroy, and there
an older man's slow but sure approach might be useful in the
government of the Empire. For the moment, it was clear that
optimism and zestful confidence were what was needed around the
throne of the Great King. Shortly afterwards Xerxes held a meeting
of the Persian senior commanders and dispensed to them those
standard platitudes that have been used throughout the ages by
kings and generals. Courage was called for, the reputation of their
ancestors must not be disgraced, utmost exertion, noble aims,
brave enemy not to be despised, and then – 'If we defeat them
there is no other army in the world which will ever dare confront
us.'

On the following day spices were burned on the bridges and
boughs of myrtle were spread along the surface that the army
would tread. The gods were being propitiated, and now Xerxes
himself waited for sunrise. He was imploring the blessing of
Ahuramazda upon the whole enterprise. The Shining One lifted
above the land-mass of Asia. The men out of the East were about
to conquer the lands that still lay in the darkness to the West. The
Great King poured a libation of wine out of a golden goblet into
the sea that he had previously chastised. He turned his face to the
glory of the sun and prayed 'that no chance might prevent him
from conquering Europe or turn him back before he reached its
utmost limits'. He threw the goblet into the sea, its shining flight
to be followed a few seconds later by a golden bowl, and then a

Persian scimitar. All due rites had been attended to. Nothing now remained but to equal promise with performance. The Sun-God beading their swords, their spears, and their armour, the 10,000 Immortals, wreaths of victory on their heads, began the crossing of the upper bridge.

3

THE PERSIANS

THE NATION AND THE EMPIRE that Xerxes was now leading to the invasion of Europe represented a concentration of military and political power such as the ancient world had never known before. Like all empires it was founded on the ruins of others but, unlike those that had preceded it, instead of remaining confined within the territorial limits of the Near East the Persian Empire was still expanding. From 547 B.C. onwards it continued to do so for some seventy years. Its first real check was in Greece, but despite even this it was not until the campaigns of Alexander the Great that its power was finally broken. Even then, when Alexander's empire splintered after his death, the world and culture of Iran, in the shape of the new Persian Empire, revived and continued the later struggle against Rome. It did not finally collapse until the seventh century when the Arabs, always unconquered, overthrew it. For over a thousand years, the East challenged the West, and the most crucial of all these challenges was that which was now set in motion by Xerxes. Had it succeeded, the Zoroastrian creed might have been imposed upon the pagan Greeks. There would have been no fifth-century Athens, and all European history would have been very different.

The Achaemenid Empire had been founded by the elder Cyrus in 550 B.C. and there is a strong case to be made out for the theory that the whole of ancient history (which determined the history of Europe) sprang from the conflict between Persian (Iranian) culture and that of the Greco-Roman world. Although there can be no doubt that Greek culture was infinitely superior in many respects to that of Persia, it is only from the Greek Herodotus that we gain any real idea about the Persian Empire, the Persians themselves leaving only the self-aggrandising monuments of monarchs. The Persian contribution in the political and administrative sphere can never be dismissed. The fact is that the Greeks, from whom we have our only over-all picture of the time, did not understand the nature of this contribution. Xerxes, as we have seen, was merely regarded as an overbearing autocrat – instead of a thoughtful and far-planning ruler intent on building an empire that would embrace Europe as well as the East. It was enough for the Greeks to refer to the Persians and 'the Medes' (a generic term used to encompass both strains of the Iranian race) as 'barbarians' – people who go 'bar-bar-bar' and do not speak Greek.

The Medes had appeared on the scene of world history in 612 B.C. when Nineveh, the capital of the Assyrian Empire, had fallen before a combined attack of Medes and Chaldeans. For centuries the Assyrians had dominated the Near East with their formidable war-machine. Now, out of the powers which rushed in to fill the vacuum caused by the collapse of Assyria, it was the empire of the Medes that was to prove the most enduring. It reached its limit in Anatolia, where it came into conflict with the Kingdom of Lydia. A line was temporarily drawn, but the Iranians had advanced sufficiently far into Asia Minor for it to be only just a matter of time before they came into contact – and conflict – with the Greeks who were established in that area which was known from the language and race of its settlers as Ionia.

This was to occur in the sixth century B.C. when Cyrus, the son of a Persian vassal-king and a Median princess of the ruling house, raised the standard of revolt against the hegemony of the Medes. Cyrus, whom the Athenian Xenophon was to extol some years later as the model of what a ruler should be, was not content with the stagnation that had fallen over the Medes under its recent ruler, and determined to advance the existing Iranian empire even further. Following his Median predecessor into the Kingdom of Lydia, Cyrus defeated the Lydian King Croesus and took him prisoner in 547 B.C. The importance of this Lydian defeat was soon felt by the Greeks in Asia Minor and throughout the Aegean for, both as subjects and supporters of the Lydian king, they had long maintained friendly relationships with his empire. Their influence was paramount throughout Lydia and their cultural supremacy had long been recognised and appreciated. The relationship had not been all one-sided, for the Greeks had been swift to adopt the Lydian invention of coinage, and, as merchants and sea-farers, had been quick to see how this transformed the whole economy of the Mediterranean.

Cyrus for his part was well familiar with the Greeks and with their presence in Ionia and was also aware that the Greeks were formidable warriors, even if politically divided. His first diplomatic attempts to win Greek support without recourse to arms failed signally, with the exception of the powerful city of Miletus at the end of the Meander valley which came out in support of the Persian monarch. The other Greeks, dismayed at the situation in which they found themselves, decided to appeal to Sparta as the strongest military power on the Greek mainland. The Spartans were not to be drawn into supporting the Ionian Greeks but nevertheless sent envoys to visit Ionia, and also to pay an unexpected call on Cyrus at Sardis. Clearly they were interested to discover the strength and the intentions of this formidable new Persian ruler. In view of what was to happen in subsequent years in the conflict between Persian and Greek, the first reaction of the great Cyrus to the presence of these envoys in his court is not without an ironical twist: 'Who *are* the Spartans?' he asked some other Greeks who were present.

At this moment in his career, Cyrus was more concerned with Babylon and other countries, including Egypt, which he intended to bring under Persian rule, and he left the affairs of Lydia and Ionia in the hands of a governor and tax-gatherers. It was only a short time before a revolt was raised against the Persians which ended with the imposition of a military occupation force, the colonisation of the area, and the swift realisation by the Greeks that, while they had managed happily enough under Lydian kings, the dominion of Persia was another thing altogether. The inhabitants of one Greek city, Phocaea, emigrated to Corsica rather than submit, but the majority adopted the classic strategy of retiring within the walls of their towns. Unfortunately for them the siege-engines and firepower of the Persian archers brought up against them by their commander Harpalus proved too formidable for the Ionians' defences. One by one over a brief period the Greeks were forced to accept the rule of Persia. In all of this it cannot be said that the famous oracle at Delphi encouraged Greek resistance. Submission to the inevitable was the advice given. Persian gold may well have had some honeyed effect upon the oracle's tongue.

The conquest of Lydia, which had confirmed the power of Persia was but the beginning. Within eight years Cyrus had carried all before him, even as far as the borders of India, and he was now ready for his major thrust – against Babylon. In October 539 the empire of Babylon and all its adjacent lands acknowledged Cyrus, king of the Medes and Persians, as 'King of the world, great king, legitimate king, king of Babylon, king of Sumer and Akkad, king of the four rims [of the world]'. His immediate policy of religious tolerance towards the former subjects of Babylonia meant that Syria and Phoenicia readily paid him homage, while his popularity with the Jews was assured for all time by his restoration of the Temple of Jerusalem.

The adherence of Phoenicia to the Persian throne also meant that from now on the foremost mariners of antiquity, with all their ships and trading posts throughout the Mediterranean, were available for the expansion of Persian power, far beyond the confines of the homeland. Eight years later Cyrus, one of the world's rulers who assuredly deserves the term 'Great', met his end in battle against the Massagetae on the north-eastern frontier of his empire. Herodotus (and many other intelligent Greeks) always retained a great respect for Cyrus and the characteristically Persian qualities that he embodied. He concludes his account of his life with the story of how one day a rich and influential Persian came as spokesman for the people to the Great King and suggested that, since Persia was now the most powerful country in the world, it would be a good idea if they were to emigrate from their poor and mountainous country and occupy some rich and fertile lowland.

Cyrus did not think much of this suggestion; he replied that they might act upon it if they pleased, but added the warning that, if they did so, they must prepare themselves to rule no longer, but to be ruled by others. 'Soft countries,' he said, 'breed soft men. It is not the property of any one soil to produce fine fruits and good soldiers too.' The Persians had to admit that this was true and that Cyrus was wiser than they; so they left him, and chose to live in a rugged land and rule rather than to cultivate rich plains and be slaves.

His son Cambyses, having avenged his father's death, then set about the conquest of Egypt, the last remaining independent and imperial power in the ancient world. It is significant that the Greeks of Cyprus and of Samos – both considerable naval powers – went over to the side of the Persian king and were willing to ally themselves with their old rivals the Phoenicians in the expansion of empire. The victory over Egypt was assured and, with the death of the last native Pharaoh, Persia was triumphant. Only in Africa, whither the ambitions of Cambyses also extended, was he unsuccessful. He died while in Syria on his way to suppress a revolt by a pretender to the throne. The pretender Gaumata (who may even have been what he claimed, a true son of Cyrus) was himself a Magus, a member of the Median priesthood, and had their support in what amounted to an attempt to overthrow the military aristocracy and restore the dominance of the Magi. A counter-revolution by the heads of the great families was led by Darius, an Achaemenid of an older branch of the family to that of Cyrus, and himself young enough to have both father and grandfather still alive. Gaumata was killed by Darius and the conspirators established Darius as king. All the conspirators were Persians and began an immediate purge of the Magi. It was hardly surprising that trouble soon stirred throughout the Empire and a determined counter-revolt was organised by the Medes. It took Darius twelve months and nineteen battles to suppress the insurgents and it remains astonishing that the fabric of the empire survived. The fact was that Darius commanded the better troops and that he was a determined and perennially cool personality. The strength and ruthlessness which he brought to his years as monarch were in evidence from the very beginning.

Now, when 'all the dwellers in Asia were subject to him, except the Arabs', Darius determined to set about the reorganisation of the empire. His attention to detail, his concern with economic affairs, and his inauguration of the first Persian coinage laid the foundations for the long-enduring structure of the Persian Empire. Scoffers might say that 'Cyrus was a father, Cambyses a master, and Darius a shopkeeper', but it was the very practicality shown by Darius that transcended the achievements of the old-style warrior-kings. In his use of coinage Darius was quick to see the value of propaganda. As A. R. Burn points out:

. . . in Darius's empire, his golden *darics* with the device of the running archer – a *crowned* archer, so it represents the Great King himself, armed and swift – circulated wherever trade was considerable, and did away with the need for use of the scales when the king paid his armies. Armed and swift: this was the image of the king to be borne in the memory of millions who never saw the king or his likeness otherwise . . . Also, and most important, the financier-king regulated the taxes of the empire and laid down clearly the amount that each province had to pay.

The vast empire was divided into 'provinces' or, as they came to be known, 'satrapies', since each was under the rule of a satrap or provincial governor who was responsible for paying the requisite tribute to the Great King. Babylonia, for instance, which was accounted the richest province, paid an annual tribute valued at one thousand silver talents which was composed of precious metals, cattle, and fine clothing. Egypt, which paid largely in the form of grain and cattle, was reckoned to produce a tribute worth seven hundred silver talents. The royal inscription at Behistun lists twenty-three satrapies in all, ranging from Persia itself to Ionia and Scythia on the Black Sea. At a later date Libya and Nubia were added to these provinces of empire and, after Darius' expedition into Scythia, his first holding in Europe was added – Thrace in the far north of the Grecian mainland.

The establishment of this bridgehead into Europe followed upon Darius' determination to establish a northern frontier-limit to his empire. This was in effect unnecessary, for the Scythians were no threat to Persia or its satrapies, but the fact is, most probably, that Darius like so many great conquerors could not stop. He had established the limits of his empire to the south-east, south-west, and north-east. Only to the north-west, where he wished to secure the shores of the Black Sea, were the boundaries of his powers undefined. In 513–512 Darius marched north on his Scythian campaign. Like that of his successor Xerxes, this was a well-prepared and carefully executed invasion in which the Ionian Greeks and the Greeks of the adjacent islands co-operated. The Bosporus was bridged under the orders of a Samian architect Mandrocles, thus linking Asia and Europe, and Darius had the satisfaction of watching his army march over on to a shore hitherto unknown to Persians. A rendezvous between the army and the fleet of the Ionian allies was arranged at the Danube, where the Greeks constructed with their ships a pontoon bridge for the army to cross. Behind them the tribes of Thrace were left subdued and acknowledging the suzerainty of the Persian monarch.

When it came to the Scythians inhabiting the steppes of Bessarabia, however, even Darius found himself at a loss. He was confronted by the immensity of southern Russia and its great rivers – as well as by the fact that its inhabitants pursued a scorched-earth policy, refused to give battle, and merely retreated into their endless rolling country. Finally, Herodotus tells us: 'Darius returned through Thrace, and came to Sestos in the Chersonese, whence he crossed over in his ships to Asia. . . .' He left behind him, however, a large section of the army under one of his best generals, Megabazus, who proceeded to ensure that the coastline of Thrace was thoroughly subdued. Thus the Persians secured for themselves a permanent foothold in Europe. The limit of Megabazus' campaign was the frontier of Macedonia where Amyntas, the king of the country, formally offered him those age-old tokens of submission: earth and water. The Greek states to the south regarded the Macedonians as hardly Greeks at all, barbarians almost; yet to the far-sighted it should have been clear that, under ambitious leadership, the power of Persia would hardly stop next time at the edge of the Greek world.

Darius was not content with his preliminary venture into Europe and now, with the whole of the East united behind him and with the Phoenicians and Egyptians providing him with a large navy, he set about an elaborate investigation of Greece itself and the world that lay yet farther to the west. The master-mariners of Sidon, renowned among the Phoenicians themselves and recorded as such by Ezekiel in the Bible, were commissioned to take two warships together with a supply ship and make a thorough reconnaissance of the areas in which the Great King was interested. The fact that the expedition ended ignominiously with the storeship being seized in southern Italy, and the two warships wrecked in the stormy straits of Otranto, did not alter the fact that it indicated Darius' desire to expand his empire westwards. Herodotus, who tells the story, was far from being in a position to know everything. He certainly knew of this one 'spying' venture that came to grief, but this in no way means that there were not others which were unobtrusively successful.

One thing that the Persian monarch will have been swiftly apprised of, now that the Phoenicians were willing servants of his imperial aspirations, was the long-term enmity between Phoenicians and Greeks. Western Hellenism in Sicily and southern Italy was under great pressure from the great Phoenician foundation of Carthage, as well as from the Etruscans in Italy. Furthermore, true to their egocentric and individualistic nature, the Greeks in their new colonies were as divided against one another as they were in their own homeland. Syracuse, one of their greatest foundations in Sicily, was bedevilled by party struggles while most of the other cities were in the grip of tyrannies; and successful tyrants, in order to maintain their hold upon their own city states, almost invariably made war upon one of their Greek neighbours. In 511–510 B.C. the city of Croton in southern Italy attacked its rich rival, Sybaris (which has become synonymous with luxurious living), and completely destroyed it – even going to the vindictive length of diverting the River Crathis over its site so that even its memory should perish from the earth. From the reports of spies and from information readily given by expatriate Greeks in his court Darius observed and digested all the information that he needed. Cyrus, Darius and, in his turn, Xerxes must never be confused with the simple Asiatic and Northern warlords of later centuries, for whom to conquer, loot and enslave was the prime object. The Persian monarchs, served by an efficient army and bureaucracy, were – whatever the Greeks may have called them – in no sense barbarians.

The major event that triggered off the great Greco-Persian wars was a revolt against Persian rule that had its origins in Ionia. One of the principal causes was undoubtedly the economic suffering that formerly rich and tranquil Ionia suffered under Persian hegemony and taxation. Their trade in the Black Sea area had been blocked ever since Darius had gained control of the Dardanelles, and their colonies in Sicily and Italy were either at loggerheads one with another or (as in the case of Sybaris) were being destroyed by fellow Greeks. But the deciding factor was almost certainly the loss of liberty that the Ionians felt under the interference of Persian satraps. Even more distressing than this was the Persian system of putting local government into the hands of Greek 'tyrants'. Such men, hated by their fellow Greeks and dependent entirely upon maintaining sycophantic relations with Persia, were liable to be harsher in their dealings with the Ionians than the Persian satrap.

The rebellion flared up in 500 B.C. and a mission was sent to the Greek motherland asking for help. It is significant that only Athens and Eretria on the island of Euboea promised to send naval contingents. The Spartans held aloof because they were on the verge of war with their neighbour Argos, and they were further-more always averse to foreign entanglements. The revolt opened with an attack on the great Lydian capital of Sardis which was burned to the ground, although the satrap and the Persian garrison managed to hold out in the acropolis. This early success inspired the other Greeks throughout Ionia, from the Bosporus southwards, to rise up against the Persian yoke, even the island of Cyprus joining in the rebellion. The Great King looked north and saw not only Ionia in flames but his new colony in Thrace cut off and his com-munications with the Black Sea and its settlements in danger.

The efficiency and the strength of the Persian Empire was quick to show itself. Starting from the south, Cyprus was first of all recaptured, its last stronghold capitulating in 496. A year later the fleet of the Ionian confederation was decisively defeated in a battle off the coast near Miletus. This city itself, which had been the main-spring of the revolt, was besieged and destroyed in 494, and the inhabitants – to prevent any further trouble in the area – were deported to the interior of the Persian Empire. In the mopping-up operations that followed, off-shore islands such as Chios and Lesbos were brought under Persian rule. The small Athenian force which had been sent to Ionia had been withdrawn as early as 498, but their action in giving encouragement, if little help, to the Ionians was not forgotten in the court of the king. Athens and Eretria were high on the list of mainland Greek states to be punished in due course.

Mardonius, a nephew and son-in-law of Darius, was the com-mander selected to carry out Darius' designs after the revolt itself had been quenched. He captured the important northern island of Thasos, secured Thrace and accepted the submission of Macedonia. It was clear that these actions were all prior to an invasion of Europe proper. Unfortunately for Mardonius his fleet ran into a violent gale on its way round Mount Athos and a great many ships and their crews were lost on that rocky and inhospitable coast. (This disaster was something that the Persians did not forget and which was why Xerxes took such great care to circumvent it.)

'The expedition returned to Asia after a disastrous campaign,' wrote Herodotus, but he was exaggerating. The northern Aegean coast was completely occupied and the shipbuilding capacity of the Persian Empire was such that in every port not only were the losses made good but also a whole new fleet was being constructed. This was clearly intended for an invasion force, since it included a great many transports designed for carrying horses. Darius was not to be deterred by one attempt against mainland Greece, especially since it had been aborted not by the Greeks but by weather and natural hazards. As evidence of his intentions he sent heralds to demand formal submission from the islands and city-states. All the islands, menaced by the overriding seapower of Persia, submitted, as did most of the mainland states – Athens and Sparta being notable in refusing. Sparta, as has been seen, treated the envoys with contempt and threw them down a well 'to get their earth and water from there'.

When the Persian invasion force sailed for Greece in 490 Mardonius was still incapacitated from a wound received in the previous expedition and his place was taken by Datis, a Mede, who is credited with having evolved a new plan for the attack on Greece. This was to ignore the north and strike directly across the Aegean, securing those outriders of the mainland, the Cyclades islands, and then descending upon Athens and Eretria to punish them for their behaviour during the Ionian revolt. Proceeding from Samos the fleet passed barren Ikaros and fell upon Naxos, where the inhabitants fled before them and took to the hills. Since Naxos was one of the largest islands and renowned for its pride and courage, the destruction of its capital and its easy conquest had an immediate effect upon the other Cyclades. All, within a short time, surrendered to detachments of the Persian fleet. Only sacred Delos, home of Apollo and Artemis, was treated with the greatest respect by Datis. He would not even allow his ships to anchor there and sent word to the Delians, who had taken refuge in nearby Tenos, to return and assist him to pay homage at the great altar of Apollo. The priests of Delos came back to witness the frankincense brought by the Persian general flare and fume before the giant statue of the god Apollo. All this was a very clever piece of politics, for the priests of Apollo and the oracle at Delphi were then, and later, to prove themselves of considerable help to the followers of Zoroaster. It was not difficult to equate the sun-god Ahuramazda with Apollo. Propaganda is not a twentieth-century invention.

Euboea, the long fish-like island that guards the coast of Attica, was the next target, and within six days its city of Eretria was reduced, the inhabitants like those of Miletus being deported into the heart of Persia. The disastrous news from Eretria was carried from Athens to Sparta by a professional runner, Pheidippides, who covered some 140 miles of rough road, goat-track and scree-covered slopes, reaching the unwalled city in the Eurotas plain on the second evening. Unfortunately the Spartans could not march at once. It was the feast of the Carneian Apollo, the most sacred part of a sacred month when no Spartan might go to war. 'When the moon was full', they said (that was in about one week's time), 'their army would march to the assistance of the Athenians.' Some moderns have suggested that this was no more than a cynical ruse to keep the Spartan army for the defence of their homeland. This is to ignore the strict rules and regulations imposed by ancient religious cults. It could, in any case, in no way have availed the Spartans to lose their only powerful ally, and the only one possessing a fleet that could be any defence against the Persians.

Possibly to the surprise of the Athenians, who may have thought that the Persians would land in Phaleron Bay to the south of the city, Datis had decided to disembark his forces at Marathon. It was a sensible choice, for the plain afforded plenty of space for the deployment of his troops, and the fact that it was over twenty-five miles from the city would, in theory, give them time to get the men in order, fed, and ready for action – all very necessary measures after a sea-voyage in the rough and cramped conditions of those days. The most forceful personality among the ten Attic *strategoi* (generals) was Miltiades, and it was he who, in a debate of the Athenian Popular Assembly, prevailed upon the others to march out at once and engage the enemy on Marathon plain. It was a bold decision and contrary to the thinking of many, who would have preferred to wait for the enemy to advance upon the city itself. Athens was already walled at the time, but the decision of Miltiades and the agreement of the Assembly to engage the Persians at

Marathon suggests that it was not sufficiently strong to be able to withstand a well-conducted siege – and they knew what had happened to the cities in Ionia.

The story of the classic battle that followed has been often told, has inspired poets, and has passed enduring into the history of the western world. Among those who took part in the battle was Aeschylus, one of the greatest poets and dramatists of all time, whose brother was killed at Marathon. The battle itself has no part here, except in so far as the defeat of the Persians led to the later meticulously planned expedition of Xerxes – designed to wipe out for ever the memory of that fateful day in mid-August 490. Better arms and better training gave the 10,000 Athenians and their allies, the 600 or so Plataeans, a victory over a much larger army – but one which, it must be remembered, had been under the ugly conditions of shipboard for some time. It was in fact the hoplites, the heavily armoured Greek foot-soldiers who established a dominance over the archers, lighter-armed men, and a number of hastily deployed cavalry (the horses, again, not at their best after a sea voyage). Less than 200 Athenians had fallen, but the Persian dead, which were carefully counted, numbered 6400.

To the Greeks this was an amazing figure, and indeed the disparity in losses remains remarkable. To the Persians, however, it was comparatively insignificant. The greater part of their army was re-embarked aboard their ships, out of which, although exposed on a hostile shore, only seven were lost. In the Greco-Persian wars it is always important to remember that the available manpower of the two principal Greek states, Athens and Sparta, must be numbered in only a few thousands. The Persians, however, as the campaign of Xerxes was to show, could count on forces running into hundreds of thousands. A hundred dead fighting men was a more serious loss to the Greeks than several thousand to the Persians and their allies. (The situation was very similar in these terms to that of the Israelis versus the Arab states in recent years.)

Worsted at Marathon, the Persians still had no intention of conceding defeat. Rounding the southern tip of Attica, their fleet made for the Bay of Phaleron where the Greeks had originally expected them to land. Miltiades had anticipated this secondary move and – just as he had brought his troops so rapidly from Athens to Marathon, 'running to the battle-cry', – he now led them back at a similar pace. Nothing can better attest to the fitness, discipline and physical endurance of the Attic hoplites than their advance to Marathon, their triumph over a far larger enemy force, and then their immediate return to confront the enemy. When the Persian fleet appeared off Phaleron Bay they found the victors of Marathon drawn up in order and ready to receive them. They were not about to beach their ships and disembark in the face of those grim, visored men, their long spears a thicket of death, and their bronze shields and corselets gleaming in the triumphant sun of Greece. Datis turned the fleet about and made sail for Asia.

Three days after the full moon, the Spartans, in a notable feat of forced marching, arrived at Athens – possibly on the very same day that Datis had withdrawn. The Spartans open-heartedly congratulated the Athenians on their victory, and then 'desired to see the Medes'. They went out to the battlefield at Marathon and viewed the dead. The Spartans had never engaged the Persians, and no doubt they wanted to inspect the quality of their arms and armour. They must have suspected (as indeed did the Athenians themselves) that this was not the last that the mainland Greeks would be hearing of the Persians.

Marathon was, indeed, a victory of the greatest significance for all of Greece. It had strengthened the resolution of Athenians and Spartans alike; it had proved the superiority of the hoplite over the Persian foot soldier; and it had confirmed the authority of Greek leadership. (The news that the Spartans were on the march, which almost certainly must have reached Datis via his scout-ships to the south, may well have hastened his retreat.) While the Greeks everywhere rejoiced, and while Marathon assumed for all time in their history the same mystique as Waterloo in that of Britain, the Persians had time to ponder over the campaign. They had lost a battle, but they had not lost the war. Their defeat at Marathon was to lead to the infinitely careful war-plan of Darius' successor, Xerxes, and the studied preparation of an immense army and fleet designed for the conquest of Greece and of all Europe that lay beyond. In the workshops of Persia, on the slipways of the East, and out of the almost inexhaustible manpower of the empire, would be forged the hammer to crack the small stone of mountainous Greece.

4

THE ATHENIANS

THE ATHENIANS, who had saved all Greece at Marathon, were for the moment, and very understandably, imbued with optimism. They, and they alone (although they never forgot the heroic contribution of the little city of Plataea), had been successful in routing the awesome Persians; the conquerors of Ionian Greece and most of the Aegean islands; the army and the navy which had hitherto been considered invincible. This heady triumph was to prove of immense value to their morale when, in due course, the Persian Empire under the direction of Xerxes returned for the second round. To Athenians their triumph seemed all the greater because it had been achieved on land rather than their familiar environment, the sea. It was Attic hoplites who had defeated the Persians without any help from Sparta – normally considered the masters of land warfare.

The hero of the hour was inevitably Miltiades, whose policy of marching out from the city and engaging the enemy at Marathon had been amply justified. It was natural under the circumstances that considerable attention should be paid to his advice as to the further conduct of Athenian policy. The islands of the Cyclades lying like a circling shield to the south were, he pointed out, essential to the defence of Athens. All of them were now under Persian control, representing a dangerous threat to the Greek mainland and, above all, to the shipping routes of the Aegean. 'Attack at once!' was his advice, to reinforce the security which Marathon had, for the moment, given them. This was strategically very sensible but there were many who did not approve of the venture, not least because they sensed in Miltiades a potential tyrant. The cost of such an expedition was also a deterrent, but this objection was overruled when Miltiades more or less guaranteed that he would make it pay its way by exacting indemnities from the islands which had medised. Herodotus casts a bad reflection on the motives of Miltiades, implying that it was no more than personal ambition which drove him to propose the Cycladic expedition. This seems highly unlikely, and the judgement of the historian stems most probably from hindsight – from the fact that the whole affair proved a costly failure. In the siege of Paros, the primary objective (for it was felt that if Paros, one of the richest and most important islands, was captured, then most of the others would automatically yield to Athens), Miltiades himself was seriously wounded. The fleet returned to Athens and the enemies of Miltiades seized their opportunity. He was accused of 'deceiving the people', and the death sentence was demanded. Marathon, however, and the part that Miltiades had played in that brilliant campaign, could not easily be forgotten. Miltiades himself died from gangrene, but not before he was sentenced to pay the large sum of fifty talents – a fine which left his son financially ruined. Athenian politics was always ruthless.

Ultimately they were to prove no less harsh in the career of the man who became Miltiades' successor – perhaps the greatest Greek politician who ever lived, and the man who was destined to save Greece from the far greater threat that was posed by Xerxes. This was Themistocles, who was to become the most prominent figure in Athenian political affairs during the years in which the fate of Europe was decided. He was unpopular with many of his fellow citizens, particularly those of the conservative caste of mind, for he was a radical, who saw far in advance of his other educated contemporaries that the future of a city-seaport like Athens lay in her navy and, therefore, in the men who commanded and manned her ships. This was a policy that was unlikely to prove palatable to the richer, land-owning classes, for it was they who would have to foot a large part of the bill for the ship-building, victualling, and maintenance. The armoured knight, or hoplite, who had seen the victory of his class at Marathon, was hardly likely to be sympathetic towards a policy that favoured sailors and oarsmen who, even though they might indeed be free citizens of Athens, were a long remove from the great families like the Alcmaeonids and the Peisistradids.

The picture that one gains of Themistocles from most Greek historians, including Herodotus and Plutarch, is of a conniving and self-seeking man who was always concerned with his own interests and was even ready to do a deal with the Persians at the moment of Greece's greatest peril. As a Greek and an Athenian, it was unlikely that Themistocles did not have some degree of self-interest at heart: he would have been totally unlike his race if he had not. But even Plutarch, who accused him of 'malignity', and in any case was writing long after the events, was forced to admit that a bust-portrait which he had seen of him showed a man who appeared to be noble and heroic. (A copy of this portrait made in Roman times shows a thick-necked, rather flat-faced man, with a large sensitive mouth and an open-eyed 'bulldog' appearance. Except for the beard and the moustache, Themistocles has a Churchillian aspect.) Thucydides, one of the greatest and most impartial historians of all times, described him in the following terms:

Themistocles was a man who most clearly presents the pheno-menon of natural genius . . . to a quite extraordinary and except-ional degree. By sheer personal intelligence, without either previous study or special briefing, he showed both the best grasp of an emergency situation at the shortest notice, and the most far-reaching appreciation of probable further developments. He was good at explaining what he had in hand; and even of things outside his previous experience he did not fail to form a shrewd judgement. No man so well foresaw the advantages and dis-advantages of a course in the still uncertain future. In short, by natural power and speed in reflection, he was the best of all men at determining promptly what had to be done.

Had he lived in the twentieth century he might have been a Greek guerilla-leader in the Second World War, a ship-owner subse-quently, and then – possibly – Prime Minister. In any case, he would finally have been banished, exiled, or assassinated. The Greeks, the only people in history who have made four major contributions to human culture and civilisation (the spring of Minoan Crete, the summer of fifth-century Athens, the golden autumn of the Alexandrian empire, and the wintry splendour of Byzantium), have so competitive a spirit that they cannot tolerate for long the exceptional brilliance of one man. Nevertheless, it was Themistocles above all others who was to give the lead to his people and to other Greeks in the struggle that was soon to be renewed against Europe by Persia.

Themistocles was not slow to see (like the maligned Miltiades before him) that a powerful navy was essential for the salvation of Greece. Fine though the Attic hoplites had proved to be at Marathon, outstanding the warriors of Sparta, the strange and rocky land of Greece with its small population could never compete in the long run with the immense manpower of the Persian Empire. Bravery, superior technology, the 'last ditch' attitude of men who are defending their homeland against a foreign invader – these were qualities that the Greeks possessed in plenty. But their enemy was numbered 'as the sands of the sea'. Furthermore, the Phoenician and Egyptian navies, as well as the ships of Cyprus, Ionia, and most of the Aegean islands, far outnumbered the Athenian navy and its allies. It seemed that Greece, and Athens in particular, could only be saved by a miracle: something in which the pragmatic Greeks, unlike the Hebrews, found it difficult to believe.

The miracle occurred, although in no spiritual form, but in the discovery of a rich vein of silver in the mining area of Laurium near Cape Sunium in 483. The mines were all state-owned and, under normal conditions, the profits from them were shared out among the citizens. The unexpected windfall of the new seam, which would have given every citizen about ten drachmas (a small sum), was diverted by the persuasive powers of Themistocles into building one hundred triremes – a new type of three-banked warship which would for some years give the Greeks command of most of the Mediterranean. It is evidence that the hard-headed Assembly whom Themistocles had to convince were sensible enough of the impending threat to Greece to be prepared to divert the 'silver windfall' from their own pockets and those of their fellow citizens into such a vast expenditure on defence.

Since the name of Athens herself, as well as of the far-sighted Themistocles, will always be associated with the word 'trireme', and its importance in the forthcoming Persian invasion would affect the whole issue, the vessel and its crew are dealt with separately. For the moment, however, what mattered was that the brilliance of Themistocles and the intelligence of the Athenian Assembly led to the construction of a great new fleet. Themistocles had an additional argument with which to convince those in the

Assembly who were sceptical of a further Persian invasion, and therefore demurred at such an expenditure of money. He could point across the water at Athens' ancient enemy, the island of Aegina, and remind them that the Aeginetans were hostile as ever to Athens and that their navy was even larger.

5

THE SPARTANS

THE SPARTANS were something of an enigma even to their fellow Greeks. They formed the most powerful state in the Peloponnese, and later in all of Greece. Their capital Sparta was situated at the northern end of the central Laconian plain on the River Eurotas. It commanded the only land-routes into Laconia as well as the two principal valleys from Arcadia to the north and the main pass over Mount Taygetus leading to Messenia. Tradition has it that the city was founded by Lacedaemon, a son of the god Zeus. Unlike the Ionian Greeks, however, including the Athenians, the Spartans came of a different branch of the Greek stock known as Dorians, who had invaded the Peloponnese in waves about 1000 B.C., dividing into several branches, one of which pushed on south down the Eurotas valley to found their capital at the point south of the junction of the Eurotas river with the Oenus. Thus was Sparta born.

The language of these Dorians was Greek like that of the Ionians, but with some differences, including a broader accent. The nation that was to become known as Lacedaemonia or Sparta (after two place-names) settled the fertile hill-girt plain which had been described earlier by Homer as 'hollow Lacedaemon'. Of a different temperament to the Ionians in many respects, being less lively and considerably less individualistic, they were destined to evolve a strange and austere state-system unlike that of other Greeks and, indeed, unlike almost any other that has followed in human history. Notwithstanding this, the Spartan values and disciplines were to arouse the admiration of a number of later Greek philosophers for the very reason that they were so different from the anarchy that so often prevailed in other Greek states.

The expansion of Sparta entailed securing the upper Eurotas valley, then the land to the south, and ultimately the whole of

Laconia. This inevitably brought them into conflict with the ancient city of Argos whose territory had included the whole of the eastern coast of the Peloponnese and the island of Cythera. The Argives, formidable though their history was, were driven back. They were never to forgive or forget and, as their conduct would later show during the Persian invasion of Greece, they were prepared to stand aside and even come to terms with the Persians rather than fight together with, let alone under, Spartan command. By the middle of the sixth century B.C., after a series of other local wars, some fought with savage intensity, the Spartans had come to be recognised as the foremost state in all Greece and the bulwark of Hellenism.

From the very start, having conquered the native peoples of the Eurotas valley, the Spartans, unlike most other Greeks, do not seem to have intermingled with the subject people, not intermarrying, and holding themselves curiously aloof, except in their role as masters. In this very beginning lay the seeds of their future state. Some Greek writers, Herodotus among them, thought that the institutions of Sparta derived from those of the Dorian city-states to be found in Crete. Plutarch and others were also of this opinion. It seems perhaps more likely that a similarity of structure was due to common racial origins and a shared outlook.

At the head of the rigidly stratified society which evolved in Sparta there were at the top the Dorian conquerors, the 'Spartiates'. They formed, as it were, 'The Master-Race'. They were the only people to have the vote, and they lived in military messes in the capital. Below them came the *Perioikoi* or Neighbours – free men who marched and fought along with the Spartiates, but did not have voting rights. The third stratum of the society was formed by the Helots. These, who may well have been descendants of the indigenous inhabitants, worked on the farms that belonged to the Spartiates. They were not slaves in the classical sense of the word but cultivated the land and gave half their produce to the Spartiate citizens. That they were a proud, even if subject, people is shown by the fact that the Spartiates had to keep a close eye on them and be on their guard against a Helot uprising. Nevertheless many of them fought at Thermopylae and again at Plataea. Long after the campaign of Xerxes there was, indeed, a big Helot revolt (which the Spartans put down ferociously), but at the time that Greece was in such danger relations between the rulers and the ruled seem to have been basically amicable. But the threat, however veiled, was always there, and for this reason and because of the other conquered people around them the Spartans had always to keep a proportion of their army at home. They could never field all their fighting manpower.

Something else which made the Spartans an inward-looking warrior-race was that, being a land-power, they did not, like the other Greek city-states, solve population problems by sending out emigrant ships to the new-found lands of Sicily and Italy. It was true that Sparta had done so in a few cases, most noticeably Tarentum (Taranto). But their real solution was war, as when they turned on their next-door, western neighbour of Messenia and, after two long and bitter wars, finally annexed the land and enslaved the population. This gave them a further problem: quite apart from the Helots, and the other conquered lands, they now had the hatred of the Messenians to deal with. The conclusion must be that, apart from any inborn qualities, they became a warrior-race largely because it was essential for them. (Grundy calculated that the proportion of Free to Non-Free in the Spartan state was 1:15.) To maintain a ruling class out of such a disproportionate relationship meant that the citizen of Sparta, the Spartiate, must of necessity have made himself so hard and fine a soldier that his efficiency outweighed the balance.

As the poems of Alcman (*circa* the mid-seventh century B.C.) reveal, there had been an earlier Sparta. It had been aristocratic, certainly, but far from the Sparta that we hear of later, and which figured so prominently in the fight against the Persians some two centuries later. Even then, it must be noted that Alcman was a foreigner, and there was only one Spartan poet of whose work a little is known and that consists of injunctions to the warrior – martial poems set to music in fact. It seems that the wars against their neighbours eliminated a Sparta which, although not much of a producer of fine pottery and artefacts, certainly imported them from other Greek states.

The famous discipline of the Spartan warrior caste was attributed to Lycurgus and the laws he impressed upon these people. Nothing is known about him as a man, and even in classical times speculation existed as to whether he was a man, a myth, or a god. The fact remains that some two centuries or more before the Persian invasions the Spartans had adopted their iron code of rules which set them apart from all other men. For one thing, no Spartiate was permitted to own gold or silver. They were compelled to turn their back upon coinage, which was to open up all the trade throughout the East and the Mediterranean basin. No silver coins were even issued until two centuries later than the Persian wars. Such metal for transactions as was required was cast in iron spits – certainly an unwieldy commodity and, in any case, no Spartiate was allowed to engage in trade.

These same laws also forbade him from indulging in agriculture, craft, or indeed in any kind of profession – except that of arms. Many military castes over the centuries have despised the tradesman or the artisan, but none has ever carried it to the same level as Lycurgus demanded of the Spartiate. To ensure that this Master Race maintained its sound stock each child was examined shortly after birth by the Elders, the seniors of the city. They either passed it as suitably fit and strong or, if it was reckoned at all weakly, they had it exposed or thrown over a cliff. At seven or eight years of age boys were taken from their mothers and were enrolled in a group of their year. It is not clear whether at this age he still lived at home but, in any case, he now came under the discipline and control of a senior Spartiate. Similarly, at thirteen he was transferred to yet another group under similar control, but presided over by a magistrate. Their whole life was devoted to the state. (Except for this latter qualification, or the incredible harshness of their lives, it is not difficult to feel that something of the Spartan system had been ingested by the classically educated headmasters who helped form Britain's nineteenth-century public schools.)

The boys slept in dormitories on rush-beds, rushes they had to cut without the aid of a knife – presumably on the banks of the Eurotas. Their rations were kept to the minimum, so much so that it was expected that they would steal food to supplement them but, if caught, they were severely punished. From the very beginning, it can be seen that those qualities required in a soldier – cunning, audacity and just plain 'scrounging' – were encouraged. As might be expected, their training was largely designed to toughen their bodies; so the military arts were taught; drill, weapon-training, and of course athletics. Other forms of education were not, however, entirely neglected and A. H. M. Jones writes in his book *Sparta*: '. . . there was singing of traditional songs, and no doubt Home and the Spartan poets were read'. One suspects that it was the battle-scenes of the *Iliad* rather than the wanderings of the wily Odysseus that engaged their attention. One aspect of education that amazed other Greeks was that, apart from the military side, girls received a very similar training. Greeks were well enough used to seeing men appearing naked in running races or wrestling, but the sight of young females doing so both amazed and disgusted them. Their own women, whether in Corinth, Athens or elsewhere, were kept very much in the tradition of the East and rarely seen outside the home.

Very few Greeks from other states knew much about everyday life in Sparta, nor indeed much about Sparta at all. The little they heard seemed to them almost incomprehensible and unattractive. Outsiders were not encouraged, in any case, and for the slightest transgression were summarily sent beyond the Spartan borders. (It is not difficult to think of modern parallels in this respect.) What little we do know about the Spartan state is very important in order to understand something of the nature of the men and the constitution that lay behind them. They were prepared to fight to the last against all their enemies: even against the apparently limitless hordes of 'The King with half the East at heels'.

Although at a later date the constitution gradually changed it always remained conservative. H. D. F. Kitto in *The Greeks* has succinctly summarised it:

> There were two kings – reminiscent of the two equal consuls in the Roman Republic. The origin was probably different, but the desired effect was the same: in each case the duality was a check on autocracy. At home the kings were overshadowed by the Ephors ('Overseers'), five annual magistrates chosen more or less by ballot: but a Spartan army abroad was always commanded by one of the kings, who then had absolute powers.

Aristotle describes the kingship at Sparta as a 'kind of unlimited and perpetual generalship'. Kitto continues: 'There was also a Senate, and there was an Assembly, but the Assembly could not debate, and it expressed its decisions – to the amusement of other

Greeks – not by voting but by shouting: the loudest shout carried the day.'

This astonishing compendium of almost every kind of government from monarchy, aristocracy, oligarchy to democracy was quite unique. Other Greeks, who were always engaged in trying out one or other system, usually with great bitterness and bloodshed, just could not understand how such a ramshackle affair could work. The fact is that it did; one reason, perhaps, why a number of Greek writers and philosophers admired these strange soldiers of the Eurotas valley. Some of their other characteristics appealed to them far less: their strict religious celebrations, as binding as their military discipline, which led them to be late for the battle of Marathon, only to send a comparative handful of men to Thermopylae. Their religious conceptions, some possibly deriving from old beliefs of the indigenous natives and others brought with them from the various invasions of centuries before, seemed strange indeed to the citizens of Athens. Some indeed were primitive and cruel. One of these was a test for manhood, in which boys had to run the gauntlet to try to steal cheeses from the altar of Artemis Orthia (a very ancient image of Artemis, possibly a wooden statue, and a far remove from the Artemis of later Greeks). As both Plutarch and Pausanias record, during this ritual some of the boys literally died from the beating they received.

When a Spartiate became eligible for one of the clubs or dining messes, at the age of twenty, he had become a fully fledged citizen-warrior. These clubs carried the same distinctions as those of later centuries, some having more *kudos* than others, and the equivalent to one blackball precluding entry. The food in all of them would seem to have been equally monotonous and unattractive, consisting of the 'famous' Spartan black broth, barley bread, a limited ration of wine (no treating), and dessert of figs or cheese. The food was cooked by Helots or slaves. It is recorded that a visiting Greek with a palate for food was once entertained at a Spartan mess and remarked afterwards: 'Now I understand why the Spartans do not fear death.' The two kings were each members of a mess, the only difference being that they received double rations – but only if they attended the mess. Spartan eating habits, like almost everything else, derived from the austere laws of Lycurgus which taught a contempt for pleasure. Based on the theory that the men must be prepared for war at any time and the exigencies of campaign food, they must not be allowed to grow soft or self-indulgent at any time. It is easy to scoff, as many other Greeks did, at the wintry hardness of the Spartan manner of life, but there was another effect which all this discipline produced – not only superlative warriors but excellent-mannered citizens. This began in early youth when all young men were taught to walk through the streets of the city with their eyes down-cast out of respect for any citizen they might pass on the way. The old were revered, the women respected, and the young warriors admired.

While the Greeks of other states were (not unlike the Greeks of today) immensely volatile, individualistic to the point of anarchy, and imbued with the feeling that it was every man for himself, the Spartans were famous for their ordered behaviour. A good illustration of this is given in a tale told by Plutarch. In the crowded throng at the Olympic games an old man was looking in vain for a seat from which to watch the events. His stumbling attempts to find one were noticed by many Greeks from other states, who mocked him for his age and fruitless endeavours. When, however, he came to the section where the Spartans were seated, every man among them rose to his feet and offered him their seats. Somewhat abashed, but nevertheless admiringly, the other Greeks applauded them for their behaviour. 'Ah', the old man is reported to have said with a sigh, 'I see what it is – all Greeks *know* what is right, but only the Spartans do it.'

Spartan marriage customs fascinated other Greeks, who knew so little about them anyway. There was even the tale that there had to be a symbolic rape and that, not until a child was conceived or even born, was the marriage considered consummated. In fact, in sexual matters, the Spartans, true to their conservative outlook in every-thing, seem to have had the highest rate of monogamy in all Greece. They undoubtedly had a high respect for their women and regarded them as having a greater equality than the Oriental approach to be found in Ionia, Athens, or Corinth. Also, contrary to the attitude that might have been expected among a warrior caste, homosexuality seems to have been little known – quite unlike the Thebans in northern Greece who were to make a cult among their soldiers of couples fighting side by side together, as in the famous 'Theban Band of Lovers'. The only exception to this monogamous rule would seem to have occurred where a man was perhaps too old or otherwise incapable of fathering children. In this case a woman was permitted to have sexual relations with a man chosen by her husband and, if children ensued, they probably took the husband's name. In general, the young women, receiving much the same education as the youths, probably shared a life with their men far closer than did those of Athens.

Despite the fact that all Spartiates were supposed to be equals there can be no doubt that, although they received the same training and lived and fought together, some were, in Orwell's words, 'more equal than others'. Some had big farms and an equivalent amount of Helots to work them, some much smaller farms, and others had hardly enough money to pay their mess bills. From early days an attempt had been made to equalise the size of pro-perties, but it was in the nature of man that lands should pass by bequest or gift and some landowners in the period after the Persian wars became extremely rich. A. H. M. Jones has the following comment upon the subject in *Sparta*: 'The common education, however, and the common meals produced a genuine equality, and poor and obscure Spartiates could readily rise by merit. Lysander of noble – indeed Heraclid blood – descent, but too poor to pay his own school fees, rose to be the leader of the Spartan state. . . .' On the other hand, through sickness or other deprivation, some Spartiates inevitably reached the point where they could no longer pay their way and relapsed into the position of 'non-citizens'. The exclusive nature required of being a pure Spartiate meant that, although there were probably 8000 Spartiate adult males at the time of Xerxes' invasion, within about one hundred years, in the time of Aristotle, they had sunk to 1000.

Despite this decline, the Spartans still excited the admiration of Xenophon, who was also writing at some distance in time from the same events. In his somewhat incomplete account, which does not tell us as much as we would like to know, it is nevertheless evident that he found a society that was little changed since the time of Leonidas. He comments upon the difference between the education of the Spartan youth and the youth of other Greek states:

In the other Greek states parents who want to give their sons the best education place them under the care and control of a moral tutor as soon as they are old enough to learn. They send them to a school to learn letters, music, and the exercise of the wrestling ground. Moreover, they soften the children's feet by giving them sandals, and pamper their bodies with changes of clothing. It is also customary to allow them to eat as much food as they can.

Xenophon then goes on to describe the training of the Spartan youth which, as has been seen, was the complete reverse side of the coin. However, some were able to see both sides and an anecdote about Diogenes, the great Cynic philosopher, living some seventy years after the invasion of Xerxes, illustrates this. On one occasion at Olympia he was asked what he thought of some extravagantly dressed young men who were passing by, and replied: 'Mere affectation!' A little later, his attention being drawn to some young Spartans in their torn and threadbare garments, he snorted: 'More affectation!' Yet Diogenes' own outlook on life, one suspects, was more akin to that of the Spartans than to that of the well-dressed pleasure-lovers.

Some thirty-six years after the death of Leonidas, King Agesilaus of Sparta, as Plutarch recounts, showed that the essential Spartan spirit, which distinguished her citizens from all others in Greece, still had not changed. At that time there was a war between a coalition led by Athens against Sparta and her allies. The latter had been complaining to Agesilaus that it was they who provided the bulk of the army. Agesilaus, accordingly, called a council meeting at which all the Spartan allies sat down on one side and the Spartans on the other. The king then told a herald to proclaim that all the potters among the allies and the Spartans should stand up. After this the herald called on the blacksmiths, the masons, and the carpenters to do likewise; and so he went on through all the crafts and trades. By the end of the herald's recital almost every single man among the allies had risen to his feet. But not a Spartan had moved. The laws of Lycurgus still obtained. The king laughed and turned to his allies, remarking: 'You see, my friends, how many more soldiers we send out than you do.'

The whole Spartan attitude is contained in those words.

ARMS AND THE MAN

THE STORY OF XERXES' INVASION of Greece, the story of its ultimate failure, cannot be understood without relating it to the arms borne by the opposing sides. Technology, sometimes neglected in accounts of early history, played its inevitable part. The modern military historian, whether of the First or Second World War, hardly omits from his narrative such things as the development of the tank, radar, sonar, the fighter or bomber aircraft, the submarine, or the torpedo – to mention but a limited number of the devices with which one side achieved ascendancy over the other. To some extent the same was true of ancient wars.

No scientific analyst of warfare had yet appeared upon the human scene; there was no Clausewitz, and even Thucydides was long unborn. Wars could still be conditioned by ceremonials, and religious rites, such as the Spartans' unwillingness to march at the time of a lunar festival. Over and over again in ancient history the modern reader is amazed to see how opportunities could be thrown away, or avenues of initiative left unexplored, because of some custom or religious taboo. We do not think like our distant ancestors. Nothing is going to prevent a modern army from advancing because it is the full of the moon – except that it might be inconvenient in a practical sense, whereas a murky night would be preferable.

The Greeks' superiority in their arms was due not only to their more advanced technology but also to the fact that the type of warfare that had evolved amongst them had produced the heavily armoured hoplite. When one city-state engaged another, the crucial battle would usually be fought on a plain by citizen-soldiers. The enormous army of the Persians, culled from all quarters of the empire, embraced every form of weapon from the almost neolithic weapons of the Ethiopians to the comparatively sophisticated arms and armour of the Persian Immortals. The typical Greek army, curiously enough, was composed of a force which could only be effective in one fifth of the area of Greece. It may seem surprising that Greece, a country – as later generations have discovered – so suitable to guerrilla warfare, with lightly armed men holding down whole areas where heavy troops cannot move, adopted the set-piece battle somewhat akin to that of the Middle Ages and even later. The psychology which led to this type of warfare being the accepted norm probably derives from Homeric days where, as also in the chronicles of the Jews (with the notable exception of David and Goliath), armoured champions met one another in single combat with the opposing armies looking on. The mixed engagement between the armoured forces of both sides came later.

The Persians, too, came from a mountainous country, but even Xerxes' spies and Greek collaborators can hardly have prepared him, or his army, for the real nature of the country he was about to invade. 'Those who know the slopes of the limestone hills of north Derbyshire,' wrote G. B. Grundy,

will be able to appreciate to some extent the nature of the slopes of the Greek mountains. But they cannot realise it. The ruggedness is accentuated to an enormous extent by the effects of a climate which is almost rainless for two-thirds of the year, but for the remaining four months is liable to torrential rainstorms which sweep everything before them, and carry away from the hill-sides the earth which has been cracked and disintegrated by the intense heat of the summer season. . . . The rocks are closely set together. All are pointed and sharp. There is no soft vegetation on which to tread. What vegetation there is consists for the most part of low scrub some twelve to eighteen inches high, of which much is of a thorny character, and whose marked characteristic is that it will, when the wayfarer is making his way through it, support his foot at that moment in the step when support is most inconvenient, and let it through with an unexpected suddenness which is equally inconvenient and upsetting. Passage up, down, or along a Greek hill-side is a severe labour even for a man in light marching order, and cannot be maintained for any length of time under a Greek sun, unless the traveller follow the narrow goat tracks. This state of things, bad as it is, is sometimes complicated by the fact that the hill-sides are covered by thick bush, as, for instance, above Thermopylae, some ten feet high.

The narrow pass below the Hot Gates of the sulphur springs was a natural choice for men to stand and fight a battle in heavy armour.

The hoplite force, against which Xerxes was to throw the flower of his army, relied on two basic qualities, solidity and weight. The Spartans and their allies stood in a close, almost unbroken, wall of armour, the shield being held on the left arm, and each man protecting the right side of his neighbour. The hoplites thus presented a line of shields and breast-plates to the advancing enemy. Under normal circumstances, which did not apply at Thermopylae, the right-hand side was naturally the weak point, so the best troops were always put in this position of trust and honour. Thermopylae, however, was an ideal situation for a hoplite battle because this weak side was guarded by the sea.

In the battle that was to follow, the force under Leonidas stood firm in the opening phase. There was no need for them to do other than stand like a rock, and let the seemingly inexhaustible waves of the enemy break themselves to pieces on their spears and shields. Later, when advancing troops turned and ran, the Spartans adopted other tactics. They advanced at a slow step, and then broke into the rapid march, hardly a run but more like the slow determined movement of a rugby pack. This was part of their highly disciplined training and it was to enable them to dominate the battlefields of Greece. The same fifes that led them to war were also used to give orders during battle itself and – although we have no knowledge of the musical notation – it is attested by Thucydides that strict control of army movements was ensured by various notes of the fifes.

Although not so complete as that of the medieval knight, the armour of the hoplite was extremely heavy; far more so than that of most of his later successors on the battlefields of the world. The helmet in general use was of the type known as Corinthian, named after the city which is credited with having first developed it. In earlier days it had been made out of bronze and was beaten out of a single sheet of metal. The whole of the head, including the collarbone (so vulnerable to a sweeping sword-cut) was completely covered. The cheeks were also guarded by an extension of the lower rim of the helmet which left only a narrow slit, shaped like a T, for the eyes and nose. To protect the head from bruising or concussion there was an inner lining which was secured to the bronze or iron by leather laces that passed through a series of holes in the helmet. A legacy from the past was the horse-hair crest which ran along the line of the crown and was often made to seem even more formidable by being given a forward tilt. To beat a complete helmet out of a single piece of iron was a highly developed skill, requiring many hours of patience and expertise. Indeed, as with the 'lost art' of granulated gold, perfected by the Etruscans, it is doubtful if many modern workers in metal could achieve the perfection and the resilience of the Greek Corinthian helmet.

The principal parts of the body, the shoulders and trunk, were protected by a composite corselet. This consisted of two shoulder-pieces (again as a protection against the overhand cut of a sword or the descent of a spear or arrow) which were laced together at the chest. Chest and stomach were covered by one or two sheets of leather which extended down below the waist. This flap was usually, though not invariably, covered by oblong metal scales made of bronze. A number of vase paintings show Greek warriors arming for the fight in this style of corselet, but it would seem likely that in this case the Greeks had borrowed from their eastern enemies. A very similar type of body protection was worn by the Persians.

Another type of corselet, which it is possible that some of the Greeks wore at this period (armour, as in later centuries, may have passed down from father to son), resembled a bell. This consisted of two bronze plates, covering front and back, and laced together down the sides. Somewhat like the ceremonial armour to be found as late as Renaissance Europe, it was moulded to fit the torso and often carefully modelled to reproduce the shape of the chest and stomach. Below this hung a leather kilt to which were stitched protective oval or palm-leaf-shaped pieces of bronze similar to those in the more usual protective body-armour.

The other and indeed the main form of protection for the Greek hoplite was the shield. This had evolved from a crescent or round shield carried in earlier days (and still used by lightly armed troops) known as the *pelta*. Whereas this shield usually had a wickerwork base and was covered with leather, the hoplite's shield was wood covered with bronze. In order to give the arm a firm grasp there was an arm-band (*porpax*) in the centre, through which the hand and arm were passed, the hand grasping a stout cord just inside the rim. This cord was separately knotted at about half a dozen stud points. If a cord should break, the hoplite could shift his hand around and obtain a further grip upon the next corded section. It was from this great round shield known as a *hoplon* that the Greek hoplites took their name. An average diameter of a shield was about three feet, although, to judge from one example (four feet across), shields, like the armour itself, were made to individual specifications. The outer cover of the shield, and almost invariably the rim, was made of bronze, wood only forming the base.

In Homeric and indeed much later days, the armoured warrior would have his personal blazon or device upon his shield. If the shield was primarily wooden, then this was attached in bronze to the wooden facing. Later on, this was engraved upon the bronze covering itself. As individual hand-to-hand combat declined and men became marshalled into organised and disciplined units, it was no longer necessary to know the personal identity of your opponent. Sparta (Lacedaemon) had forgone the self-aggrandisement of the personal 'hallmark' by the fifth century. What the troops of Xerxes would have seen as they approached the armoured Spartiates in the pass of Thermopylae was a row of almost identical round shields each bearing the same sign, the Greek Λ (Lambda or L) standing for their state Lacedaemon. In this way, the Spartans with their disciplined unity foreshadowed the organised regiments of later centuries.

In the first stages of any encounter the primary weapon of the hoplite was his spear. The shaft was either of ash or olive, and the typical spear used by the hoplite was about six feet long. It was not a javelin to be hurled, but was designed to form, like the Swiss pike of later centuries, a formidable fence against which the enemy would tear themselves to pieces. Bronze spear-heads have been found dating from as late as the fifth century, but the majority undoubtedly favoured the more efficient iron tip. Early vase paintings show hoplites armed with two spears but, by the time of Xerxes' invasion, it would seem that one long spear was the principal equipment of the hoplite. The Spartan poet Tyrtaeus describes a typical battle-line such as the Persians were to encounter at

Thermopylae: 'Standing foot to foot, shield pressed on shield, crest to crest and helmet to helmet, chest to chest engage your man, grasping your sword-hilt or long spear.'

The long iron sword, which had survived from the distant past, was still in use. Like the slashing sword of the Normans, this was a two-edged weapon. By the time of the Persian wars, however, a new type of sword had begun to emerge, one-edged, and designed for a cutting stroke. Although the heavy two-edged sword with its cruciform handguard and swelling blade still existed, it was gradually superseded by the smaller cutting weapon. For the hoplite, whose left arm was engaged in holding his shield, the shorter sword with a slightly curved blade (somewhat similar to a Gurkha *kukri*) was far more efficient. It seems very probable that the Greeks had adopted this from the Persians or other Eastern peoples. Snodgrass in *Arms and Armour of the Greeks* describes it as follows:

> Both the cutting edge and the back were convex, weighting the weapon heavily towards the tip; the hilt had a handguard and pommel which projected on the cutting side only, and was frequently shaped like a sitting bird with the head serving as a pommel. . . . Harmodius struck down the tyrant Hipparchus in 514 B.C. with a sword of this type, and with its characteristic overhand stroke.

Although there is no definite proof, for bodies do not necessarily lie where the arms are found, it can be accepted that most of the armoured men who fought under Leonidas used a sword of this type. Spears would finally break, or be cut to pieces by advancing enemy swordsmen, but in the final stage of battle (although Thermopylae must be considered as having gone beyond what that was normally considered to be) it was the curved and relatively short cutting sword which held the line until the end of things.

Curiously enough, the Greeks had never regarded the bow and arrow as an important weapon in warfare. This seems strange, for clearly this very early method of killing beasts or men was a most efficient weapon. The bow is not very difficult to make, and even in a land where suitable wood is not easily available there was sufficient in Greece to make the 'self' bow, which is formed out of one piece of wood. In the Near and Middle East, on the other hand, the bow had long been established as the principal weapon for hunting and for warfare. Out of the Black Sea area of Asia there had arrived waves of invaders, horsemen who were skilled in the use of a short man-made bow. This was the famous and classic 'Cupid's Bow', which has passed into literature and painting. When this bow was strung, but not drawn, it was kept, together with the arrows, in a special bow-case that hung over the archer's back. This was the bow used by the famous Scythian horsemen which discharged arrow-shafts little more than eighteen inches long. The most efficient weapon that the Eastern peoples possessed in the war against the Greeks was the composite bow. This had originated in Asia, and was made out of strips of animal horn which were set into a wooden stave. Dried sinew was carefully flexed around the completed bow and the result was an easily portable weapon that suited horsemen and lightly clad troops. (As late as the Crusades, Arab horsemen with this traditional type of bow were to cause havoc among the armoured European knights.)

While the Greeks, quite apart from their corselets, wore greaves, carefully moulded to fit their wearer's legs to protect them against a slashing blow under their shields, the Persians wore comparatively little armour. Although a warlike people, their methods of fighting, which had secured for them the largest empire in the world, had hardly required more than a leather corselet, proof enough against most dropping arrows and thrown spears. The javelin – which the Greek had largely abandoned in favour of the long pike-like spear – was still their principal weapon after the arrow. Only the famous Immortals, the 10,000 men comprising the king's personal body-guard, wore anything approaching the armour of the hoplite. Their leather corselets were covered with bands, or platelets, of bronze or iron. It was rare for them to have any head covering other than a loose cloth – rather like a *burnous*, designed more for protection against the sun than anything else – and they had never adopted the metal greaves for the legs, but wore skin trousers.

They carried a leather or wickerwork shield and, apart from the bow and arrow, used a dagger for close-quarter work. Although admirably equipped and trained for the type of warfare that they normally encountered – for instance, in their recent action against Egypt – they were not a match for the heavily armoured Greek hoplite. In the great plains of Asia, where mobility was all-important, they would easily have proved their efficiency and capability against any army that the Greeks could muster. But Thermopylae, the narrow pass between the mountains and the sea, was an area that might have been specifically designed for the kind of warfare for which the Greeks – and especially the Spartans – were trained.

SHIPS OF WAR

THE BIREME or two-banked oared vessel, which had been the principal warship in the Mediterranean for centuries, was superseded in the sixth century B.C. by the trireme. Thucydides, who is the first writer to provide us with any real information about them, says that the Corinthians were the first to have built triremes 'in Greece'. This suggests that they may have originated elsewhere, for he goes on to say that 'triremes in large numbers were first owned by the tyrants of Sicily and the men of Corcyra'. One thing that is certain – despite controversy which still exists as to the exact construction of the vessels – is that the trireme was rowed at three levels and there was one man to each oar. Evidence for this comes again from Thucydides who, in a passing remark, says: 'It was decided that each sailor, taking his oar, cushion and oarstrap....'

In order to achieve the third bank of oars, what the designers had done was to provide the vessel with an outrigger: an extension beyond the ship's side that gave the top level of oarsmen (*thranites*) a greater leverage. The total crew of a trireme consisted of about 200 men, of whom 170 were oarsmen. The *thranites* at the top numbered 31 on each side. Below them came the second bank (*zygites*) with 27 rowers to each side, and at the bottom, also with 27 men each side, came the *thalamites*. Both the two lower decks of oars were worked through holes or ports in the side, and it is clear enough that the least enviable position in the ship was that of the *thalamites*. They had little enough chance of escaping if the trireme was holed or otherwise overwhelmed. Aristophanes also makes the joking comment that it could be very unpleasant to be on the bottom tier if someone above decided to relieve himself. The remaining members of the crew consisted of fifteen deck hands, fourteen soldiers (some of whom were archers), and a flautist who piped the time for the oarsmen. The helmsmen, whose job was all-important on the 'run-in' towards an enemy trireme, steered by means of two broad-bladed steering-paddles as had been the fashion for centuries. In command of each trireme was a *trierarch* (master, and sometimes owner). Trierarchs were usually rich men of some consequence, and the competition between them to produce the finest and the most efficiently worked trireme was intense. True, they gained no financial reward for having the best ship and the best crew, except for a simple wreath or *stephanos* – as treasured then as medals in later centuries. Although the all-important oarsmen came from the poorer classes, they were free citizens – quite unlike the galley-slave labour of later years in the Mediterranean. It was the oarsmen, in fact, who by their predominance in numbers over the rich land-owning citizens were to provide the basic substratum upon which Athenian democracy was to evolve. Sometimes, as in modern days, they were no more than the tools of demagogues, but on rare occasions, as under men like Pericles, they formed the fertile sub-soil for the brief but golden age of Athens.

The Greek trireme, like the bireme before it, and like the single-banked galley that survived in the Mediterranean as late as the eighteenth century, was almost entirely dependent upon manpower. Under favourable conditions with the wind from abaft the beam – preferably as far aft as possible – the trireme could be propelled by its simple squaresail which was set upon a short mast. Under fair-weather conditions, then, the trireme's oarsmen could be given a respite, but in the fickle Mediterranean Sea it would rarely be for long. In any case, when it came to action, the trireme was entirely dependent upon manpower, for the cumbersome mast, sail and attendant rigging were stowed away or sent ashore before an engagement. This was why a fleet defending its home coastline would usually pick a place near a shelving beach where the unnecessary gear could be left behind. On the other hand, a fleet advancing, say, across the Aegean from the coastline of Ionia or elsewhere, might have come all the way under oars. The defensive fleet, therefore, even if outnumbered, always had an advantage over the attacker in the fact that its men would have spent less time at the oars before battle commenced.

From an inventory found in the dockyard of Piraeus it would seem that even the longest oars did not exceed four or four and a half metres in length. The ship itself, whose ancestry went all the way back to the hollowed canoe of primitive times, was long and narrow-gutted. On a beam of three metres at the bottom, which extended to six metres at the level of the *thranites* on the outriggers, the trireme would have been about 37 metres long. Such a vessel was clearly unsuited for heavy-weather work and, indeed, there were only about four, or at the most five, months of the year in which the trireme could safely operate. 'The limitation factor in ancient warfare', as I have said elsewhere, 'was determined not only by the harvest season, when most of the nation's population was engaged in ensuring the bread supply, but also by the fact that armies could not be transported, garrisons maintained, or sea battles fought, except in calm weather.'

The principal weapon of this period, as of the centuries before, was the vessel itself. It was the great underwater ram in the bows which was the forerunner of the cannon and guns of later days. The trireme was in fact launched at its opponent like a giant arrow. The moment of impact was 'the moment of truth' for all aboard. In order to withstand the shock, the vessel had to be specially constructed, and all-important – as of course in all ship construction – was the vessel's keel. This was usually made of oak (with a false keel of some softer wood that could be replaced when it wore out through the constant hauling up, and launching from, a beach). The wooden ribs forming the supports on to which the vessel's planking was set were firmly imbedded in the keel. The trireme's planks, usually of pine, were laid one on top of another in what is called carvel fashion. They were fastened to the ribs by bronze nails or wooden dowels. The average thickness of a trireme's planks would appear to have been about three inches.

The extreme length of the hull in proportion to the beam meant that additional longitudinal strength was necessary, and this was provided for by *zosteres* ('waling-pieces', in nautical terms), which were strong wooden planks extending from bow to stern designed to prevent the vessel from sagging in the middle. There were often as many as four of these *zosteres* to strengthen the weakness inevitably left by the oar-ports for the rowers. The lowest of them was the strongest and had a different purpose altogether. This waling-piece was cut and fashioned in such a way as to dip downward towards the bows, at which point it was firmly bolted from

77

side to side through the great projecting beak of the ram. The ram itself was also made of wood but was sheathed with bronze. Since the whole 'firepower' of the galley consisted in ramming the enemy, it was essential that provision should be made for the 'recoil' or shock on the moment of impact. To reinforce the basic additional strength already provided by the *zosteres*, the hull was further strengthened by a series of heavy rope cables known as *hypozomata*. These encircled the whole hull from stem to stern and gave even further longitudinal strengthening.

Some war vessels, and in particular those of Egypt, tended to carry a large number of heavily armed soldiers to board the enemy immediately after the ramming had taken place. This concept of, as it were, fighting a land-battle afloat was discarded after some time by most of the more experienced naval powers such as the Athenians and the Phoenicians. At the time of Xerxes, however, boarding parties were still all-important. The tactical use of the ram later became the paramount factor in any sea battle. Ideally, of course, the objective was to catch the enemy beam on, breaking clean into his ship's side and holing him. But the ram could also be used by clever manœuvring to run right down the side of the opponent snapping off the oars like matchsticks (the looms of the oars leaping back under the impact and killing or maiming the rowers). Having thus disabled the opponent, the trireme could then back off and, almost at leisure, come in and administer the *coup de grâce* by holing the stricken enemy. It was, one might say, the far-distant, man-impelled, precursor of the torpedo.

Early representations of galleys from the sixth and seventh centuries show the ram as a long single spur projecting a considerable distance out from the bow. Such a single-headed long ram clearly had the disadvantage that it might well snap off in the enemy's side, tearing open the bow of the attacker. At a later date it was found that a shorter but stronger ram, involving in some cases three separate points – rather like a trident – was more effective and could be better braced into the trident's stem and sides. (This is shown on the prow of the famous *Victory of Samothrace* – about 300 B.C.) Further additions to the prow of the vessel were projections above the water-line on the stem itself, as well as heavy wooden catheads projecting on either side of the bows which protected the forward oars after the ram had penetrated, as well as serving to tear away the enemy's upperworks as the trireme swept past in a sweeping blow.

During the years after Marathon, as the Persians girded themselves for the second round, the whole of the eastern and central Mediterranean saw a phenomenal increase in shipbuilding activity. It was not only in the Levant and Greece and the Aegean islands that the impending conflict made its presence felt. In Sicily the Greek colonies were only too well aware that the threat to Greece was a threat to themselves, and that the Carthaginians were enlarging their fleet not only to protect their colonies in Sicily but to evict and destroy the Greek colonies, most of which were planted on the eastern side of the island. Carthage, the offspring of Phoenicia, was determined to assert its claim to the control of the central and western Mediterranean. The whole of the ensuing conflict united such strange bed-fellows as the far-distant Ethiopians, and the mountain men of the Persian Empire, with the seamen of the Levant, Egypt and north Africa, as far afield as the great Gulf of Tunis where Carthage dominated the waters. In the face of such apparently overwhelming might it was hardly surprising that those Greek islands and mainland city-states which had not already medised were actively considering doing so. The only hope for Greece and for the future of its people and its culture lay in those two disparate states, Athens and Sparta. Now that Themistocles had largely committed the Athenians to being the naval shield of the country, it was clear that the brunt of an attack by land should be borne by the Spartans and other allies.

DISPOSITIONS

ON THAT DAY IN EARLY MAY 480 when Xerxes watched from his marble throne the Immortals begin their crossing of the bridge over the Hellespont and the fleet exercises in the blue strait below him, the Greeks were still in a turmoil. Although they had had not months, but even years, in which to prepare themselves for the inevitable second round against the Persians they were still disunited. As always, it was the independent nature of the Greeks, coupled with the rivalries of the numerous city-states themselves, that prevented a real cohesion, even in the face of so overwhelming a threat to the freedom of all Greeks. The very individualism that they cherished was the greatest danger to their continued existence.

In the autumn of 481, after Xerxes' heralds had made their demands for the tokens of earth and water from the Greeks, it became plain which states were prepared to accept the challenge and which had already submitted or medised. Ambassadors from the majority of the mainland states met in a congress on the Isthmus of Corinth held under the aegis of Sparta. An alliance was proclaimed between all the states attending, with Athens and Sparta universally accepted as the leaders. This, the Greek Isthmian League, was the first occasion that the Greeks had shown anything approaching a semblance of unity or of national feeling. But almost as significant as those who attended the meeting were those who abstained. It was hardly surprising that Argos, traditional enemy of Sparta in the Peloponnese and quite recently defeated by the Spartans, was in no mood to accept any secondary place under them. They made the unacceptable demand that Argos should have an equal share in the high command. This was impossible, and was no more than an oblique way of saying that they had no intention of fighting. It was also true that the Argives had been privately approached by the Persians, who had offered them a most-favoured-nation status in

the Peloponnese if they remained neutral. The Argives clearly saw
this as a means of dominating Sparta in due course, and of regain-
ing their ancient position of leadership in southern Greece. If they
had need of any excuse, they had also consulted the Delphic oracle
and had received the advice to sit tight within their walls and 'let
the head save the body'.

The cities of Crete, far removed from the new development of
Greece, and only too conscious that the Persian-serving Ionian
Greeks and the Phoenicians ruled the seas that had once been
dominated by their distant ancestors, were determined not to be
involved. Other states equally – like Achaea – were more concerned
about their own problems, and did not see the impending struggle
as of any concern to them. Quite apart from these, there were states
like Thessaly where its rulers, the Aleuadae, were openly friendly
with the Persians, while once-famous cities like Tiryns and Mycenae
had suffered too much in the past from Argos, and particularly
Sparta, to feel any desire to help them out.

The Greeks of the mainland had long been in consultation with
their prosperous colonies, or former colonies, in rich Sicily and
southern Italy, but little help was to be expected from these direc-
tions. Gelon, the tyrant of the great city-port of Syracuse, had, it is
true, offered his services with that of his considerable fleet – but
only if he had the high command. This had been turned down,
because it was unthinkable that a 'mere colonial' should hold such
a position. In any case, by the time that the great invasion of Xerxes
was on the point of being launched, Gelon, like the next most
important ruler in Sicily, Theron of Acragas, realised that they too
were under threat of attack. The Carthaginian colonies on the
island, with the aid of their founders and in concert with Persia,
were about to launch a major blow against the Greek settlements
as soon as the invasion of Greece got under way. Xerxes and his
staff had largely anticipated that additional help might arrive in
Greece from the cities of Sicily, and had prepared to circumvent
it by a flank attack on the island. (Gelon of Syracuse alone had
promised 200 triremes and well over 20,000 men for the defence
of the Greek homeland.)

Something that added to the disunity and dismay of the Greeks
was the oracle at Delphi itself. In the years prior to the invasion
the various inquiries sent by agitated cities had received little

81

comfort in return. It was not only to Argos that Delphi gave the dismal news of a Persian victory and advised neutrality or friendship with the enemy. Gelon of Syracuse covered himself, after the attack had begun, by sending an emissary to Delphi to watch events and, if necessary, to offer submission. The Delphic oracle never at any time advised him to allow his rich city to become involved. Throughout this period it is possible that Delphi was either bribed by Persian gold or it was *Pétainist*, in the sense of making as reasonable an accommodation as possible with the apparently inevitable victors. (It was, in any case, well enough known to the priests at Delphi that Xerxes would always spare their shrine, just as he had that of sacred Delos.) The Cretans, for instance, were not only following their natural inclinations, but were also advised to stay neutral. The Athenians, as might well be expected, received the grim warning that 'they should fly to the ends of the earth'. The Oracle was explicit:

Do not stay here, you who are doomed. . . . Leave your homes and the heights of your wheel-shaped city. . . . All is ruined and the swift God of War, hurtling in a Syrian chariot, shall destroy it. He shall lay low many a tower – not yours alone – and burn to ashes many shrines of the gods. Even now they stand dripping with sweat and shake with terror. From the topmost roofs drips dark blood, which foretells your inevitable ruin. Arise and leave the sanctuary, and prepare your hearts to meet misfortune.

Delphi was not only 'The Navel of the Earth', but was also the centre best equipped to receive information from all over the Greek and Mediterranean world. Merchants, travellers, scholars, ambassadors, mystics and plain 'spies', all passed through the glowing illuminated home of the sun-god Apollo. (As has been seen at Delos, the fact that Apollo almost equated with Ahuramazda of the Persian religion gave his worship and his priests a foot, as it were, in both camps.) If Athens was doomed, it could hardly be expected that the arrogant Spartans ('They dared to throw the Great King Darius' ambassadors down a well!') could expect any comfort. They were told that either their city 'of the wide places' would be sacked or 'The whole of Lacedaemon shall mourn the death of a king of the house of Heracles [from whom the kings of Sparta claimed descent]'. This last of the many Delphic oracles certainly held a kernel of truth. A king of Sparta would indeed have to die in an effort to check the apparently invincible march of Persia.

The politics of both Athens and Sparta during the years immediately preceding the great invasion inevitably has considerable significance. In Athens, the political struggle which had ended with the triumph of Themistocles had been bitter in the extreme. His principal opponent in later years had been Aristeides, a dignified conservative who was known because of his incorruptibility (rare indeed in Greek politics) as 'the Just'. Whereas Themistocles represented the 'navy party' which, as has been said, meant the poorer classes, Aristeides represented the 'hoplite party': men who could afford to provide their own armour, men of substance, and men furthermore who had already proved their worth at Marathon.

The curious Athenian process of ostracism, whereby voters annually wrote on a piece of potsherd the name of the man whom they felt the state could best do without, was the means whereby Aristeides was finally removed from the chessboard. (It is significant that the discovery of a pile of shards all bearing the name 'Themistocles' and dating from this period show how bitter was the struggle between the parties.) Ostracism meant banishment, and a sufficiently high count of votes meant exile for ten years. Political opponents of Themistocles who had been banished during this period included Hipparchus in 488–7, Megacles a year later, and Xanthippus two years after him. In 483–2 it was the turn of Aristeides, who was prominent among those who did not agree with the use of the Laurium silver to build the new triremes. A well-known anecdote records how, on being asked by an illiterate citizen to write his own name on a potsherd, he courteously inquired why the man wanted Aristeides banished. Back came the unexpected, but very human, reply: 'Because I'm sick and tired of hearing him called "the Just".'

If Athens had had its problems and close political in-fighting, so had Sparta. While the political scene in Athens seems not too unfamiliar to a modern, that of Sparta (like the state itself) is obscure and confusing. All this stems from that strangely muddled constitution which had grown up among the Lacedaemonian master-race. Grundy, like others, finds Sparta's actions in international affairs difficult to interpret:

There is such an extraordinary *consistency* [my italics] in that "unambitious", "vacillating", "dilatory" policy, which even her friends and admirers condemned in the fifth century before Christ, and less passionate critics have condemned in the nineteenth century after Christ, that a thoughtful student of history may well feel some doubt as to whether that policy was dictated by an innate, unintelligent, selfish conservatism, or was due to motives of such a compelling character as to condition rigidly the relations of Sparta with the outside world.

The situation in Sparta was curious enough, to say the least. The dark struggle for power had taken place at a different level from that of Athens and had been considerably more primitive. Kleomenes, who had been one of the two kings of Sparta until his death in 489, had been responsible for the banishment of his fellow-king Demaratus, on the grounds that the latter was illegitimate. Herodotus has much to make of this story and tells it well; for the intrigue involved, and that which was to follow, was worthy of Shakespeare (with *Macbeth* in mind). Demaratus had gone across to the Persians and was now one of the advisers on the staff of Xerxes. It was Demaratus who cautioned Xerxes against underestimating the Spartans in warfare:

When the Spartans fight singly they are as brave as any man, but when they fight together they are supreme above all. For though they are free men, they are not free in all respects; law is the master whom they fear, a great deal more than your subjects fear you. They do what the law commands and its command is always the same, not to flee in battle whatever the number of the enemy, but to stand and win, or die.

It is clear that despite the embitterment which had driven him to the court of Xerxes the former king never forgot the Spartan virtues.

The death of Kleomenes has sinister undertones. After his twin-king Demaratus had been exiled, it is said the Spartans found out that lies had been told about the latter's paternity, and that the whole thing was a put-up affair by Kleomenes. He fled from Sparta, visited Thessaly and Arcadia, and tried to get a league of chieftains to support him. It is possible that he had in mind a return to Sparta at their head and – with the aid of the Helots – the establishment of a completely new regime. The Spartiates were quick to see the danger to their own privileged position if Kleomenes succeeded in his aim, and invited him to return. 'But when he did come back', says Herodotus, 'he immediately went mad; he had always been somewhat unstable. . . .' It appears that he was a heavy drinker, drinking his wine undiluted 'in the Scythian fashion', and he now became violent and uncontrollable. His half-brothers, the elder of whom was Leonidas, had him arrested and put in irons. Then one morning he was found in his cell with his body hideously cut up by a knife. The official story given out was that he had bribed his Helot jailer into giving him the knife so as to commit suicide – but it does not ring true. Some complicity between his half-brothers, even if not outright murder, seems more likely. It is possible that when Leonidas led out his small force to Thermopylae – to his eternally remembered death at the Hot Gates – he had something on his conscience to expiate.

ACTION AND REACTION

FORTY-SIX NATIONS, under thirty Persian generals, were assembled for the invasion of Greece. Over and above them were six chief marshals, five of whom were sons of the royal house. Among the infantry generals were princes of the royal blood, while Otanes, father of Xerxes' queen Amestris, commanded the crack Persian Guards. The latter was not responsible to any marshal but took his orders directly from the king himself. 'Why, O God,' a countryman is reputed to have asked Xerxes, 'have you taken upon you the form of a Persian man, changing your name to Xerxes, in order to lead the whole world to conquer and devastate Greece? You could have destroyed Greece without all that trouble.'

The crossing of the whole army by the bridges took about a week and Xerxes, who passed over with his royal bodyguard behind the sacred horses and chariot of his god, was now able to see from the European side of the Bosporus the full magic of this display of imperial might. Herodotus says that the men 'crossed under the lash', but this seems improbable. It is merely another instance of his painting a portrait of an oriental tyrant whose reluctant soldiers – unlike the Greeks – had to be forced into action. That the lash was applied to the pack animals is more than likely, for otherwise, if we accept the figure of something like 75,000 beasts, ranging from horses and mules to camels, there would have been an inevitable congestion on the bridges.

There was in any case a very good reason for the army to press on into the alien territory of Europe as fast as possible – water. The Persians with their excellent organisation had set up food-dumps and supply organisations throughout Asia Minor and the northern part of Greece, which already came under their control, but they certainly could not organise the streams, rivers and other sources of water-supply. Herodotus asks the question: 'What water did not fail them except for that of the great rivers?' On the salient question of the water-supply of the invasion army no authorities can equal Maurice, with his practical military experience as well as his personal knowledge of all the terrain covered by it in the long march. To paraphrase his conclusions after the forces had left Asia Minor – limited quantities of water could have been obtained by boring 'but this was beyond their resources'. At the point where the columns crossed, although there was water at Maidos near the bridges this was not on their route, so throughout this stage the army would have had to carry its own water with it. Except for occasional springs and wells, it seems that the troops would have had to take four days' supply with them in water-skins. It is possible that, along with the careful preparations of food depots, water-troughs had been erected for the animals in open ground around Gallipoli and at the northern end of the marsh midway between Melas and Aenos, which could have been kept filled by regular convoys from the Melas itself. The allowance for the troops would have worked out at about two quarts per day, 'not an over-generous allowance for men marching in hot weather, whose food is dry grain'. Taking the estimate of the grand army's numbers as 210,000 this would have amounted to 420,000 gallons of water. Presuming that much of this was carried by the camel corps, something like 15,000 camels would have been required (a good camel being capable of carrying 300 lb of water). It is the essential matter of water-supply which disproves the Greek tradition of the army being composed of three million men.

It was not until the whole force assembled at Doriscus near the large River Hebrus that they could be ensured of a really adequate supply. It is very probable that, as Herodotus describes, the army was marshalled here to be regrouped in preparation for their further advance. There was also a food depot at this point, and the animals would have found ample grazing-land along the banks of the river. Doriscus was an ideal place for the pause before the advance. There was, furthermore, a convenient fort, which had been founded by Darius, to serve as a general headquarters.

While the Persians prepared themselves for their assault on northern Greece, the threatened Greeks, at this last stage before the invasion of their homeland, were still in disarray. Having failed to secure the naval assistance from Gelon of Syracuse, with the abstention of the Cretans from any involvement, and with doubts existing as to whether Corcyra would send a squadron to the defence of the Greek mainland, the navy party under Themistocles was at a considerable disadvantage. It seemed clear from reports on the strength of the Persian navy that, even after the new ship-building programme, the Athenians and their allies would still be heavily outnumbered. There was considerable difference of opinion among the high command at Corinth, the Peloponnesians arguing that the best solution was a land-defence line to be drawn across the Isthmus. This, of course, could hardly appeal to Themistocles, or indeed any Athenian, for the suggestion implied that, if the worst came to the worst, all of northern Greece including Athens itself would be abandoned. He took refuge in an additional answer that the Delphic oracle had given to the Athenian delegates, after they had returned with the first dark prophecy that Athens was doomed and that her citizens 'should flee to the ends of the earth'. (It is possible that he himself had some hand in ensuring the second more favourable, even if ambiguous, response.) This said that 'all-seeing Zeus' had listened to Athens' prayer and that, despite a dire outlook, 'the wooden wall alone shall not fall'. It went on to say that 'divine Salamis would bring death to the sons of women after the corn is scattered or the harvest gathered in'.

Although the Delphic oracle took its usual care to make double-ended pronouncements (for instance, which nation's women's sons would die?), the mention of Salamis and of the wooden wall are quite specific. Pessimists took it all as a further warning of defeat, while others maintained that the wooden wall must mean the palisades of the Acropolis. The policy of Themistocles, how-ever, had long been centred around Salamis. He saw the island as not only the place to which the government and army of Athens must withdraw if their city was captured, but also the area in which his new navy might best take on the Persian fleet in constricted waters, where the greater numbers of the enemy might well prove of no advantage but even a hindrance. It was up to him to convince the people, in the great debate that followed the second Delphic pronouncement, that his interpretation was the correct one. It is evidence of the powers and skill of this remarkable man that, despite his many enemies among the conservatives, despite the fact that his argument was a somewhat thin one, he somehow managed to win the day. His oratory was Churchillian as he pointed out that it was freedom which mattered above all. Cities could be rebuilt, but they were nothing in themselves. The essence of the state lay in its citizens. Themistocles appealed to the people over the heads of his opponents, and the people responded. His war-policy was overwhelmingly approved.

Troezen in the Peloponnese, which was reputedly the birthplace of the legendary King Theseus of Athens, was chosen as the place to which the women and children of Athens should be evacuated. The people of this comparatively insignificant city-state responded magnificently to this renewal of the ancient blood-tie. The old people together with household goods were to go to Salamis, while the treasurers and priestesses were to remain on the Acropolis (this for the sake of public morale). General mobilisation was pro-claimed, the fleet was to be manned, and all men under fifty were expected to serve. The salient aspect of policy was that, when the triremes had been manned and furnished for war, one hundred of them were to proceed to meet the enemy at Artemisium off Euboea, while the other hundred were to cruise off Salamis and Attica. The point that must be remembered was that this whole operation, as conceived by Themistocles and approved by the Assembly, applied to the Athenians only. What the reactions of the Peloponnesian allies would be was an unknown factor. They might think very differently.

Themistocles now had the hard task of persuading the Pelopon-nesians against their 'defence of the Isthmus' policy. The Spartans, the Corinthians, and the inhabitants of Athens' old-time enemy, Aegina, had to be made to realise that a forward defence of Greece was essential. It is not difficult with hindsight to see that a strategy which rested upon a defence-line across the Isthmus would certainly have failed. All the Aegean islands opposite the coast had either medised or in any case could easily be rendered ineffective by the Persian fleet. Nothing would have been easier with the weight of sea- and land-power to isolate the Peloponnese and then invade it. The Isthmus of Corinth defence-line would have proved in those days as easy to turn as that of Maginot in this century. A combination of Greek military skill with naval power, if most judiciously used, might just turn the scales against the Persians. The unlikelihood of success if one operated without the other had to be made clear. (Events were to do so in any case.) The shadow of Marathon, somewhat naturally, haunted all discussion. If the Greek hoplites had triumphed before on land, why should the same not happen again? The answer should have been plain to all but the most conservative-minded. The expedition of Xerxes, on its vast scale, was designed to conquer Greece and all the Grecian West. First Greece, then the Ionian islands, then Sicily, and then the rich colonies in Italy – this was the intended progression of conquest.

Part of Themistocles' strategy was inevitably dictated by the very natural Athenian suspicion that the Spartans might let them down, might rely on the defence of the Isthmus, might (for whatever given reason) procrastinate and turn up late – as they had done at Marathon. If the worst came to the worst and northern Greece was overrun, the Spartans might come to the conclusion that they could stay secure in the Peloponnese. They and the other allies had to be convinced that, on this occasion, it was all or nothing for every state which had declared to hold their ground against the might of the invader. For the first time in their history the Greeks had to learn to co-operate with one another. In only one respect did the Athenians have an advantage over the Spartans. If Attica fell and Athens was overrun, they would – even if worsted in a sea-battle – still have some ships left. The survivors could 'do a Dunkirk' and (after collecting women and children from Troezen), they could abandon Greece, sail south and then west across the Ionian Sea, and plant a new colony in Sicily or Italy. The Spartans, with their small fleet, were condemned to fight on the land – with no escape.

The agreed strategy of the Congress at Corinth had originally been for the Greeks to fight as far forward in Greece as possible. In the spring of 480, before Xerxes had crossed into Europe, they had acted on an appeal from Thessaly and sent a force of 10,000 hoplites to hold the 'Mount Olympus Line' at the coastal pass of Tempe. The idea of holding a line as far to the north as possible was sensible enough in itself, but the pass at Tempe could easily be turned. Themistocles himself had commanded the Athenian contingent and a Spartan named Euainetos the Lacedaemonian. It is significant that the latter was not a member of the royal family, and therefore that the Spartan contingent was not a major one – or one of the kings would have gone at its head as was the custom.

The Athenians must have provided the main body of the force. It had become obvious from early on that the chosen position was impossible to hold. Not only was it bypassed by two routes to the west of Olympus, but the local tribes, far from being co-operative, had already determined on a Persian victory. Agents of the Great King had been active in the area for some time, offering inducements to the northern Greeks not to put up any resistance. Quite apart from that, it was well enough known that the Aleuadae were pro-Persian, while Alexander of Macedon was in fact a vassal of Xerxes.

The latter, a smooth charmer, and ostensibly attached to the Greek cause, had a brother-in-law who was a Persian general (somewhat difficult to explain away) and had no intention of being involved in what he clearly saw as a coming victory for the Persians. However, he was trusted by the Greeks (possibly because he had once run in the Olympics and nearly gained a crown) and they went to him as a reliable source of information. So he was – up to a point – for naturally he knew the northern area far better than the Athenians or the Spartans did. He demonstrated the grave defects of the Tempe pass as a holding-place, and advised them to pull back while there was still time. The Spartan Euainetos was convinced, and Themistocles must have felt relieved. The loss of 10,000 hoplites, as well as about the same amount of lightly armed men who accompanied them, would have been an intolerable blow at the very start of the campaign.

Although he was in favour of an action, even if only a delaying one, as far north of Attica as possible, Themistocles must always have held to his original conception of a fleet engagement at a point carefully chosen to the Greek advantage. The Greek force accordingly had withdrawn, sometime towards the end of May, and marched south. Both the hoplites and their accompanying soldiers were no doubt pleased to be moving back nearer to their homes. Greeks at that time rarely engaged in battles outside their local known territory. The inhospitable and treacherous northern mountain area (full of semi-barbarians and Greeks who had 'sold out' to the enemy) could never have induced in them the instinctive patriotism of Marathon.

10

ULTIMATE DECISIONS

THE WITHDRAWAL FROM THE PASS OF TEMPE provided the background to the thinking of the League Congress when it met for the last time before 'the thunder of the chariots in the north' had made itself ominously heard. It was hardly surprising that the return of the hoplite force had resulted in the immediate defection of nearly all the northern Greek states, especially Thessaly and Boeotia, which now saw themselves as having been abandoned. Alexander of Macedon had long ago made his choice, for he had seen from the beginning that, if the Persian host was held up on his territory by a delaying action, it would strip his own land barren. Better by far that they should pass swiftly through Macedonia.

It seems astonishing that even at this late hour the spokesmen should have been bickering and politicising (but modern Greeks under somewhat similar circumstances have done so to this day). Athens had earlier made the greatest concession of all: she had agreed that her fleet should come under the over-all command of a Spartan. Since Athens represented by far the greatest naval power in Greece, her action in doing so was admirable – even if it was largely forced upon her by the fact that the Peloponnesian allies would not accept an Athenian in charge. Themistocles most probably made this concession because he knew that, in the end, it was his strategy that would have to be adopted, and that the size of the new Athenian fleet in comparison with the composite numbers of the Spartan and others would, when it came to action, determine the tactics. 'Realising that if they quarrelled about the command, Greece would be lost', Athens (which almost certainly means Themistocles) was prepared to swallow her pride.

Green comments:

Most of July was wasted. . . . The Spartans, in particular, had their usual religious objections to campaigning at such a season. Their chief festival, the Carneia, fell on or about 20 August, at the time of the full moon; so, that year, did the quadriennial Olympic Games, during which all warring Greek states sank their differences and competed together in relative friendship.

As had been said before, although these religious, or quasi-religious, obligations may seem odd to a modern, they were far from so to an ancient Greek, who lived in a world surrounded by totems and taboos that often obfuscated his thinking. One definitely rational piece of thinking that had marked the Athenian decisions promoted by Themistocles was to recall those who had been exiled under the system of ostracism – although possibly not to home itself, but only to the island of Salamis. It seems clear, at any rate, that in her hour of need Athens was prepared to use all the brains that she could summon – even if they were hostile to the man or party in charge. Aristeides responded (as might be expected from what one knows of his character) and so did Xanthippus. Hipparchus, on the other hand, had joined the 'Quislings', who sought their future with Xerxes and looked for revenge – and power – when both Athenians and Spartans were beaten into the ground.

Old Artabanus in the wise counsel that he had given to Xerxes – and for which he had been sent back home – had summarised the problems which would follow upon an invasion of Greece. Since the Greeks clearly thought along the same lines, and since their thinking determined their strategy in the face of this apparently overwhelming threat, his words, as given by Herodotus, are worth repeating:

> I warned your father – my own brother Darius – not to attack the Scythians, those nomads who inhabit a land without cities. He would not listen to me. Quite confident that he could overcome them he invaded their land. Before he returned home many brave soldiers who had accompanied him lay dead. But, my lord, you intend to attack a nation infinitely superior to the Scythians: one with a reputation for immense courage, both on land and sea. . . . The Greeks are reputed to be great fighting men – something one can well judge from the fact that the Athenians on their own destroyed the large army that we sent against them. . . . I strongly urge you to abandon this plan.

Artabanus' advice was based sensibly and primarily upon logistics. The Persians would be far from home, their lines of communications extravagantly extended, and, as he reminded Xerxes, 'God tolerates pride in no one but himself. It is always the large buildings and the tall trees that are struck by lightning. This is God's way of bringing the lofty to their proper level. Often a great army is destroyed by a small one. . . .'

The Greeks in their councils, quite apart from the formal League at Corinth, had already seen that their best hope lay in allowing the Persians to over-extend themselves. There could be no hope of defeating so vast an army in a pitched battle. However superior the hoplites had proved themselves at Marathon, this time sheer weight of numbers would overwhelm them. The Greeks had little in the way of archers and the same could equally be said of their cavalry. Their only chance lay in finding a suitable defensive line to check the invaders, for however brief a period, while the main engagement took place at sea in a position which they had carefully selected. Tempe had proved too far forward, the surrounding inhabitants pro-Persian, and their flank easily turnable. Geography determined the line which they finally decided to hold.

Greece is a mountainous country and, as Artabanus had already pointed out to Xerxes, its coast is singularly inhospitable. To the east and north of Athens the long fish-shaped island of Euboea lies like a defensive shield. Its eastern coast offers no harbours and any fleet finding this bleak shore to leeward in the event of a blow would be in great trouble. It was now high summer and, after the indecisive vagaries of the *prodroms*, the real 'Greek wind' had set in to blow. The *Meltemi*, as it is called, is almost as steady as the Trade Winds of the oceans. It can be relied upon throughout most of the summer to be constant from a northerly direction, as the colder air from the Black Sea and Russia beyond flows down steadily to replace the hot air which lifts over all the Aegean, the Mediterranean, and Africa. Dying away only slightly at nightfall (but still leaving a pitching and lumpy sea), the *Meltemi* can be expected to blow at anything between Force 6 to 8 on the Beaufort scale, at times even reaching gale force. Such conditions can render sailing difficult in the Aegean even for modern coasters, caïques, or well-found sailing boats. For the trireme, labouring under oars, and even the wind from astern, the *Meltemi* was hardly a friend.

Between the northern tip of Euboea and Cape Sepias on the mainland there lies a six-mile-wide strait, leading into the Euripus channel, which separates the island from Greece itself. Artemisium on the northernmost spur of Euboea took its name from a temple erected there to the goddess Artemis 'Facing the East', this attribute no doubt arising from the fact that it was from here that ships took their departure eastwards across the Aegean. It had no doubt been well endowed by mariners contemplating what was then a long and often hazardous voyage. North of Euboea from Cape Sepias to Mount Olympus the land presents an iron-bound coast – a wall of mountains where there is little shelter except for small craft, and certainly nothing that could remotely accommodate a fleet. The Persian armada, after they had traversed the ship-canal through the peninsula at Mount Athos and rounded the two other peninsulas of Chalcidice had a long haul of over sixty miles before they came to the strait between the island of Skiathos and Cape Sepias, with always this brooding and hostile coast on their starboard hand, threating them if a gale from the north blew up. Confronting them, as they emerged, lay Artemisium. It was plain that the key to the whole naval campaign lay here. At this point they might be held or even defeated. At the same time Themistocles, who possibly saw this in his grand design as no more than a holding action, was well enough aware that the fleet must act in concert with the land forces – as indeed must Xerxes himself. The Persian army would have to pass round the Malian gulf opposite the northern end of Euboea and here, at the Pass of Thermopylae, lay the ideal place for a comparatively small force to check a large one, which would not be able to deploy and take advantage of its numbers. Artemisium and Thermopylae, then, between them presented a geographically linked dual sphere for action.

At this late moment, 'as the Greek forces hurried to their stations', Herodotus informs us, 'the people of Delphi in great alarm for their own safety and that of Greece, applied to their oracle for advice. "Pray to the winds," came the answer, "for they will be good allies to Greece." ' The Delphians passed on this response to all the Greek states who had decided to fight and it gave them great comfort. Themistocles, whose strategy, as we have seen, depended to some extent on the fact that the Persian fleet would have to come down that long and formidable coast and who, like every Greek acquainted with the sea, knew what weather the winds could stir up in the Aegean must have been as comforted as any.

In the high heat of late June, having left Doriscus, Xerxes and the army marched westwards while the fleet coasted offshore headed for the Athos canal. In the coastal plain east of the River Nestus the army was able to deploy and instead of moving like a great snake could now be organised into three parallel columns. There were two marshals in charge of each column, Mardonius and the king's brother leading the column that followed along the coastline, while Xerxes himself was in the central column, and the third and most inland column marched along the foothills that hemmed the plain. Now indeed the die was irrevocably cast as the fleet with its sweating oarsmen streamed south, and the army spread out in a broad fan over northern Greece. Nothing like this had ever been seen before, nor, in the long and strife-torn subsequent history of Greece, would anything quite like it ever be seen again.

Where the hills drew close to the sea, west of the Nestus, one Thracian chieftain showed that not all in the far north were prepared to accept this invasion of their country. He refused to give the token earth and water, and fled inland to the hills. At the same time he cautioned his six sons to have no truck with the enemy but to join him. The sons, however, were pro-Persian and, as young men, probably thought it would be both fun and profitable to join the Persian army. At a much later date, when they return home among the vanquished, they found an inexorable old man who had neither forgiven nor forgotten their disobedience – he had all of them blinded. Most of the local tribesmen, however, were more amenable and either joined the host or were conscripted into it. Only a tribe called the Sacae would neither assist nor be conscripted, 'for they have never been reduced to subjection . . . living in high mountain country, well-wooded and covered with snow. They are also formidable warriors.'

Xerxes need not bother about such tribesmen in any case; they constituted no threat to his vast army, and could be left on their inclement mountainsides. Water at times still proved a problem; a small river was drunk dry, and in another place a very brackish lake (Herodotus says 'salt') was drained by the pack-animals. Later on a further hazard was to beset them, the animals, and in particular the camels, being attacked and eaten by lions. Herodotus suggests that the lions developed a special taste for camel meat. The fact was that the camels always came last in the advance because the sight and smell of them upset the horses, so it was natural that the stragglers should get taken. During the early stages, because of the nature of the country, the army's progress was slow. There were no roads, pioneer corps had to go ahead and hack their way through and, where the ground was suitable, engage in proper road-building. Long after the great invasion was over, the people of Thrace still revered this Persian road and would not cultivate the land. No doubt they found it useful.

When the army reached the River Strymon at a place known as Nine Ways the pioneers, efficient as usual, had arrived well in advance and pontoon bridges had been prepared for the crossing. The excellence of the organisation, the careful planning and attention to detail, is one of the most remarkable aspects of the Persians – and would not be equalled for many centuries. Herodotus is keen to stress the superstitious and indeed barbaric nature of the invaders and their religion. After telling us that the Magian priests sacrificed white horses to propitiate the great river, he adds that, hearing the place was called Nine Ways, they took nine native boys and nine girls and buried them alive. There is something slightly suspect in this story, for human sacrifice had no part in the religion of Zoroaster (although it had in that of the Phoenicians).

Xerxes was naturally eager to see the great canal and watch his ships passing through it two abreast. He turned aside from the main route and visited Acanthus, whose citizens had been among his warm supporters and who had helped in the construction of this masterpiece of engineering. As a mark of the royal favour he made them a present of a suit of Median clothes – presumably to be worn by the head man or hung up in a temple. One minor episode marred the Great King's pleasure in this visit and that was the sudden death of Artachaeës, a notable Persian, a relative of the king, 'the biggest man in Persia, over eight feet tall'. Renowned for his stentorian voice (always useful in a foreman!) he had been placed in over-all charge of the construction works. He was buried with great pomp and ceremony and the army heaped a large mound over his grave. He was later worshipped as a demi-god by the local inhabitants. It is curious, though, that no one at the time – nor Herodotus with the benefit of hindsight – seems to have detected any ill-omen in the death of this enormous Persian of royal blood at the very start of the campaign.

The Greeks through whose lands the king and his army were now passing found out what Alexander of Macedon had long ago anticipated – they were eaten out of house and home. It was not only the locust-like swarms of the troops and the beasts that denuded all the land around, but the senior citizens through whose townships Xerxes passed were compelled, as vassals of the king, to see that he was suitably entertained. Apart from all the food for Xerxes and his large personal retinue it was natural that they should set it all before their overlord in suitable vessels of gold and silver. To their dismay they found that, when the tent of Xerxes was struck in the morning, all the table-gear on which they had lavished so much money was moved off with it. It was a good thing, as one leading citizen remarked, that Xerxes did not dine twice a day, or they would all be totally ruined.

Following the stop at Acanthus the army and the fleet had necessarily to part. While the army made its way westward across to Therma at the head of the Thermaic Gulf, the fleet, after the passage of the canal was over, had to round the other two capes of Chalcidice before heading up north for the next rendezvous. It is possible that not even the excellent information system of the Persians had quite prepared the army for the difficulty of this part of the terrain. Something like a third of the troops had to go ahead and cut a way through the dense forest-land and it was the fleet which, possibly to the surprise of all concerned, reached Therma first. One wonders whether the warnings of Artabanus ever echoed in Xerxes' ears. It was already late July, and here he was without even having started the campaign. July would burn into August and then with September, when the Mediterranean becomes unstable and often violently stormy, he would be far from home and well into the country of his enemies. If it had taken so long to get this far unopposed it is possible that his sleep may have been troubled by the thought of what might happen when both army and fleet were deep into a hostile sea and land.

Whatever his private feelings, or those of his advisers, may have been, the fact remains that it was necessary to make a fairly lengthy stay at this point on the route. He had to wait for last reports from his heralds, despatched long in advance, as to the dispositions of the Greek states and which of them, at this late hour, were prepared to surrender and which (he certainly knew of two) were determined to resist. Xerxes' love of natural beauty, very typical of a Persian of his caste, has already been commented upon, and now from the head of the Gulf he could see in the clear early light of day the peaks of Mount Olympus and of Ossa shining to the south. The home of the Greek gods beckoned. Besides which, there was a good practical reason for his next action. He was 'informed that between the two mountains there lay a narrow gorge through which ran the river Peneus, and also a road that led into Thessaly'. The king decided to go down by sea and inspect the river mouth for himself. 'No sooner had the fancy taken him than he acted upon it. Going aboard the Sidonian vessel which he always used for any such occasion, he gave the signal for the rest of the fleet to put to sea, leaving the army behind in its encampments.'

Xerxes knew well enough from his advisers that, largely through the machinations of Alexander of Macedon, the Tempe pass had long been evacuated by the Greeks and was now free for the passage of troops. The route had its attractions for it passed straight between the mountains (thus obviating a long detour to the north-west of Olympus and Ossa). Xerxes would then have his army on the direct line south towards the head of the Malian Gulf where he must hope that his fleet, having worsted any Greek opposition at sea, would be waiting ready for the passage of the Euripus channel between Euboea and the mainland. What the Persians suffered from throughout the campaign – although they had had spies all over the place for years and although they had well-informed Greek advisers with them – was that salient thing, local knowledge. Since there were no maps or charts, local knowledge was of prime consequence in ancient wars: something which meant that the invader of foreign territory was always at a grave disadvantage. Even in the twentieth century, as has been found out in numerous theatres of war, the personal acquaintanceship with the terrain held only by native villagers gives a considerable 'edge' over any invader however numerous, efficient, and well armed.

It did not take Xerxes and his immediate staff long to see that the Tempe gorge would be useless – possibly disastrous – for the passage of a host so large as theirs. Its main attraction was obvious: it was less than five miles long, thus saving not only days of time but the exhaustion of troops and baggage train under the high-summer weather. Its principal disadvantage was immediately and equally obvious: it was too narrow. The broiling River Peneus, while it would provide them with all the water they could possibly need, took up so large a part of the pass that in a number of places there would not be more space than some fifty yards through which men and animals could pass. To take an army of tens of thousands through such a defile was to invite disaster. It was true, as Alexander had told them, that the hoplites had withdrawn, but they might return again. And could one trust Alexander, or even many of the supposedly friendly northern Greeks, not to take advantage of the Persian predicament if they were so foolish as to put their whole head, and then sinuous body, into such a trap designed by nature for the decimation of men? The answer was obvious. Xerxes admired the breathtaking view, 'that deep romantic chasm which slanted down the green hill', but recognised it as 'A savage place!' There was nothing for it. They would have to take the long northern route round by the line of the Haliacmon river and strike inland behind Olympus, Ossa, and Pelion.

The gods of Greece lay in her formidable mountains, in her harsh and largely inhospitable terrain, and in the scouring northerly winds of the Aegean Sea.

11

MARCH TO THE NORTH

THE NEWS THAT THE PERSIANS were already in Pieria and were building roads for the mass movement of their army was enough to break up the last conference of the Corinthian League at the Isthmus. The allied fleet, following the plan of Themistocles, made ready to sail for the north to tackle the Persians in the vicinity of Artemisium. The largest part of this fleet, as we know, was provided by the Athenians with their one hundred new triremes, plus over forty older vessels which had been recommissioned and refitted during the intense dockyard activity of recent months and years. Including their Peloponnesian allies the whole fleet which moved up to hold the sea line between Artemisium and Thermopylae was about two hundred ships, against which the Persians could bring down something to the amount of 650.

In the meantime, despite the fact that the most holy Spartan festival, the Carneia, was due to take place in the third week of August the Spartiates recognised the gravity of the situation and agreed to send out a portion of their army. It was no more than a token force, designed to conduct a holding action with the aid of allies whom they would pick up on their way. Although the numbers were small, the fact that it was meant to be representative of the most formidable military power in Greece and that it was the clear intention of Sparta – once the Carneia was over – to commit herself totally to the struggle, was proved by the fact that (unlike at Tempe) one of her kings went out at its head. Leonidas was now a man in his early fifties and, as had been seen, had previously been involved in the grim power-struggle around the kingship of his land. A torso statue of a Greek hoplite, wearing a Corinthian-style helmet with cheek-pieces shaped like rams' heads, has been considered by many authorities to have formed part of the memorial statue that was later erected to the memory of the king. Even if it is not of him, it is the kind of head that one would expect to find on a Spartiate warrior of the ruling caste. Bearded and broad-faced, it looks out at the world from deep-socketed eyes with defiant aggression. This was certainly the face of Sparta.

It was now late July, the fertile valley around the unwalled city shaking with heat, as the king assembled his small, picked task-force. Three hundred Spartiates in all formed the core, but there is no doubt that with them went something approaching one thousand other soldiers – either Helots who had been emancipated (certainly used in later wars), or possibly *perioikoi*, 'friendly neighbours'. Xenophon, although writing at a later date, tells us the Spartan procedure when one of the kings set out for war. Because of the innate conservatism of this strange Greek state it is unlikely that this would have changed very much, if at all, since the time of Leonidas:

First of all he [the King] offers up sacrifices at home to Zeus the Leader and to the other gods associated with him. If the sacrifice seems propitious, the Fire-Bearer takes fire from the altar and leads the way to the borders of the land. [Fire, needed for cooking, heating or light had to be conveyed in iron cauldrons.] There the King offers sacrifice again to Zeus and Athene. Not until the sacrifice proves acceptable to both of these deities does the King cross the borders of the land. The fire from the sacrifices goes ahead and is never quenched; behind come animals of all sorts which are to be sacrificed. Whenever he offers a sacrifice the King always begins the ceremony before dawn. . . . Gathered together at the sacrifice are the colonels, captains, lieutenants, leaders of foreign contingents, commanders of the baggage train as well as any general from the states who wishes to be present. . . . When the sacrifices are over the King summons everyone and gives out the orders of the day. If you could but watch the scene you would come to the conclusion that all other men are mere amateurs at soldiering, and that the Lacedaemonians are the only artists in warfare.

On this subject of 'artistry' Kitto has the very pertinent comment:

The Laws of Lycurgus were, to the Spartans, a pattern of

'Virtue', that is to say of aretē, of human excellence regarded strictly from within the citizen-body. It was a narrower conception of 'virtue' than the Athenian, and it offends modern humanitarians almost as much as its demands would scare them, but though cruel in some aspects and brutal in others, it has a heroic quality. No one can say that Sparta was vulgar. Nor would a Spartan have admitted that Sparta was artistically barren. Art, *poiesis*, is creation, and Sparta created not things in words or stone, but men.

To this one could add that modern humanitarians, as such, might well not exist had it not been for the heroic and 'Spartan' qualities displayed by men like these and those other Greeks who, nearly two and a half thousand years ago, defended the Pass of Thermopylae.

It is evidence of the awareness of Leonidas that this holding action was likely to be suicidal that (probably with the words of the Delphic oracle in his mind) he was careful to select as his kingly *corps d'élite* only men who had sons living: he had no intention of seeing any Spartiate family line extinguished. His concern here is obvious when one realises that the Spartiates could never at any time field an army of the ruling caste larger than about 8000. It was from the lack of fresh blood into the Spartiates that this small unique nation would ultimately perish.

'In other states,' to quote their admirer, Xenophon, again,

all men, I imagine, make as much money as they can. One is a farmer, another a shipowner, another a merchant, and others live by various different handicrafts. But at Sparta freeborn citizens were forbidden by Lycurgus to have anything to do with business. He insisted that they should regard as their only concern those activities which make for civic freedom. How, indeed, should wealth be considered seriously there since he also insisted on equal contributions to the food supply and the same standard of living for all, thus removing the attraction of money for indulgence's sake?

The sheer professionalism of the Spartan army was what distinguished it from the other citizen armies of Greece, since all its men (aged between twenty and sixty) had been trained for nothing but the military art since they were boys. Their arms and armour did not differ from that of other Greek hoplites but the Spartan warrior was distinguishable from his fellows because he wore a scarlet cloak; this again because Lycurgus had decreed that its colour was suitable for war and because it bore the least resemblance to any clothing worn by women. Men past their first youth were also encouraged to wear their hair long since the sage reckoned that it would make them look both more dignified and more frightening. The soldiers were organised into files (*enomotia*) each commanded by an *enomotarch* or junior officer; the files then being linked to form 'fifties' (*pentekostyles*) under the command of a senior officer. Xenophon adds the further comment that they 'carry out with perfect ease manœuvres which instructors in tactics think very difficult'. When marching in column, section followed section as they would have done now as they passed northwards through the Peloponnese, but 'if an enemy in battle array were to make an appearance they would on the orders of their officers deploy into line to the left, and so on throughout the columns until the battle-line stands facing the enemy'. It would be different at Thermopylae because of the restricted nature of the terrain, but the iron discipline was ever unchanged. When camping *en route* they formed into a circle, with their arms and other impedimenta stacked in the centre. Sentries were placed looking inwards so as to keep their eyes at all times on the military equipment, while scouts took up their positions on any elevated features of the landscape round about to see that the camp was not surprised.

As he passed north through the small cities of Tegea and Mantinea, and then through Arcadia, on his way towards the Isthmus, Leonidas gathered in other small allied contingents to the total of 2120, Arcadia itself providing the bulk of these. He now, it would seem, had a little more than 3000 men, hardly enough even for a delaying action in the pass. However, as Burn points out, tradition has it that he reached the Isthmus with 4000 and the only conclusion to be drawn is that the additional 1000 were 'emancipated Helots, armed as hoplites . . .'. We know that the bulk of the Spartan army would not march until after the Carneian Festival, which occurred at the third moon after mid-summer – towards the end of August in 480. Why the other

Peloponnesian allies despatched such small forces can only be guessed at, but the most reasonable conclusion seems to be that they still felt that to fight so far forward was not in their interests. They still clung, in fact, to the strategy which Themistocles had set his face against – that of holding a line across the Isthmus. Not even the fact that a Spartan king was on the march could drag them from their 'Maginot Line', or even isolationist, policies.

Putting the Isthmus behind him Leonidas marched north through Boeotia, where he may have hoped for some larger reinforcements, but only the small township of Thespiae came to his support with 700 hoplites. The important city of Thebes, somewhat grudgingly, sent no more than 400 men – a trivial amount and, as Herodotus suggests, 'their sympathy was secretly with the enemy'. The Locrians of Opus sent him all the men they had (some hundreds?) while the people of Phocis despatched 1000, and these of Malis possibly a further 1100. The entire force which he took with him to Thermopylae was probably a little more than 7000 men.

A Spartan king on the march, with the immense reputation of his city behind him, must have been a strong inducement to these small places to put their limited manpower under his command. The other Greeks, furthermore, and presumably Leonidas himself, told them that this was merely an advance force, and that the main body would soon be joining them. The sea, these northerners were informed, was strongly held by the fleet of Athens, Aegina, and the other allies, and there was no cause for alarm. 'The invader,' they were reassured, 'was after all not a god, but only a man. The greater the man, the greater the misfortune. Xerxes was no exception. He too was human, and could expect to be humbled in his pride.'

While the nodding horsehair-crested helmets and the scarlet cloaks marched north, picking up these reinforcements on their way, the allied fleet under a Spartan admiral, Eurybiades, had rounded Cape Sunium and was on its way up the Euboea Channel. A reserve fleet of some 200 ships had been left behind to guard the southern positions from Attica to the Argolid. There seems little doubt that the finest new ships were sent up to defend the position off Artemisium and even they, with presumably the best crews, will have made hard work of it. Under the blazing midsummer sun the oarsmen had to toil against the fast current which whips down between Euboea and the mainland, speeded at this time of the year by the fact that the northerly winds have been blowing for many weeks. Ahead of them had been sent a fast cutter with a well-known Athenian aboard, to act as liaison officer between the fleet at sea and the army under Leonidas. Sweating under the high sun, that small force made its way to a point of human destiny.

LAND AND SEA

THEY CAME TO THE PASS OF THERMOPYLAE, the sea on
their right hand to the north, crisped with the bright waves of
summer. It was a formidable place. To the left of them the heights
of Mount Kallidromos rose up stark and sheer, a defensive wall
brilliant at noon, and lit at night only by the summer starshine, for
it will have been the dark of the moon when they took up their
positions. The full Carneia moon that year was on 20 August.

Their right flank, then, lay on the sea and their left was protected
by Kallidromos, an ideal place for a hoplite line, being unturnable
at either end. It requires an effort of the imagination today to see
the pass as it was at the time when Leonidas reached it. Over the
centuries, the Malian Gulf has silted up and the modern coastline
now lies several miles away from the scene of the action. In 480,
however, the point which was chosen for the defensive line was
only about twenty yards wide. There were two other places that
were even narrower, one to the east and one to the west of the
chosen position. The reason why Leonidas and his staff eliminated
them from their strategy was that in both of them the slopes,
though steep, were far from sheer. In a massive assault, such as was
to be expected, their left flank might well be turned. The Persians,
it must be remembered, were mountain men and accustomed to
fighting over rocky conditions – far more so than any Greek
hoplite, who must of necessity fight on comparatively flat ground.
The Spartans, therefore, chose a slightly wider front, but one
where their vulnerable left was protected by a sheer wall of
rock.

There was another advantage to be gained from the site they
chose. At this point, which was known as 'The Middle Gate', the
people of Phocis at some time in the past had built a defensive wall
designed to protect them from the Thessalians to the north. It was

now in a ruinous condition, so the defenders immediately set about repairing it. The sulphurous springs which gave the place its name, Hot Gates, poured out – and still do – from the base of the mountain about a mile to the north-west from 'The Middle Gate'. They presented no hazard to anyone passing along the ancient coast road, and nowadays have been diverted into some modern baths, where those whose olfactory threshold is high can enjoy them.

Xerxes and the army were still in Macedonia when the Spartans and allies began to dig themselves in at Thermopylae. He was just on the point of moving, since reports had reached him that the way was cleared for the troops to pass over the mountains into Thessaly. Just as the first columns were beginning their advance, he decided to send a small detachment from the fleet down to inspect the strait between Cape Sepias and the island of Skiathos, and then to reconnoitre the Gulf of Pagasae. This was to lead to the first naval engagement of the whole campaign, and one which did not auger very well for the Greeks. Ten fast ships, almost certainly Phoenician and possibly specifically from Sidon, were selected for the operation.

The Greeks from their naval base at Artemisium had naturally enough despatched scouts to watch the Skiathos channel where the enemy must inevitably first be seen. There were three triremes on guard, one from Athens, one from Aegina, and one from Troezen – their task clearly being not to engage any advance squadron but to report back quickly to base. They were, however, out-manœuvred or, as seems clear, the heavier Greek vessels were no match in speed for the lighter-built and faster Phoenicians.

At the first sight of the enemy all three turned tail and fled. The Persians gave chase, and the ship from Troezen, commanded by Prexinus, was captured at once. The victors picked out the best-looking of the marines on board, took him up to the bows and cut his throat. They thought, no doubt, that the sacrifice of their first handsome Greek prisoner would aid their cause. The name of this unfortunate was Leon, which may have had something to do with his fate. [Leon means 'Lion', therefore possibly a very acceptable sacrifice?] The ship from Aegina, however, which was commanded by Asonides, put up a fierce resistance. A marine on board, Pytheas, distinguished himself in particular and, after his ship was boarded, continued to fight until he was almost cut to pieces. He fell at last but, as he was still alive, the Persian marines did all that they could to save his life, dressing his wounds with myrrh and binding them up with linen. When they got back to their base they displayed him with admiration to everybody there and looked after him well. The other prisoners from the ship, however, were treated as slaves.'

War, then as now, was an indescribable mixture of cruelty and violence coupled with admiration, in some cases, for the courage of an opponent.

The third vessel, the Athenian, its retreat cut off, fled northward and finally ran itself aground at the mouth of the River Peneus in Thessaly. The whole crew of 200, who only got clear of their pursuers by the narrowest of margins, then made their way back through hostile Thessaly to reach Athens after a long overland march. Presumably the Thessalians let them through because sailors were worthless as hostages, not worth ransoming, and had nothing with them of the slightest value. On the other hand, they may still have been temporising and have not as yet quite made up their minds as to the forthcoming issue between Persian and Greek. Three of the pursuing vessels, we learn, ran aground on a small rocky reef in the Skiathos channel which, with seamanlike efficiency, they promptly marked for the benefit of the oncoming fleet using stone blocks to form a pillar. (The Phoenicians' marker pylon has long since gone, but the place is clearly marked on modern charts, and shows itself by a breaking swell when the wind is in the north.) On receipt of a signal flashed from Skiathos the Greek fleet is said by Herodotus to have withdrawn to Chalcis (a run of some ninety miles). Some modern historians have thought it unlikely that the fleet would have done more than withdraw a few miles west of Artemisium, although they would certainly have withdrawn their lookouts and advance guard from Skiathos itself.

Xerxes and his staff had calculated that it would take the army some fourteen days to get itself down to Thermopylae. The fleet on the other hand, moving from the Thermian Gulf to that of Pagasae, could do the journey in two to three days. The fleet was therefore instructed to stay where it was for eleven days after the king's departure and then get under way for the rendezvous. If Xerxes and his staff, after all their elaborate preparations over the years and in all their efficiency on the march itself, had erred, it was in ignoring the time element. Once they had got themselves across on to the mainland of Europe there seems little evidence that they had made any great haste. Indeed, such evidence as there is suggests that Xerxes, enjoying his triumphal progress, had dallied too long. It is true that in places the nature of the terrain had delayed them (necessitating road-building, for instance), but even now, when his scouting squadron had returned with their news and he knew that the Greeks were awaiting him, he seems to have dallied. While in Thessaly he held races between his own Persian horses and the local breed, and was delighted when the Persians triumphed every time, for he had been assured that the horses of Thessaly were the finest in Greece. This seemed a good omen. In Achaea he found time to listen to local story-tellers and even diverted the army slightly to avoid a piece of ground which he had been told was sacred.

The admirals and captains of the Persian fleet may well have wished that the army could move a little faster (often a bone of contention between other navies and armies in many later years). None of them can have been ignorant of the fact that they were now into mid-August and that it would be late in the month by the time that they set sail. Even in those days without charts, written information or instruments, weather lore, transmitted orally over many centuries, will have been almost as accurate as anything that can be found in a modern Pilot for the Aegean. When vessels were relatively frail and very largely dependent upon manpower, weather conditions were all-important and none of the master-mariners in the Persian fleet can have been ignorant of the fact that, although sultry high summer was still with them, it could break at any moment. Hesiod wisely set the limit of the sailing season for sensible men to fifty days after the summer solstice. Even though the Egyptians, for example, may have been ignorant of Aegean conditions it is impossible that the Greeks from Ionia and the islands or the Phoenicians who had known the sea for centuries cannot have been aware that they were about to set out down a singularly inhospitable coast at a time in the year when the weather is likely to become unstable. Under the *grande chaleur* of summer all the Aegean has been gradually heating up and it requires no more than a slight change in barometric pressure to produce an imbalance. When this happens the hot air rises suddenly over the sea, lifting like a great balloon, and the cold air from the north roars down to replace it. The Delphic oracle (though often misleading and confusing) was at the same time the repository of most of the knowledge – including meteorological – of its time. 'Pray to the Winds' had been the last counsel given to the seemingly doomed Greeks. The Athenians accordingly offered up prayers to Boreas, God of the North Wind.

The Persian fleet sailed on time as ordered and, after one day's voyage out, 'they were off the part of the Magnesian country between Casthanea and Cape Sepias. On arrival the leading ships made fast to the land but, as there was not much room on the small beach, the remainder came to anchor and lay facing offshore in lines up to eight deep.'. All had gone well so far, but many of the captains, except for those who had arrived first and managed to beach their ships, had good reason to feel uneasy at their exposed position, but still they could remind themselves that twenty-four hours would see them in safety. 'At dawn next day,' Herodotus continues, 'the weather was clear and calm. . . .'

It was that curious bright stillness which often precedes the onset of a violent north-easter. A 'Hellesponter' was then the Greek word for it, while today it is known as the *maistro*, the 'master wind'. It can come raging out of a cloudless sky without warning, as the hot air lifts soundless to the south. (Even the modern barometer can be too slow to catch any advance changes in the air pressure.) As often as not there are no forewarning signs – no banners of cirrus or altostratus, nor any premonitory swell in advance of its coming. So it was on that day when the Persian fleet was getting under way and preparing to move on down the coast. Suddenly out of the north the wind began to pour in gale-force fury. The Persian fleet was caught on a lee shore.

Herodotus continues:

Those who realised in time that the blow was coming, and all who happened to be lying in a suitable place, managed to beach their vessels and get them hauled ashore before they were damaged and before they lost their own lives as well. The ships which were caught offshore, on the other hand, were all lost: some

being driven down onto the place called the Ovens at the foot of
Mount Pelion and others onto the beach. A number ran aground
on Cape Sepias itself, and others again were driven ashore off the
cities of Meliboea and Casthanea. It was a storm of the greatest
violence.

The Athenians had prayed to Boreas and the god had obliged
them. Herodotus maintains that the Persians lost 'four hundred
ships, at the lowest estimate'. This, like his figures for the fleet
itself, would seem to be an exaggeration. That they lost a great
many is almost undeniable, as anyone who has seen that harsh coast
can easily imagine. (It would be hard going to claw off it even in a
well-found modern sailing boat under northerly gale conditions.)
Awkward, oared triremes, with only a squaresail, would have been
extremely difficult to extricate from such a lee shore and there can
be no doubt that the loss was severe. Perhaps a quarter may have
been destroyed, but a loss of 400 fighting vessels would have
amounted to nearly half of the front-line fleet: something which
would have been unacceptable and which would have led to the
abandonment of the naval campaign. The fact that the Persians
regrouped, made good their storm damage, and later proceeded
relentlessly on their way does not suggest a shattered fleet. The
gale lasted unabated for three days – a long blow for August when
such storms, though fierce, are usually over in about twenty-four
hours. (At a later date the Athenians remembered how Boreas
had answered their prayer and built him a shrine by the River
Ilissus.)

It is clear that the Greek allied fleet sat out this storm tucked well
under the lee of Euboea, so Herodotus' statement that they went as
far south as Chalcis *may* not be wrong, although they need not have
gone anywhere near as far away to find a good lee under the island.
One suspects that they went a little south of the latitude of Thermopylae and then took shelter close under the western coast of
Euboea. Green, however, believes the Herodotean source and
thinks that Themistocles deliberately went down into the narrows
by Chalcis in the hope of inducing the Persians to follow. They
would then have found themselves in unfamiliar, constricted
waters, where their numbers would not have been able to tell, and
where the slower but heavier Greek triremes could have done to

them what they were, indeed, later to do at Salamis. This is quite possible, but what is really significant is that the 'Hellesponter', which did such damage to the invasion fleet, left the allies completely untouched.

Even before the storm had blown itself out the Greeks had informed reports of the destruction of a great number of the enemy from their watchmen in northern Euboea. No doubt much wreckage was coming down on the great rollers past Cape Sepias and through the channel between Skiathos and the neighbouring island of Skopelos – an area known for good reason to this day as the 'Gate of the Winds'. 'On hearing the news, they offered prayers of thanksgiving and libations of wine to their saviour Poseidon and made all speed back to Artemisium in the expectation that there would be few ships left to oppose them.' In this they were to be disappointed for, as they headed north for their station, they could see great numbers of ships rounding Cape Sepias and turning up into Aphetae just within the Gulf of Pagasae. It is possible that if they had been quicker in their return or had not lain so far away they could have caught the main body of the Persian fleet at this point and provided the battle that Themistocles sought. As it was, they did have one piece of luck, for fifteen stragglers coming up behind the main body mistook the Greeks for their own fleet and made to join them – only to be rounded up and captured. Since they were a mixed squadron, some of them Ionian Greeks whose triremes would have been almost identical, it is not so surprising that this mistake took place. One of the captains, who was from Paphos, admitted during interrogation that out of twelve ships from his Cypriot squadron eleven had been lost in the storm off Sepias. Greatly heartened by this news, and by the general picture that they obtained of the storm-battered condition of the enemy fleet, the allies sent back all the prisoners to their headquarters at the Isthmus of Corinth.

At the time of the great storm, the Spartans and their allies had been consolidating their position at Thermopylae. Placed as they were in that narrow pass close to the sea's edge even the most unobservant of landsmen could not have escaped noticing – and feeling – the cut of the wind and the roar of the sea. They knew that the Great King was coming, for some of the wrack of his advancing fleet must have siphoned past the north of Euboea and been reported. The gale will have struck their narrow ledge of land and hurled upwards over the mountain that protected their inboard flank. Spray will have splattered over the sea-edge, the cauldrons with their flames will have had to be protected, and the scarlet fighting cloaks drawn close over the waiting men.

FIRST ENCOUNTERS

IMMEDIATELY AFTER THE DEFENCE FORCE had taken up their position, Leonidas had set about the necessary tasks of a professional commander. While the old Phocian wall was being reconstructed he had two main objectives: first, to secure his supply-lines and, secondly, to deny the land immediately to the north of Thermopylae to the enemy. Between the pass and the city of Lamia, through which Xerxes must pass in order to attack him, there lay a fertile plain. It was practical to raid the farms, homesteads, and granaries in the area – and it was practical to do so at night so that the unfortunate locals and the people of Lamia would not be able to see how small was the force that lay in the track of the great army. Leaving the wall behind them, the troops moved up past the West Gate and spread out into the plain. Presumably, since there was as yet no threat to his position, he took nearly all his men with him. In a night that ruined many a farmer (war spares no one) granaries were emptied, buildings set afire, and even the trees were cut down. Let the lights and the noise and the shouting be heard in Lamia, and let its citizens report in due course to the Persian king that the famous Spartans were waiting to receive him! The raid had, of course, its practical aspect since cattle were driven back to their base, grain was always welcome, and a scorched-earth policy – even if only over this limited area – meant that the advance units of the enemy would find no comfort on the land. For his main supply-base Leonidas had the village of Alpeni behind his lines, but the raid enabled him to establish a useful and immediate supply-dump at the Phocian wall itself.

The other immediate consideration was the security of his chosen position. All passes can, in the end, be turned. Their tenability, even for a temporary holding operation, rests entirely upon the length of the detour that the enemy will have to make before he

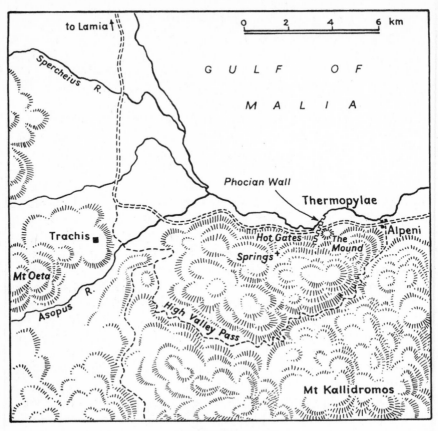

3   THERMOPYLAE

can circumvent the defence and take the opposition in the rear or –
quite simply – bypass the defenders and march forward. Leonidas,
like Themistocles, had shown that he rejected the Isthmian Line
thinking of so many of the Peloponnesians, and had proved it by
his willingness to march all the way from Sparta to this lonely pass
in the north. The very name of the mountain which protected the
landward flank of the Spartans was a clue in itself to a weakness in
the Thermopylae position. Kallidromos means 'Beautiful Running
Track'. Now it is true that such a name might well be applied by
local inhabitants in jest, or even in the sense of placating a formidable place. (Just so the Sicilians who inhabit the fertile but ever-
dangerous slopes of Mount Etna to this day call it 'The Beautiful
Mountain' – more to conciliate the volcano than to show their

aesthetic appreciation of it.) Herodotus does not use the name Kallidromos, though at a later date the great geographer Strabo does, and one senses that it is an old local name and that it had a meaning. For Kallidromos does provide a beautiful track.

'[It] was originally discovered', Herodotus writes, 'by the Malians of the area. Later they used it to help the Thessalians, leading them over it to attack Phocis at a time *when the Phocians had built themselves a wall across the pass to protect themselves from invasion.*' (My italics.) It had long been known, then, that the Phocian wall which Leonidas and his men had just rebuilt and reinforced could be bypassed comparatively easily. The men of Phocis who were serving with Leonidas knew all about this route, and so of course did the Malians. The latter were about to be overrun by the Persians, and they had no cause to love the Spartans. Herodotus comments: 'So, for a long time, its treacherous use had been known to the Malians. The track begins at the Asopus, the stream which flows through the narrow gorge. The track itself, like the mountain, is called Anopaea. It ends at Alpenos, the first Locrian settlement after one leaves Malis.'

Kallidromos, in fact, as its name suggests, was not a spiny ridge of rock (such as one might expect from a casual inspection), but along its crest there run two parallel ridges, between which lies a narrow but fertile mountain plain which at that time was fringed by dense oak forests. It was of course impossible that Leonidas should not know about this for, even if as a man from the Peloponnese he had no personal knowledge of it, his Phocian allies would have been the first to tell him of its existence. The indictment of the Greek Ephialtes (a man from Malis as one might expect) by ancient and subsequent modern historians, as the Judas who betrayed the Spartans and the Greek cause is over-severe. Indeed, one or two other names were traditionally given as the name of the *guide* who led the Persians over the mountain. The fact is that even if it was a man called Ephialtes, which one may accept, there were others who could have shown the Persians the way. Most shepherds, local farmers, or mountain men could have done so. The great secret about Thermopylae and 'the selling of the pass' is that there was no secret.

Leonidas naturally would have been the first to hear about it, and he did what one expects any commander to do. He realised at once that, since he could not abandon Thermopylae, which he had been entrusted to guard so as to maintain the strategic line with Artemisium and the fleet, he must set a watch-dog on the path that outflanked his position. Ideally, he would have chosen for such a role a Spartan contingent – men trained from childhood in war, in tracking down subversive Helots in their hideaways, men who could hear in a rustle of grass the passing of a potential enemy, and men men who had consecrated themselves by the laws of Lycurgus to stand and die. ('Come back *with* your shield or on it,' as the Spartan mother is said to have told her son.) Unfortunately, because he had no more than his 300 chosen Spartiates, Leonidas could not afford to deplete the ranks of these trained professionals who would have to stand and face the army of the Great King, and who would have to officer their mixed allied force – men of uncertain training whose morale and discipline could not necessarily be relied upon. Leonidas has been criticised, with the benefit of hindsight, by later historians for not having sent a Spartan contingent to guard the pass over Kallidromos, or at least for not having sent a Spartan handful to ensure that the leadership was resolute. It is difficult under the circumstances to see that he could have done other than what he did: he sent back the Phocian contingent, 1000 strong, to take up a position where they could deny any enemy the passage long enough for the news to get through to Leonidas that the *well-known* route over the mountain was being used. The men of Phocis were familiar with the area, had known it for many years; they had shown themselves resolute enough to be prepared to join this Spartan advance guard and face the overpowering enemy from the East. The real trouble was to stem from the fact that 'the dog did not bark in the night'.

That darkness was approaching. At about the same time as the capture of the fifteen triremes by the allied Greek fleet, the head of the Persian army was forming up in Lamia. Many historians (mostly study-bound men until this century) have written about armies just 'arriving', but armies in any century – even in the mechanised war-bedevilled one in which we live – take some time in which to arrive. Scouts must go ahead, followed by fast and lightly armed troops, a crack spearhead, and then in turn the main – however disciplined – somewhat amorphous body, followed in its turn by commissariat, baggage-train, pack animals, and sundry followers. The bulk of the army of the Great King most probably advanced in two columns, one along the coastline and the other going inland by the Othrys mountain-route. The arrival of Xerxes near Trachis between the rivers Spercheius and Asopus, and the fact that he stayed there for four days before any attack on the Thermopylae position developed, means little more than that the king and his staff were waiting for the main body of the army to come up and regroup. The first to arrive on the scene will have been the advance guard of cavalry (Herodotus says 'one man on horseback'). Xerxes now knew that it was the Spartans who were holding the pass against him, but it is likely that he knew that it was not the Spartans alone but a mixed force of Greeks. Perhaps Demaratus, who will certainly have heard that Leonidas was at their head, may have assured him that it could not be the full force out of Sparta as this would not be permitted by their strict laws until after the festival of the Carneian moon?

Like any sensible commander-in-chief Xerxes determined, even at this last hour, to try a divisive and conciliatory policy. According to Diodorus, but no more than hinted at in Herodotus, Xerxes sent heralds to the Greek lines to tell the defenders of the pass that if they laid down their arms they might depart in safety. More than that, the Great King assured them that if they did so they would be considered as allies of the Persians and would be rewarded with far richer lands than those they now possessed. It was hardly surprising that this tempting offer produced some division and argument in the Greek camp, but one must take leave to doubt that these heralds were ever allowed behind the Phocian wall. If they were, indeed, ever sent, they would certainly have been met by a Greek delegation in the pass. Leonidas could never have been so foolish as to allow any Persians to see quite how small was the force that stood waiting to oppose them. It would seem that 'the Peloponnesians', from whom one can safely exclude the Spartiates, were in favour of the old idea of falling back and holding the Isthmian wall. 'Leonidas', it is categorically stated, 'said that they must stay where they were. But at the same time they must send an appeal to all the states in the confederacy to despatch reinforcements, as their own numbers were inadequate to cope with the Persians.' The men of Phocis and of Locris very naturally were in agreement with the Spartan king, for it was their lands and their cities which would be devastated by the enemy if northern Greece was abandoned. Xerxes' offer was rejected.

Herodotus now tells the story which, famous though it is, must be repeated yet again for the brilliant light which it throws upon a small but significant moment in human history:

> During the conference Xerxes sent a horseman to find out the strength of the Greek force. . . . The Persian approached the camp and made a survey of all that he could see [evidence enough that the heralds were never allowed behind the Phocian wall] and to observe what the soldiers were doing. This was not, of course, all the Greek force, for he could not make out the troops behind the reconstructed and guarded wall. Nevertheless, he took careful note of those troops who were stationed outside the wall. At that time they happened to be Spartans, some of whom were stripped for exercise while others were combing their hair. He watched them in astonishment and took due note of their numbers, and then rode back at leisure. No one attempted to pursue him and indeed, no one took the slightest notice of him.

This truly 'laconic' behaviour must have astounded the Persians even as much as it did the Great King when the horseman came back into his presence with his report.

Demaratus cannot have failed to be concerned on hearing that a Spartan force under Leonidas was holding the pass. The latter was no enemy of the exiled king and, although Demaratus hoped to regain his throne and save Sparta through his friendship with the Persian monarch, he cannot have wanted to be responsible for the annihilation of a force composed of Spartiates. Not only did he know Leonidas but, in that small world of the unwalled city to the south, he will have known all the men, or the families of all the men, who were now (so casually, it seemed to Xerxes) preparing themselves to die in battle. Perhaps it could be avoided? He is already supposed to have sent a secret message to Sparta, warning his people of the time of the invasion – a message which passed like uncensored mail through the Persian lines because its real contents were written on the wooden tablet below the wax, where normal letters were inscribed. (This hidden message is said to have been discovered by the clever wife of Leonidas himself, bright-eyed

Gorgo.) When asked by the king who were these men outside the wall in the pass, Demaratus told him that they were Spartans. He cannot possibly have hoped to weaken the king's determination to invade Greece, but it is just possible that he may have tried to make his kinsmen sound so formidable that Xerxes and his staff would decide to leave them alone and make a detour round Thermopylae. In any case, he owed it to himself as their former king to make them sound as awe-inspiring as possible – and therefore most useful allies after his restoration.

Whatever his sources for this episode, Herodotus produces a very convincing speech by the exiled and unhappy Spartan king. 'On a previous occasion,' Demaratus said, 'you have heard me talk about these men. I told you at the time how this venture would turn out.' (The wreck of a large part of the Persian fleet may have served to give him an uneasy feeling of disaster.)

> My Lord, I only try and tell the truth when in your presence. You mocked me before, but please hear me again. These men are making ready for the coming battle and they are determined to contest our entrance to the Pass. It is normal behaviour for the Spartans to groom their hair carefully before they prepare themselves to face death. I can reassure you on one point: if these men can be defeated and the others of them who are still at home, then there is no one else in the whole world who will dare to lift a hand, or stand against you.

The Great King smiled. What was a small stone wall to a ruler who had bridged the Hellespont and driven a channel for his ships through the land behind Mount Athos? What was a scuffle of dust across a small plain to disturb the ruler of the greatest empire that the world had ever known?

BATTLE

ONE GOOD REASON for the apparent delay of Xerxes before sending his troops forward to attack the Spartan position was the state of the fleet. Had the great storm not occurred, and had the fleet proceeded as intended round to their rendezvous, eliminating any of the Greek ships *en route*, then the attack on Thermopylae could undoubtedly have begun within a day or two. Even the advance-guard of the army was sufficient to make the first exploratory probe against the walled pass and the limited number of defenders that it could accommodate. The storm damage occasioned to the ships, requiring several days to repair, seems sufficient reason to account for the Persian delay – delay which, naturally enough, the Greeks later liked to see as fearful hesitation. The idea of the Persian monarch, with his vast army, turning timorous at the very first sign of Greek resistance is absurd. Xerxes, as has been seen, had been in no great hurry since his entry into Greece and, at the beginning of a campaign, which had been years in the preparation, he was unlikely to jeopardise his opening move.

The account as given by Herodotus is confusing, but the sequence of events would seem that after the three-day storm, while the main body of the Persian fleet was sorting itself out and making good the damage in the Gulf of Pagasae, Xerxes decided on a bold move and despatched a force of 200 ships with the intention of bottling up the Greek fleet within the Euripus channel. Their orders were to proceed north-east through the Skiathos channel so as to give the impression to the watching Greeks that they were heading north. Once through the channel, they turned south making their way down the long and dangerous eastern flank of Euboea. It was a calculated risk, but one which would certainly pay dividends if they could block the Greek sea route at Chalcis while the main body of their fleet, battle-ready after its repairs, would come down on them from the north. The Greeks would have no escape and could be annihilated at leisure. The news of this daring plan was brought by a certain Scyllias, a famous swimmer and diver, who had been working for the Persians on salvage operations, during which he seems to have saved his foreign masters a great deal of money – 'as well as putting plenty aside for himself'. Either by boat, or by a ten-mile swim from Aphetae, he came ashore at Artemisium with the alarming news that this squadron was even now turning for its passage east of Euboea with the intention of outflanking the Greeks and bottling them up from their potential line of retreat. This information was immediately sent back to an Athenian squadron of fifty-three ships which had not yet started for Artemisium to alert them as to the danger. Scyllias also brought the Greeks some reassuring news: the extent of the storm damage that had overtaken the Persians.

The Greeks had a little time to reflect, for it would take this Persian task-force about two days and nights to get round Euboea. Inevitably there was a good deal of dissension among them – some being in favour of abandoning Artemisium and getting back south. Throughout the debate that followed it is made clear that Eurybiades, with his typical Peloponnesian outlook, was all for withdrawing. Themistocles, on the other hand, was for staying and taking the offensive against the Persians before they had regrouped and made good all their repairs. In the end he triumphed in what can only be called a very Greek way. The Euboeans, hearing that the Spartan commander was in favour of withdrawal and knowing that this would lead to the devastation of their island, came to Themistocles with a massive bribe to be distributed as he would, if only he could prevail on the other commanders and particularly Eurybiades to stay put. Themistocles was never averse to money, so he pocketed as much as seemed suitable for himself, passed over a sixth of the sum to Eurybiades (who changed his mind about withdrawing), and squared the other commanders. Even at this late hour, and with the fate of their country in the balance, it is instructive to see how their typically Mediterranean rationale never deserted the Greeks. Very illuminating is the story recounted by Plutarch of how Themistocles dealt with one of the commanders who was in favour of withdrawal.

Among his own countrymen the bitterest opposition he encountered came from Architeles, the captain of the sacred state
galley, who was anxious to sail back to Athens because he did
not have enough money to pay his crew. So Themistocles stirred
up the feelings of Architeles' men against him to such a pitch
that they made a rush at him and snatched away his dinner. Then
while Architeles was still nursing his indignation and chagrin at
this, Themistocles sent him a box containing a dinner of bread
and meat and under it a talent of silver. He told Architeles to eat
his dinner at once and look after his crew in the morning, otherwise he would denounce him publicly for accepting money from
the enemy.

On the day following the great debate (probably 17 August) the
decision was taken, again on the initiative of Themistocles, to
attack the Persian fleet to the north of them. It was difficult once
more to convince Eurybiades and the other commanders of the
wisdom of such an offensive move. Having agreed to stay at
Artemisium they were now in favour of letting the enemy come
down to them. What probably turned the scales was not only the
eloquence and possibly even blackmailing tactics of Themistocles
(he knew who had received bribes) but also the first-hand report
from Scyllias of the sorry state in which the storm had left so many
of the enemy. They were not all in one place, but dispersed over a
number of anchorages and it should be possible to cut out at any
rate some of them before the main body could assemble. In any
case it was high time that they took the measure of the Persian
fleet and had a chance to compare their own battle tactics with
theirs.

Late in the afternoon the Greeks made their move to the north,
taking confidence in the fact that by starting at such a time they
would, if things went against them, be able to withdraw to Artemisium towards nightfall. The Persians, for their part, could hardly
believe that so small a force compared to their own was daring to
come out to the attack. They got under way at their leisure, being
confident of annihilating them. The Greek ships were heavier and
slower and the Phoenicians and others felt sure that, with their
greater speed and manœuvrability, they would easily capture them.
However, since they were putting out from a number of harbours

at different times, while the Greeks advanced in battle-array, Themistocles' optimism was justified. His force managed to sink a number of the enemy and put several others to flight. But, as the Persian numbers built up, they were gradually able to try an encircling movement known as the *periplous*: a tactic designed to constrict the Greeks so that they would fall foul of one another, thus becoming an easy prey. (The technique was similar to that of the seine net in fishing.) To forestall this, the well-trained Athenians and their allies responded by forming 'into a close circle – bows outward and sterns to the centre'. Known as the *kuklos*, this was not only an excellent defensive tactic but it enabled the circle, at a given signal, to explode outward, each trireme striking at the nearest enemy. The Persians learned to their cost how highly trained was the adversary whom they had started by regarding with contempt. Although Xerxes had promised a reward to whoever should first capture one of the famed ships of Athens not a single Greek was taken, while thirty Persian ships were captured, among the prisoners being the brother of the king of Salamis in Cyprus, 'a man of repute in the enemy force'. As darkness came down the triumphant Greeks withdrew. It had been a satisfactory action from their point of view, enabling them to take the measure of the enemy. It also served to remind them that, in a long engagement, they would not have been able to cope with the overriding numbers of the Persian fleet.

It was on this same day, 18 August, that Xerxes had given the orders for the assault to begin on the Spartan position at Thermopylae. He could not wait much longer for the navy to achieve a victory and for the store ships to come back up the coast to bring more victuals. Although the preparation that had gone into the establishment of supply-dumps on the way had been excellent, the fact was that, once into Greece, the army was bound to go forward like a huge snake, eating its way as it moved. The raid carried out by Leonidas in the plain and the valley of the Spercheius must have left little in the immediate path of the army. The Greek fleet (until, he hoped, surprised from the rear) still faced his own navy at Artemisium. On the other hand, it would seem that only a handful of men guarded this pass between the mountains and the sea. It was clearly time to make a move by land. Early on the morning of that day, while Themistocles was still trying to convince his commanders to make an attack on the Persians in the evening, Xerxes decided to make a frontal assault on the Spartan position. It was poor tactics, and everyone on the staff must have known it, but it seemed the only action possible.

In that narrow place which lay before them across the summer-hot plain, the vast weight of the army could not be deployed. They were clearly committing themselves to an engagement that could only suit the enemy (and Demaratus with his trained eye must have recognised that Thermopylae was ideal for a hoplite action). Neither Demaratus as a southerner from the Peloponnese, nor any of the Persians, nor any of the Ionian Greeks to be found in the camp, yet knew about the 'secret' of Kallidromos. To these invading foreigners the only immediate route lay through the pass ahead. When Ephialtes came forward with the news of an alternative, it was only in this respect that he could be considered a traitor to the Greeks. The Persians, accustomed as they were to a mountainous land and able to view the country in front of them (easy to discern the hill-slopes behind the savage pass), would sooner or later have discovered the way to circumvent the Greeks. For the moment, though, it seemed that the only course was to try to overwhelm the force that opposed them.

Herodotus' statement that Xerxes was filled with rage because, although he had given the defenders of the pass four days in which to withdraw, they still made no move almost certainly reflects his sustained portrait of the Great King as an Oriental tyrant. It was only with considerable reluctance, one suspects, that Xerxes gave the order for first the Medes and then the men from Susa to attack. On the reason why these divisions should have been chosen as the spearhead Ephorus has the interesting and possibly accurate comment that Xerxes put the Medes in first either because he thought they were the bravest of his men (unlikely from a Persian monarch) or 'because he wished to see them destroyed, since the Medes had a proud spirit, the supremacy exercised by their ancestors [over the Persians] having only recently been destroyed'.

The Medes were commanded by Tigranes the Achaemenid and were equipped in the same manner as the Persians, who had indeed adopted it from the Medes in the first place. They wore dome-shaped helmets of hammered bronze or iron, a jacket of fish-scale mail with a sleeved embroidered tunic over it, long trousers, and carried light wicker shields. Their arms consisted of short spears, a dagger, and bows with a quiverful of short arrows. Although admirably suited for a certain type of warfare in the mountains, or in deserts, or in the great plains of Asia, such protection and such armament was woefully inadequate against the hoplite line which they were now about to encounter. Those were brave men indeed who now moved forward against the wall of huge bronze shields, the intimidating (and highly protective) helmets, the bronze cuirasses and leg guards which gleamed defiantly as they advanced across the plain and into the defile. It was true that the Persians' shower of arrows might 'darken the sun' (an advance report, about which one Spartan had remarked, 'Good, then we shall fight in the shade'), but when it came to close-quarter work, as it must, the weapon that would be dominant was the long Greek spear. 'The fox has many tricks and the hedgehog one good one', and at the Hot Gates the bristling hedgehog would prove more than formidable.

'The Medes charged,' writes Herodotus, 'and in the ensuing struggle many of them fell; but others took their place, and in spite of savage losses they refused to give up.' This is fair and accurate war-reporting, but his subsequent comment bears the bias of later Greek attitudes and must be dismissed: 'They made it clear enough to any observer, as well as to the king himself, that he had indeed many men in his army, but few soldiers.' It is doubtful perhaps if he had, even among the Immortals, soldiers of the calibre of the Spartans, but he had the same quality of men who had conquered a vast empire. As for their courage, it cannot be dismissed.

As man after man fell in the narrow pass so another came forward to take his place. Finally, the Medes were withdrawn. Now, even the carefully bred toughness of the Spartans was put to the test as a fresh wave – the men of Susa – came up against them. The bodies piled upon bodies may have given the fresh arrivals a shield behind which to kneel down and fire their arrows, but even so they could not break the Greek line. One must imagine the scene not as it is told in picture and story books – a simple row of grim Spartans facing the whole of the onslaught – but a regular and organised changeover of hoplites, Spartan-officered, but composed out of all the small allied force. It was growing late in the afternoon, probably about the same time that the Greek fleet was achieving its tactical if limited success against the Persians, when Xerxes and his staff decided to clear the pass before the end of the day. It was time for a breakthrough. The Immortals were ordered forward.

15

FIRST NIGHT AND SECOND DAY

THE IMMORTALS, the crack Guards division which was now ordered out against the Greeks, will have advanced with something of the same military precision as that of the Spartans. They represented the dignity of the most highly professional men-at-arms in the Persian Empire. It was the regiment into which every Elamite, Mede or Persian soldier wished to enrol. They went out across the plain with their general Hydarnes under the keen eye of their monarch. 'They advanced to the attack full of confidence that they would overcome the opposition without much trouble.'

Brave they were and disciplined they were, but they found, as had the Medes and others before them, that in the confines of the pass their numbers were a hindrance rather than a help. Once again their short spears could not penetrate that formidable bristling line of the Greeks, nor their arrows pierce the great bronze shields. As countless wars have shown, courage is not enough. Against superior weaponry even the bravest must fail, and when those better weapons were wielded by men whose whole life had been nothing but a preparation for war the outcome was inevitable. Herodotus memorably describes one of the Spartan battle-tactics that caused havoc among the Immortals.

One of the feints they used was to pretend to turn and fly all at once. Seeing them apparently taking to their heels, the barbarians would pursue them with a great clatter and shouting; whereupon, just as the Persians were almost upon them, the Spartans would wheel and face them, and in this about-turn they would inflict innumerable casualties upon them. In doing this, the Spartans had some losses too, but only a few. In the end, since they could make no headway towards winning the pass, whether they attacked in companies or whatever they did, the Persians broke off the engagement and withdrew. It is said that Xerxes, who was watching the battle from his throne, three times sprang to his feet in fear for his army.

To watch his finest troops, who came under his own personal command, suffering such savage losses, must have been intolerable and dismaying to the Great King. No doubt Demaratus found it a convenient moment to be absent from the royal circle and to hold his tongue.

The Spartans and the allies could now withdraw, bandage their wounds, eat some very necessary food and take their rest. Even for the hardest of men it had been a hard day and, although the sight of the dead in the pass served to remind them of the heavy losses they had inflicted on the enemy, all of them knew that tomorrow would be an inevitable repetition of the day that was over. The night, too, was to prove a savage one. Yet another storm blew up, 'with torrential rain and with loud thunder from Mount Pelion'. The fact that Herodotus mentions the rain and the thunder indicates that this storm was of quite a different vintage from the 'Hellesponter' that had caused the damage to the Persian fleet before. Some scholars in the past have confused or combined these two storms into one, but it is abundantly clear that they were of a completely different nature. When the Persian task-force had been despatched to round Euboea and cut off the Athenians from the south the *first* storm had blown over. No doubt it was reckoned, on a good average estimate of Aegean conditions, that several days or more of clear weather might follow upon this first hard gale. It is not all that unusual, however, after the first imbalance in the weather has taken place, for subsidiary bad weather to follow as the barometric levels sort themselves out and the air temperatures over land and sea re-adjust. Herodotus remarks, as with some surprise, that 'it was now the middle of Summer' – that is, that it was a very strange thing to happen. But this was not so; it was the third week in August and, as the meteorological tables show, the continuity of the good weather associated with the *meltemi* is no longer to be relied upon. The wind that now blew up, with its accompanying torrential rainfall, was a typical sirocco from the south-east. (Somewhere down over Egypt the *khamsin*, the hot desert wind, had started to blow and, picking up water-vapour from the sea on its way, now discharged it as the swollen air struck the mountainous flanks of Greece.)

The result was yet another disaster for the Persians at sea. (Rightly had the Delphic oracle advised the Athenians to 'pray to the winds'.) The 200-ship force which, showing remarkable speed, had nearly rounded Euboea was caught off the area known as 'The Hollows' near Carystus, at the very southern end of the island. A few hours more and they would have been into the Euboea Channel but, as it happened, they could not have been in a worse place when the roaring southerly struck. 'It found them in the open sea – and miserable was their end. The storm and rain caught them . . . and every ship, unable to see where they were going for the rain, was forced to drive before the wind and ran upon the rocks.'

The claim of Herodotus that every ship was destroyed seems suspect. If the sirocco did indeed strike the ships while they were off the series of bays at the head of which Carystus stands, it seems unlikely that none of them will have been able to make port in Carystus itself – and Carystus was pro-Persian. If, on the other hand, the Persians were still off the eastern end of Euboea (more likely in view of the time factor), then some of them will certainly have been able to run back north with the wind under their sterns. But of one thing there can be absolutely no doubt; they never rounded Euboea. The southerly gale finally put paid to the clever, but always risky, stratagem of despatching the 200 ships to take the Athenians in the rear. Of this we can be quite certain, for the fifty-three Athenian ships which had been guarding the approaches by Chalcis picked up some of the storm-shattered advance-guard of the Persians, interrogated them and, having discovered the extent of the disaster, the Athenians promptly sailed north to join Themistocles at Artemisium.

'It's an ill wind. . . .' The southerly that had wreaked havoc on their enemies boosted the Athenians up the Euripus Channel to give Themistocles fifty-three new vessels at the very moment that he most needed them. Emboldened by this great good news the reinforced Athenian fleet (and this time, one imagines, there were no protests from Eurybiades) proceeded to adopt the same hit-and-run tactics they had found fruitful before. Once again in the late afternoon or early evening they swept up from Artemisium. They found an enemy almost totally demoralised by this second gale.

They had huddled in Aphetae, thinking they were doomed, as the wind and the rain had swept up from the south. Themistocles and his commanders fell upon them like a lightning bolt that evening, attacked and destroyed the Cilician squadron, and moved back to Artemisium before a major action could possibly take place. Once more their withdrawal was covered by the swift fall of darkness. It was another brilliant small victory, boosting the pride of the Greeks at the same time as their confidence was reassured by the news of the destruction of the Persians off Euboea.

On the morning of this day, 19 August, Xerxes threw in fresh crack troops, encouraging them with lavish promises of the rewards that would be theirs if they succeeded, but dire warnings of what would happen to them if they failed. He had calculated also that since the Greeks 'were so few in number, they would be too exhausted and too worn down by wounds to put up much of a resistance'. The Great King was to be bitterly disappointed. The Greeks, as we have seen – with the exception of the Phocians guarding the pass – were organised in divisions according to their states and, in the intervals between the attacks, were able to replace the narrow front line with men who had come up fresh (or as much so as possible) from behind. To judge from a later observation of Herodotus, it seems likely that even by this second day the Persian morale was so low that they had to be driven forward by the whips of overseers (military police have never been over-popular!). In the confusion of those in front trying to turn back from the bronze wall bristling with spears and those at the back running forward to escape the blows across their shoulders the chaos was complete. Yard upon yard in front of the Greek line was piled with slain and wounded while the sickly sweet smell of death was everywhere on the air. 'So, finding that they were doing no better than on the previous day, the Persians once again withdrew.'

Xerxes was in despair and had no idea how to deal with the situation. As has been said, the Persians would no doubt within a matter of days have found the way over the mountain and down to take the Greeks in the rear, but what was the pressing cause for concern was the provisioning of the army. By this time, one imagines, except for a straggling 'tail', the whole host must have been up and encamped around. No store-ships had come up from the south and, although one can only guess at the amount of communication there may have been by sea between the fleet and the army, such news as did come through from the south will all have been bad. Indeed, at about this time when Xerxes and his staff were debating their next move, Themistocles was making the second of his lightning raids on the demoralised Persian fleet.

It was at this moment of gloom in the Great King's camp that Ephialtes so opportunely put in his appearance. Like many others he had no doubt expected the pass to have fallen on the first day, and certainly on the second. The sight of the bedraggled troops returning yet again defeated across the plain must have prompted him to come to the Great King in person (possibly before someone else did?). It will have been clear by now that such information had acquired a real value, so 'in hope of a rich reward' he made his way to the king. Burn comments: 'What the guide Ephialtes had to show his masters was not the existence of a route leading east on top of the mountains, which was locally common knowledge (Hdt. 7, 175), *but exactly where to turn east.*' (My italics.) Ephialtes was not only prepared to tell them where to cross the Asopus, so as to begin their climb to the easy ground between the two ridges of Kallidromos, but he was prepared to act in person as their guide. It was this that made all the difference. It was one night before the full moon – that Carneian moon which had held back the full Spartan army – so that the Persians and their guide would have the benefit of it all night long, as they made their way by the track about which this man from Malis was now telling the Great King.

Xerxes wasted no more time. He sent for Hydarnes, commander of the Immortals. The Persian Guards may have suffered fairly heavy losses and a blow to their morale the day before, but the losses will have been made up and their morale could now be restored. In the pass of the Hot Gates they had been fighting under conditions that were thoroughly unfavourable to them. But these were men familiar with another kind of warfare, and their training and their weaponry were ideal for hard, fast marching under mountain conditions.

Xerxes was sending them where they could prove to all the army that they were indeed the Great King's chosen Ten Thousand, and he was sending them where they could take their revenge.

16

OVER THE MOUNTAIN

At 'about the time that the lamps are lit' Hydarnes and the Immortals moved out with their guide from the camp. They had an all-night march ahead of them and the reason they delayed until nearly dark was most probably to ensure that their movements were unseen by any of the watchful enemy. There are almost more theories as to their approach route to the saddle of Kallidromos than there are possible approaches. The simplest, and therefore as so often in ancient history perhaps the best, was that they crossed the River Asopus early in their march and took the shorter but harder way up the mountain than that offered by a longer but easier route. While the men were fresh it would have seemed wise to take a more taxing route for, once up in the narrow plain along the mountain's top, the going would have been relatively easy to hardened soldiers who were, it must be remembered, inhabitants of a mountainous country. (The words of Cyrus come to mind.) The steepness of the track that leads up by this route will almost certainly have been less so over two thousand years ago. As all over Greece, the soil erosion during the centuries has changed many a contour, and the oak-forests which once lay up this way will themselves have contributed to hold earth that is now long since gone.

'By this path, then,' Herodotus continues, 'having crossed the Asopus, the Persians marched all night. They had on their right the mountains of the Oeitians and on their left those of the Trachinians. By the time they reached the top of the mountain dawn was just breaking.' All this, of course, is just reconstruction – and certainly, by the evidence of his words, Herodotus never came this way himself. He did, as others have pointed out, clearly come to Thermopylae and examine the site of the battlefield and he certainly – as always – went to the best possible source of information that he could find. There can be little doubt that it would have been round about dawn that the Persians, moving at a good disciplined pace, will have put the hard climb behind them and have entered on the relatively easy part of their passage over the mountain along its spine. At some point along here (and speculation is endless) the Phocians were encamped, detailed off by Leonidas for this very purpose, to guard the approach route and to make sure that no one got through without a struggle. Unfortunately, the Phocians, like many citizen armies of that time, seem to have been ill-disciplined soldiers – compared, that is, to professionals like the Spartans or the Immortals.

Despite the fact that the battle had raged in the pass for two days, the Phocians seem to have set no sentries and to have been taken completely by surprise. They had volunteered for this duty 'to watch the track and protect their country', and Leonidas must be forgiven for not anticipating that such volunteers would not have shown the slightest traces of professionalism. The first thing apparently that the Phocians knew of the approach of the Persian force was the sound of 'the marching feet which made a loud rustling and swishing sound in the fallen leaves'. The oak-trees will have become somewhat dry by this time in August, and the recent gales will undoubtedly have sent down thousands of leaves to join the detritus that already covered the mountain track. It was a windless night, we are told, and this vivid description contains all the elements of truth. The Phocians were asleep with no outposts to their position, no guards set, and, of course, without their armour on. (The expression 'caught with their trousers down' might serve as their monument.)

'When the Persians caught sight of men in front of them seizing their arms they were amazed, for they had not expected any opposition. Now they seemed to have run into an armed body of men. Hydarnes, afraid that they might be Spartans, asked Ephialtes who they were; and on hearing the truth, prepared to engage them.' There is something a little curious in this part of the story about 'the dog that did not bark in the night-time'. If it was only dawn or early light how could Ephialtes have been so sure that they were not Spartans – except by their sheer incompetence? Hoplite armour throughout Greece was very similar, no distinguishing signs would have been readily visible, and even if the alarmed men were shouting out to one another in a dialect of Greek other than Doric one does not imagine that Ephialtes was an expert in linguistics. Again, the phrase 'on hearing the truth' suggests that Ephialtes or others had been scouting up this way before, seen the Phocian camp, recognised them for whom they were and had kept to himself the confident knowledge that the Persians would be more than a match for them. But, if this had been the case, surely he would have told Xerxes, and Hydarnes would have been forewarned and fore-armed? There is an element of mystery here.

The Phocians, in any case, seem to have behaved in a most in-competent and even cowardly manner. True, there were only one thousand of them and this body of men who were now advancing were clearly far greater in number, but an organised and determined resistance in a comparatively narrow area was what had been expected of them if the worst should happen and the enemy find their way through by the 'secret' of Kallidromos. As the Persians drew up in battle order, knelt and began to open fire on this sur-prised enemy, the Phocians fled under the hail of arrows and made for the safety of a nearby peak. 'They thought themselves', writes Herodotus, 'the main object of attack.' How could they? They had been placed to keep watch and ward over this mountain passage so that the main body of the Greeks below should not be surprised and taken in the rear. Perhaps, with over two millennia intervening, one tends to think in too sophisticated a manner. It is somewhat like the modern astonishment that a full-moon festival could have delayed the movement of the body of the Spartan army at this time when their country was threatened. (Over sixty years later, a sophisticated Athenian general was to lose his army in Sicily through failing to move at the right time because there was an eclipse of the moon.) In any case, the Phocians find, and have found, no credit. They clung to the safety of their hillside while the Immortals, having driven off this undisciplined party of Greeks, passed almost contemptuously on their way through the mountain-side.

Hydarnes could afford the luxury of a smile. This Greek Ephialtes had shown them the correct way over the mountain (none of that Greek duplicity), or it would not have been guarded at all – how-ever inefficiently. If all the Greeks were like the Spartans, even the Great King would have had to consider the wisdom of his advance.

But this body of men who had been caught unprepared, and had then been unwilling to stand and fight, must have given him considerable confidence. Possibly the majority of the Greeks were as undisciplined and as incompetent as these? The Persians passed on, 'going fast'. They knew that it could not be long before the news that they were up on the mountain would reach the defenders of the pass. But in any case, whatever happened now, the Immortals could feel in the morning air the dawn of triumph. They were through.

The news, it would seem, had already reached Leonidas. 'The Greeks at Thermopylae heard from their seer Megistias that death was coming with the dawn.' He had been taking the omens and saw their fate written in the sacrifice. Deserters also came in during the night with the news of the Persians outflanking them over the mountain. One of these Ionian Greeks, who had developed a conscience about being in the Great King's ranks, is named by Ephorus as Tyrrhastiadas of Cyme and, since this was also the birthplace of Ephorus, the story may well represent the genuine and proud tradition of a local family that their ancestor had been the man who brought the news to Leonidas. By then the Spartan king had become a hero for all time, and such associations will have been treasured. Diodorus and others also tell a tale, which most authorities have considered suspect, that Leonidas, knowing all was lost, personally led a suicidal attempt on the Persian lines to try to kill Xerxes. We can be sure that this is untrue, for we know that Leonidas stayed to the last at Thermopylae, as was his duty and as befitted a Spartan king. It is most probably no more than one of the many accretions of legend which came to surround that last day. On the other hand, it is just possible that a small group of Spartans were sent forward by their king to try to locate the tent of Xerxes and assassinate him. Green makes the good comment: 'To dismiss the tradition out of hand is perhaps a little rash. How credible are historians a thousand years hence likely to find the Long Range Desert Group's attempt on Rommel's life in 1942?'

A last council of war was held and it seems clear that opinions were divided. There are two versions of what took place at this meeting and Herodotus gives them both.

Some urged that they must not abandon the post, others the

opposite. The result was that the army split, with some contingents returning to their various states while others prepared to stand by Leonidas. It is said that Leonidas himself dismissed them in order to spare their lives. As for the Spartans it would be not in their code for them to desert the post which they had been entrusted to guard.

There can certainly never have been any possibility of the Spartans having been undecided as to their course: they had been sent to hold the pass to safeguard the fleet at Artemisium and they would do so to the end. It is clear enough that there was some dissension, and that the Thespians and Thebans stayed with Leonidas of their volition, but that the confederate troops from the Peloponnese, who had possibly fallen back upon that old strategical concept of defence of the Isthmus, were sent home. Some have argued that Leonidas sent them back so that they could live to fight another day, others that he dismissed them with contempt because they were unwilling to stand and die. There can be nothing but speculation. One thing is certain: if Leonidas did not order them back against their will, they would always afterwards have said that it was only at the king's express command that they had left him.

The force that stayed is unlikely to have numbered more than 2000 out of the original strength of 300 Spartiates, some 900 Helots, 400 Thebans and 700 Thespians (2300). Over the past two days of savage fighting it would be reasonable to assume that some 200 to 300 of these must either have been killed or too gravely wounded to stand any more in the line. Leonidas most certainly had in his mind that response which the Delphic oracle had earlier given at the outset of the Persian campaign:

Hear your fate, O dwellers in Sparta of the wide spaces;
Either your famed, great town must be sacked by Perseus'
  sons,
Or, if that be not, the whole land of Lacedaemon
Shall mourn the death of a king of the house of Heracles,
For not the strength of lions or of bulls shall hold him,
Strength against strength; for he has the power of Zeus,
And will not be checked until one of these two he has
  consumed.

138

Some indication that Leonidas would have been prepared to receive volunteers from the departing men is proved by the case of the seer Megistias whom he expressly ordered back. Megistias from Acarnania, said to be a descendant of Melampus (who understood the langauge of all creatures), outrightly refused to obey the king but instead sent back his son with the other Acarnanians. If a seer, a holy man who was not expected to stand in the front line and fight, was allowed to volunteer and die, one suspects the later tale of the confederate allies that they only returned because that was the king's command. But they were withdrawing now, contingent by contingent, marching homeward down along the track southward – on to which, later in the day, would debouch Hydarnes and the Immortals. Was it with jeers or with indifference that those who stayed watched them go? With both perhaps, and also a little envy, however deep-concealed. In the light of the early morning the last of the defenders made ready to eat. The Spartans no doubt, their great helmets laid aside until the first attack came on, found time to comb their hair. Leonidas looked at them with the dour affection of all last-ditch commanders: 'Have a good breakfast, men, for we dine in Hades!'

17

END AND BEGINNING

XERXES NOW CELEBRATED the rising of the sun. Just as he had done at that golden moment when he had crossed the Hellespont, he poured a libation to the god. Ahuramazda, like the sun itself, came out of the East, and today would ensure that his believers had the victory. The Great King waited until 'about the time that the market-place is full' before giving the order for the army to move forward. The evocative phrase has the distinction of an age before time-pieces: it meant that hour or so, long after the farmers and the carts have come in from outlying villages to the town, when the citizens and women and slaves have attended to their household duties and have time to go out. Shopping and conversation are now the order of the day, before the sun rises too high and all sensible Mediterranean people retire into the shade like lizards. It was, there-fore, between nine and ten in the morning that Xerxes ordered his troops to cross the plain. The humidity of the night had worn off, the men had eaten, and now, before the heat of the day began, was the time to send them into action. The conclusion was obvious, in any case: within a few hours Hydarnes and the Immortals would be round at the rear of the pass.

The Spartans and their few allies waited to die. One must admire the amazing courage of the Thespians and the Thebans – and, indeed, of the Helots. Since childhood the Spartans had been conditioned by the iron laws of Lycurgus that this was the moment for which a man was born. The others had not. This makes their bravery to some degree more formidable and, though (as we later learn) a number of Thebans ultimately surrendered, the luminous glory that shines around the last stand of the Spartans at Thermo-pylae falls also on these other men. Leonidas, as soon as scouts reported that the Persians were on the move, changed his tactics. Knowing that it was only a matter of time before he was overwhelmed, he determined to inflict as many casualties as possible on the Persians before the end. With this in mind he ordered his small force out from the narrowest part of the pass, which they had been holding on the previous two days, and deployed it on a broader front where the path opened out.

Many legends were to spring up, as was only natural, about the last hours of the Greeks after they had heard that the Immortals were up on the mountain above them. Two of the Spartans were suffering from inflammation of the eyes (probably akin to acute 'pink-eye' and caused by the dust kicked up in the dry air) and had been sent back to Alpeni. One of them, hearing of the last-ditch stand, told his Helot servant to lead him to the front rank where, nearly blind as he was, he would still be able to strike out and take at least one or more of the enemy with him. The other stayed behind and returned home with the Peloponnesians. On his arrival in Sparta he was received with silent contumely by his fellows, nicknamed the Trembler, and would never have been forgiven if he had not rid himself of his disgrace by his subsequent death at Plataea. (It was better to die than return home partly blind, when your fellows had fallen with their faces to the foe.) Leonidas wanted to send a last message to Sparta, so he asked one of his Spartiates to take it back for him. 'I came here to fight not to act as a messenger,' was the reply. The king turned to another and put the same request, only to receive the laconic answer: 'I shall do my duty better by staying here, and in that way the news will be better.' Presumably a Helot was sent back with Leonidas' last despatch.

The first attack now developed and 'many of the invaders fell, while the company commanders behind them drove them forward, plying their whips relentlessly'. Once again, as throughout his history, Herodotus emphasises the free and voluntary nature of the Greeks in war, as against the sheeplike servitude of the Persians. One suspects exaggeration, although on this last day, after the previous demonstrations of the Greeks' prowess, it is quite possible that the enemy did have to be driven forward against the murderous 'hedgehog' of spears. 'Many of them were driven into the sea and drowned, while still more were trampled under foot by their own comrades. No one could count the number of the dead.' As the attack carried on relentlessly, many of the Greeks' spears were broken, and it was now that they drew their swords and came up hand to hand against the enemy. Helmets and shields dented and cut about, the brave plumes slashed away, the Spartans still fought on. 'During this part of the action Leonidas was killed, having fought most gallantly. . . .'

A savage battle now developed over the king's body, the Persians being determined to seize so valuable a trophy while the Spartans were even more determined to deny it to them. Four times the Greeks drove the enemy off, finally managing to drag the king back within their ranks. Among the many Persian dead 'of high distinction' who fell fighting over the body of Leonidas were two brothers of Xerxes, sons of Darius. Then came the moment which the Greeks had long been anticipating, the cry from a sentry at their rear: 'Here they come!' Hydarnes and the Immortals were in sight. Herodotus tells of the very last stand:

> They drew back again into the narrow neck of the Pass and formed themselves into a compact body all together – with the exception of the Thebans – and took up their stance on the Mound. This is the hillock at the entrance where now stands the stone lion in memory of the Lion's Son. In this place they defended themselves to the last, with their swords, if they still had them, and if not even with their hands and teeth. Then the Persians from in front, piling over the ruined wall, and those who closed in from behind, overwhelmed them with missiles.

The last word is significant; in Greek literally, 'thrown things', presumably arrows, javelins and even lumps of rock. To the very last the Persians kept their distance from these dying and indomitable men.

The Spartan Dieneces (he who had made the remark about 'fighting in the shade' if the arrows of the invaders darkened the sun) is especially singled out for praise, as well as two Spartan brothers, Alpheus and Maron, and above all a certain Thespian with the Bacchanalian name of Dithyrambus. The Thespians, like the Spartans, died to a man. One Spartan who, most unfairly, found himself in disgrace when he returned to his city was named Pantites. He had been sent by Leonidas with a message to Thessaly and was still away at the time of the battle. It is just possible that he had loitered, though, knowing the Spartan code, one doubts it. In any case, when he got back to his homeland he was treated as if he had been a coward and, unable to bear the imputation, hanged himself. The ruling caste of Spartiates enjoyed their privileges in Lacedaemon, but *noblesse oblige* is an expression that they might well have coined.

One may suspect Herodotus, with his pro-Athenian bias, of denigrating the Thebans, who had no love for Athens, but it is quite possible that – as he says – upon the final withdrawal to the mound they decided that they had done quite enough in the aid of a cause that was clearly hopeless. Their own city would now be overrun in any case and they and their leader may have felt that, even at this late hour, a show of submission would earn Thebes some respite. Throwing what weapons they had aside they came forward with open outstretched hands in the traditional gesture of surrender. Some of them were inevitably killed by men who were still hot for blood, but it says something for Persian discipline that the majority of those who gave themselves up were taken prisoner. They were branded with the King's mark – not, as has sometimes been suggested, an ignoble sign but, rather, one of some distinction.

By midday it must all have been over. Xerxes was now free to inspect the battlefield, noting as he did so the immense number of men the Spartans and their allies had cost him. He ordered them to be buried so that the troops following up behind would not suffer a loss of morale through the evidence of what a handful of Greeks could do. Only at one point did the royal sense of dignity and fitness yield to simple passion: the head was struck from the identified body of Leonidas and displayed before the troops on a pole. It was not a savage act, human enough under the circumstances, and the Great King had good reason to make a humiliating display of the Spartan leader. At some considerable cost he had proved that even these supposedly unbeatable Greeks were as mortal as all other men and the head of their king was evidence of it.

The assessment of the battle and its long-term effects will be apparent later. For the moment, all that mattered was that the Persian army was through and the hinge of the pass, upon which turned the whole situation of the Greek fleet, was broken. It can be no coincidence that on the same day that Thermopylae fell the Persian fleet gathered itself together for a concerted attack upon the Greeks at sea. Messengers had undoubtedly gone ahead even before

Hydarnes had come down off Kallidromos, and long before the final battle was over, giving the orders to strike by sea. It was essential to the Persian master-plan that army and fleet should work in concert together and, once it was clear that the pass would be breached that day, the word had gone to the fleet to take action against the Greeks at Artemisium. The failure of the force sent to round Euboea and take them from the south had been a considerable setback; what was now needed was a major fleet action where the Persian superiority in numbers must, so it seemed, inevitably win the day. By now they will have completed their re-fitting and, even if it is correct that none of the Euboea squadron returned to join the fleet, the Persians still had a considerable edge in numbers over the Athenians and the allies. Allowing for losses on both sides, the Persians would still seem to have had some 450 ships (possibly more) while the Greeks, even after the squadron from the south with its 53 fresh triremes had joined them, can scarcely have had more than 300.

Herodotus, unfortunately, with all his virtues, was not a naval historian and when he comes to actions at sea he is inclined to be as vague as any landsman. It is not difficult, however, to reconstruct the strategy and tactics of the day since it is obvious that the Persian objective must have been to clear the Greeks out of their way in order to secure the Euripus (the Euboea Channel) while correspondingly the Greek objective must have been to deny it to them. The Greeks will not have been 'by Artemisium' as Herodotus says, but farther west where they could oppose the enemy in the strait, most probably with their lead ships pointing towards the Gulf of Pagasae and their wings laid back so as to form a crescent-moon formation. At about noon – somewhere near the hour when the Spartans were making their last stand on the mound – the Persian fleet, having completed their preparations, moved out from Aphetae. They were also in a crescent formation but, with their superiority of numbers, they will have been able to throw their wings *forward*, the object being to envelop the Greek wings and constrict the smaller fleet in upon itself.

On that hot bright summer afternoon the initial collision must have exploded across the bay. Trireme met trireme head on, the great bronze rams crashing against one another like prehistoric beasts in combat, the forward oars snapping off as an enemy insinuated himself down one side, and the marines on both sides standing ready to board, or fighting across the interlocked bows of their ships. As has been seen, at this stage in naval warfare, once the initial manœuvring was over and the ships had been engaged, what developed was a miniature land-battle between ship and ship. Burn has pointed out: 'The sea-fights of 480 were largely marines' battles, for the press of ships rendered impossible much manœuvring for favourable position to use the ram.' Under these circumstances the heavier Greek ships, while not so fast or so dexterous as those from the Levant, had the advantage of solidity. Again, although the Greek marines were outnumbered by those carried by the enemy (somewhere in the ratio of 2:1, or 30 enemy marines to 14 Greeks per ship), the Greek armour was far superior. As Leonidas and his hoplites had just proved, one hoplite was worth a number of lightly armed men in hand-to-hand combat. Only against the Egyptians do the Greek marines seem to have fared rather badly, for the Egyptian marines were as heavily armed as they were, with large shields and – eminently practical – 'boarding pikes and heavy axes'. They also carried heavy swords while even their rowers at the bench, unlike the naked Greeks, were protected by a kind of corselet and carried long daggers for close-quarter work. Before the afternoon's fighting drew to a close the Egyptians had carried five Greek triremes, capturing them together with their crews. This was a serious loss in itself, quite apart from which the Athenians, who were naturally in the thick of the battle, had half their ships disabled in some degree. Nevertheless, things did not go all one way for, if they had, Artemisium would have gone on record as the Greek defeat that led to an over-all victory for Xerxes. As it was, a fact which is well commemorated by Plutarch and Pindar, Artemisium – though something of a stalemate – had produced the desired effect of compelling the enemy to withdraw. 'Both sides were glad when they parted and made all speed back to their moorings.' Far from being pursued, the Greeks even seem to have found the time on the way back to their station to collect their dead from the water and to salvage some of the wreckage. The fact that the Athenians and their allies were well outnumbered, and the Persian fleet was as happy to draw off at evening as they were, confirms Pindar's commemorative words about Artemisium: 'that great battle where Athens' brave sons planted the shining cornerstone of freedom'.

On their arrival back at Artemisium Plutarch records the elegiac verses which were later engraved on a commemorative tablet set up near the temple at Artemisium:

Here, by this arm of the sea, the valiant children of Athens
Sailed their ships into battle and shattered the fleets of the
    Mede,
Conquering a many-tongued host from the farthest confines
    of Asia.
These are the tokens of thanks to victorious Artemis paid.

The Greeks found that the people of Euboea had decided on evacuation and, with this in mind, had driven their sheep down to the shore. Themistocles wasted no time, but told his men to 'kill as many sheep as they pleased, for it was better that they should have them than the enemy'. Wreckage was burned, great fires were lit for funeral pyres; at the same time, with practical sense, the sheep of the Euboeans were roasted to put heart into the exhausted oarsmen and the battle-weary marines. It was at the end of this hard-fought day while all were busy at their base that the news came in from Thermopylae. Habronichus, the trusted lieutenant of Themistocles, who had been acting as liaison officer between army and fleet, had waited by the pass until the last possible moment. When he saw that all was lost he had slipped and made off fast up the channel in his thirty-oared cutter. With Thermopylae lost, Artemisium to the north was no longer tenable. It was the end of the Themistoclean strategy of the land–sea defensive line to the north.

AFTER THERMOPYLAE

AFTER THE WAR WAS OVER, the Amphyctionic League (the association of northern Greeks whose meeting-place had always been at the Hot Gates) set up a plaque to commemorate the last stand of Leonidas and his men:

> Tell them in Lacedaemon, passer-by:
> That here, obedient to their laws, we lie.

This lapidary and suitably laconic inscription reminded all Greeks for generations to come of the debt owed to the men – and to the code – of that strange and often violently disliked state in the Peloponnese. Its message has carried on even into our own remote world and time. It has been celebrated by William Golding in his essay 'The Hot Gates':

> It is not just that the human spirit reacts directly and beyond all arguments to a story of sacrifice and courage, as a wine glass must vibrate to the sound of the violin. It is also because, way back and at the hundredth remove, that company stood in the right line of history. A little of Leonidas lies in the fact that I can go where I like and write what I like. He contributed to set us free.

To this one can only add that there are today vast areas of the world where the autocracy of a Persian monarch like Xerxes is far exceeded by modern tyrannies. Even the self-perpetuating bureaucracy of our modern Western, self-styled 'democratic', world would have seemed to the Spartans who died at Thermopylae an unacceptable thing.

Thermopylae, which has been wrongly compared in recent times to the evacuation of Dunkirk, can be counted a victory in moral terms. The right men had been there, in the right place and at the right time – but far too few of them. Had Sparta sent a thousand men instead of a king's bodyguard of three hundred, the Phocian force guarding the pass over Kallidromos could have been stiffened by a leavening of Spartan officers who would have made sure that it was, at the very least, hotly contested. In the end, in view of the size of the Persian army, there can be small doubt that the result would have been much the same. In the past it was the natural human tendency to elevate the battle at the Hot Gates to an almost superhuman dimension and, having done so, to let the purpose of it be forgotten. Quite unlike Dunkirk, which was a withdrawal, Thermopylae was a deliberate self-sacrifice by a handful of men who died so that the fleet at Artemisium might stay in being. The very fact that, on the same day as the storming of the pass, Xerxes gave orders for his fleet to attack the Greeks proves how important to his strategy was the shattering of this linchpin.

The importance of Thermopylae was understood in the times that immediately followed this great battle for the West. Some later commentators have confused the issue. The death of Leonidas and of the three hundred chosen men from Lacedaemon was seen at the time for what it was: a torch, not to light a funeral pyre, but to light the hitherto divided and irresolute Greek people. If, as some have regarded it, the chosen death of the Spartan king was an act of devotion, a sacrifice to appease the gods and to ensure that, if a Spartan king must die, his city would be spared on that score, then Leonidas chose wisely. As has been suggested, it may well be that he had something to expiate. At the same time, no student of history should ever forget that, without Thermopylae, there would hardly have been that extraordinary surge of pride throughout Greece which produced the spirit that was to lead to Salamis and Plataea. For the first time in their history a distinct sense of 'Greekness' far overriding the almost eternal (and fratricidal) squabbles of their city-states served to unite this brilliant people. It was true that the unity was far from total (Argos is but one example), yet for most of the Greeks, who still remained free or had not already medised, the example of Thermopylae provided a common bond of pride and honour. Eurybiades, uneasy as he may have been in his position of command over a predominantly Athenian fleet, could find in the example of Leonidas and the Three Hundred an inspiratory proof that Sparta kept her word. They had died to a man and a king had been sacrificed, not in some local war in the Peloponnese but far to the north, in a battle to preserve the freedom of all Greece.

Herodotus tells us that he took pains to ascertain the names of the Three Hundred, something that was relatively easy to do since they were all recorded on the memorial for Thermopylae which was erected at Sparta. In this same vicinity has been found the fifth-century head and torso of a warrior which has been credibly identified as a statue of Leonidas, which Pausanias informs us was set up along with the commemorative Roll of Honour. Simonides, who wrote an encomium on 'those who died at the Hot Gates', set the tone for all subsequent tributes to a self-sacrifice that Greece never forgot, while the Spartiates held annual games in their honour at which a speech was delivered in memory of the fallen and the battle. It was Simonides also, who had been a personal friend of Megistias, who wrote a tribute to him that was set up among the monuments in the Pass:

> Here lies Megistias, who died
> When the Medes crossed Spercheius' tide.
> A great seer, yet he scorned to save
> Himself, and shared the Spartans' grave.

In the aftermath of the battle, Xerxes was mindful of what their ex-king had told him about the Spartans' prowess in war and their 'Kamikaze' code of honour. He sent for Demaratus, who gave him some very good advice which – fortunately for the Greeks – the king did not (or could not) take. After inquiring as to the number of similar fighting men there might be in Lacedaemon the king asked him what he thought was the best way of overcoming such a people. Demaratus replied:

Suppose you divide your forces and send three hundred ships from the fleet round to Lacedaemon. There is an island off the coast there called Cythera . . . which your ships can use as their base, and from which they can spread terror all over Lacedaemon. With a war on their own doorstep you need not worry that they will go to the help of the other Greeks, whom in the meantime your army can proceed to conquer. The rest of Greece will be crushed first of all, while Lacedaemon will be left helpless on its own.

This was sound and sensible. With marauding troops in Lacedaemon itself, and with the Persian fleet harrying the coastline, the Spartans would have been forced to keep their army at home to protect their city and to keep an eye on their neighbours, as well as the Helots, who might all have risen if Sparta itself was threatened. Xerxes' brother Achaemenes, who was in command of the Egyptian fleet, remonstrated. He had already seen the great Persian armada depleted by storms off the rocky coastline leading to Cape Sepias, and then the loss of the advance squadron sent to round Euboea, and here was this Spartan renegade – a soldier not even experienced in nautical matters – advising the king to despatch over half his ships to the south of Greece. 'This man is probably a traitor,' he told the king bluntly. 'He's a typical Greek. . . . We have already had four hundred ships wrecked, and if you despatch another three hundred from the fleet for a voyage round the Peloponnese, the enemy will be on equal terms and a match for us.'

What determined Xerxes' compliance with his admiral was the straightforward fact that he could not afford to divide his fleet at this stage in the campaign. Achaemenes was right: the winds, weather, and ironbound coastline of Greece had already taken too much toll. Furthermore, from the reports that had reached him, the Greeks had shown themselves more than competent at sea. The aggressive policy of Themistocles in being the first to seek action, and then the hard-fought battle of Artemisium, now paid dividends. The value of Thermopylae has been challenged by some critics. 'Too little and too late' is perhaps fair comment – at any rate as regards the poor Peloponnesian response in terms of manpower, although the force itself arrived in good time. If the Phocians and other allies had been the only ones at the pass, one can confidently say that it would have fallen on the first day. Later generations of Spartans had a right to be proud of their ancestors. Without Leonidas and his Three Hundred putting the steel into the Greek core there would have been no Artemisium.

The Greeks had learned during that sea battle, as Plutarch puts it, how they would behave in the face of danger [and] that men who know how to come to close quarters and are determined to give battle have nothing to fear from mere numbers of ships, gaudily decorated figureheads, boastful shouts, or barbaric war-songs; they have simply to show their contempt for these distractions, engage the enemy hand to hand and fight it out to the bitter end.

Now, after the fall of Thermopylae and with their landward flank exposed, there was nothing for the Greek fleet to do but retreat under cover of darkness. They banked up the fires so that they would last through the night and lead the Persians to believe that the fleet was still at Artemisium. There was no time for the rest that the men needed, nor for anything but the most immediate and simple repairs to the ships.

Themistocles and a fast squadron were the first to leave. It is strange that there is no mention of Eurybiades, technically the commander-in-chief, but one can only presume that what Themistocles had certainly assumed in advance had taken place: Eurybiades was largely a token figure to hold the divided loyalties of Greeks and Peloponnesians together. The Corinthians led the main body and the Athenians brought up the rear. It was upon them that any Persian attack might fall so it was natural that, as the best seamen, they should take this position. Many of the triremes must have been in a poor state after that hard-fought day in which the Athenians had borne the brunt and suffered so much damage. Some oars will have been ported because their rowers were dead; forward planking abaft the rams opened up; timber ribs cracked or even broken; and in many cases, of course, the bronze-clad rams had been torn off or forced back against stems that barely held together. The men themselves will have been little better than their ships, marines wounded and without even the primitive medical help of the day, rowers exhausted and salt-stained from their long hours over the looms of the oars, and all sadly conscious that despite their efforts the strategy of checking the Persians in the north had failed. At least this time they did not have to battle against the current of the Euripus Channel, which served to boost their flagging oar-strokes and their damaged ships southwards, where they could effect repairs and wait again for the advance of the enemy.

No sooner had they gone than a man of Euboea, a native of

Histiaea to the west of Artemisium, set off to carry the news to the Great King. No doubt he hoped by ingratiating himself with the Persians to save his township from the wrath that must inevitably fall upon all the long island. The Persians, who seem to have had a healthy mistrust of the Greeks, 'even if bearing gifts', kept him prisoner while they sent out some fast ships to investigate. At dawn the following day, having learned the truth, the whole fleet sailed across to Artemisium where they found nothing but burned-out wreckage, smouldering fires, and the bones of Euboean sheep. It is significant that they did not at this moment set off in hot pursuit of the fleeing enemy – the natural thing to do for a successful fleet. Clearly Artemisium had not been a victory for the Persians and they needed, quite as much as the Greeks, some time to make good their ships and reinforce them with fresh marines and oarsmen. Quite apart from this, their progress was necessarily tied up with the advance of the army on the mainland shore. The man from Histiaea reaped no reward. 'They stayed there [at Artemisium] till mid-day, and then sailed on to Histiaea which they occupied before overrunning all the coastal villages in the area.'

Xerxes still seems to have been in no hurry. He delayed at Thermopylae for a whole day while his troops buried the Persian dead (20,000 according to Herodotus), leaving only about a thousand of them on the battlefield but conspicuously, of course, leaving all the Greeks unburied. He then sent word to the fleet that all might have a day's leave and come across to Thermopylae, 'to see what the King does to the madmen who thought they could oppose him'. Clearly the warships were not involved in this day-trip for sailors, for we learn that 'so many wanted to avail themselves of this offer that the supply of boats ran out'. Herodotus comments that 'the ludicrous attempt of Xerxes to conceal the number of his own dead deceived no one'. This statement must be suspect, for it is impossible after the lapse of time when the historian was writing that he could have known what simple sailors and marines thought or said about their guided tour of the battlefield. Once again, one feels, Xerxes is being portrayed as anxious in his *hubris* to impress his fellow mortals with his omnipotence. It is more likely that this was yet another exercise in propaganda, in which the Persians both during and in the years immediately preceding the invasion had shown themselves extremely adept. In this vast combined operation it was essential that the fleet and the army should both have trust in one another's capability. What better than to show the fleet – whose morale, he must have judged, was somewhat low after their recent mauling – that they had an invincible army behind them?

Themistocles, that master of political mechanics, was also awake to the value of propaganda. As his advance squadron made its way down the channel he put in at all the places where there was fresh water, knowing that the Persians must necessarily do likewise, and left behind messages scratched or cut on the rocks. These were of course designed to be read by the many Ionian Greeks serving in the Persian fleet, and called upon them to remember that they too were Greeks and that they should not be making war upon their fellows.

> The best thing for you to do is to join us, but if this is impossible you should at least remain neutral. On the other hand, if you are under such constraint that you can do neither of these things, at least, when it comes to battle, remember we are of the same blood – that our quarrel with the Persians originally began on your account – and make sure you fight badly.

There is no evidence that this early example of 'pamphlet propaganda' had any effect, but it may possibly have caused some of the Ionians not to give of their best. One day later, after the battlefield inspection was over, the bulk of the Persian army began its march southward into central Greece.

IN ANOTHER COUNTRY . . .

IN THAT SUMMER OF 480, while Xerxes moved south into Greece, the carefully co-ordinated attack upon Sicily had begun. The importance of this western flank in the double-horned advance upon Greece and Mediterranean Europe has sometimes been a little neglected, all attention being concentrated upon events in Greece itself. But Xerxes and his staff had not been years in the planning of his great invasion without ensuring that the threat from Carthage to the Greek-dominated areas of Sicily should develop at the same time.

Western and north-western Sicily were largely controlled by Carthaginian colonies while the Greeks were mainly on the eastern and south-eastern coasts. Hamilcar, the leading Carthaginian general, had laid his plans accordingly and a vast flotilla of transports escorted by 200 warships had been assembled to carry a force of some 200,000 men, together with horses – for the Carthaginians relied largely on cavalry in warfare as well as the outmoded chariot. This was natural enough, for in the great expanses of north Africa the cavalry arm was supreme and even in Sicily the mounted men had an advantage over the hoplite, and the Sicilian Greeks also made much use of cavalry. Special horse-transports were constructed, no doubt somewhat similar to the *gaulos* (literally 'tub'), the half-walnut-shaped merchant-ship of the time which was principally dependent upon sail rather than oars. Once again the elements were to prove the Greeks' best friends. While the oared warships could advance well enough from the Gulf of Tunis across the midsummer Mediterranean the transports inevitably lagged behind, dependent largely upon a favourable southerly wind to waft them on their course towards the coast of Sicily. Unfortunately for the Carthaginian hopes the *maistro*, the 'master wind' (modern *mistral*), elected to blow hard from the north – something which to this day has upset the plans of many a sailor, and which nearly ruined the Allied invasion of Sicily in the summer of 1943. The wallowing transports were scattered and many of them sunk, thus leaving Hamilcar in a worse position than Xerxes who, at least, had all his army and baggage-train safely on dry land.

The main body of the fighting fleet successfully rounded the north-western cape of Sicily, leaving behind them the great shoulders of Mount Eryx with its temple to Astarte crowning the peak, and headed east towards the Bay of Panormus (Palermo) where they could regroup and make ready for the campaign. The first objective was the city of Himera to the east of Panormus, on whose account the campaign had been largely initiated. Its capture by Theron of Acragas had provoked its former Greek ruler Terillus, who was a personal friend of Hamilcar, to ask for aid. Nothing had suited Hamilcar and the Carthaginians, and indeed the Punic–Persian alliance, better than this providential *casus belli* – although there can be no doubt that the invasion would have taken place in any case. To eliminate a powerful Greek threat to Carthaginian colonies, and then in due course to move east and one by one take over the Greek cities, was the long-term strategy. Beyond that, but still well within the planning capacity of the time, was the ultimate move up into southern Italy where prosperous colonies beckoned, from Rhegium on the toe of the continent to Crotone and Tarentum on the sole, and northwards as far as the pearls of Cumae and Neapolis. Beyond that again lay the rich territory and the metals of Etruria. It is significant that both Corsicans and Sardinians, who had long cast envious eyes on Etruscan richness and envied their technology, were among the vast army who accompanied Hamilcar on his expedition.

Xerxes' invasion of the West, as has been seen, was no small thing: no reprisal raid on Athens and Sparta for their refusal to offer the tokens of submission (or for Sparta's treatment of the Persian ambassadors); no simple vengeance on the mainland Greeks who had assisted the Ionians in their revolt; nor was it merely the desire to lay low these proud, warlike people and add them and their rocky land to his empire. However the Greeks at the time saw it, the ambitions of Xerxes far exceeded the ones that inevitably preoccupied his immediate enemies. His aim, with the aid of the Carthaginians, was the conquest of all the Mediterranean lands. Yet again, it is significant that among the forces which Hamilcar led against Sicily were Spaniards and Ligurians, and tribesmen from the Riviera. The Greeks in their subsequent history, poetry and drama somewhat naturally saw everything in terms of an attack directed against themselves and their proud little city-states. Xerxes' aims and ambitions, on the other hand, were as wide and far-reaching as those of Alexander the Great in a later century – and had, on the surface at least, a better chance of success.

Having disembarked and beached their ships in the grand Bay of Panormus, the invasion force rested for three days. The loss of so many transports, of food, provender and general stores (and especially of horses), had left the great army somewhat depleted but – as Hamilcar was swift to assure them – the sea had been their greatest danger. Now that they were landed, the war was as good as over. It is somewhat difficult for the modern visitor to Sicily to comprehend the importance of this large island to the ancients. To the Greeks and Phoenicians who first competed as colonisers of the island it was indeed a place of almost miraculous richness.

> Sicily [as I have written elsewhere] had everything to commend it: Good vine-growing country, land for pasturage and for agriculture, water, harbours, quarryable stone, trees for fuel and for boat-building, and craggy uplands where goats could pasture. Wherever the land could not support cereals or the vine, the hardy olive flourished. Before it was ravaged by thousands of years of occupation by man, Sicily was a garden of Eden, floating on the water south of Italy and bridging the worlds of Europe and Africa.

This current Carthaginian invasion led by the Suffete Hamilcar was triggered by the desire for land and its grain, mineral wealth and power. It had no religious or ethnic cause: Hamilcar himself was half Greek, having a Syracusan mother.

Unlike the invasion of Xerxes, where the route of the army could be fairly easily foreseen, the invasion of Sicily could have started at several points, the most likely perhaps being the city of Selinus in the south which was allied to Carthage. Gelon, therefore, whose main fleet-base was Syracuse and whose sphere of naval operations extended little farther than Theron's Acragas, had no means of knowing where the blow would fall, nor of attacking the enemy at sea. Furthermore, even when it became known that Hamilcar's army had landed in Panormus Bay the Greek fleet could not head north and make its way through the Messina Strait, for Zancle (Messina) and Rhegium (Reggio) were both pro-Carthaginian, Anaxilas of Rhegium being the son-in-law of Terillus the deposed ruler of Himera, while his own son Leophron was ruler of Zancle. It can be seen that, with this combination of alliances, the Carthaginians had a good chance of boxing in the Greeks on the east coast of the island and eliminating them at their leisure. As it was,

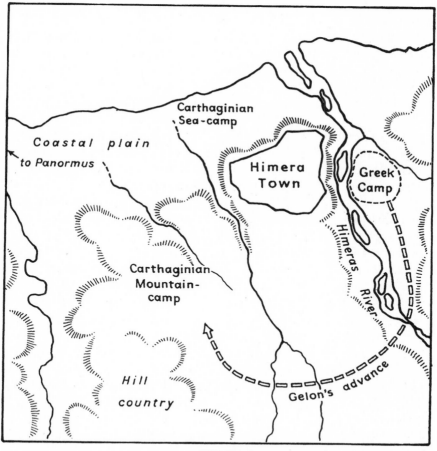

4 HIMERA

the news of Hamilcar's descent on Panormus only just gave Theron sufficient time to cross the island with a strong force and reinforce Himera before the Carthaginians were ready to attack.

Himera (Termini Imerese) stands on rising ground above the narrow coastal plain with the Himeras torrent directly protecting its eastern flank. Hamilcar, having beached the fleet immediately facing Himera, leaving only twenty triremes to patrol the coast, fortified his camp and extended its defences inland so that they reached the hills to the west of the city, thus leaving Himera cut off except for its southern and eastern approaches. Hamilcar made the first move and sent a powerful detachment of troops to test the walls and defences of the city, in the course of which the defenders were rash enough to sally out, only to be beaten back with the loss of many men. Theron, realising that it was upon the western walls that an attack must fall, promptly had the city gates on that side blocked up. He also sent off a message calling for help from his son-in-law, Gelon of Syracuse, richest of all the Sicilian tyrants and the man who had promised the Athenians such massive naval and military support if he were made commander-in-chief of all the Greeks. The latter had already mobilised all the forces at his command, which most probably included the 20,000 hoplites that he had promised for the defence of Greece, as well as several thousand archers, slingers, light infantry, and 2000 cavalrymen. (The wealth of Sicily always astounded mainland Greeks, and the fact that one city could produce so many men rich enough to own the armour to form such a vast body of hoplites was beyond the resources of Sparta and Athens combined.) Taking the swift overland route via Enna, having been reinforced by Hieron of Gela on the way, the number of troops that finally reached Himera from the south-east amounted to about 50,000 men. The joy of the besieged was re-inforced by the immediate proof of the abilities of this considerable army. The Greek cavalry, now some 5000 strong, bypassed the western flank of Hamilcar's defences and captured or cut down hundreds of his troops who were out foraging in the countryside.

Hamilcar still had a numerical advantage over his Greek opponents but he was sadly hampered by the fact that he had lost so many horses in the wrecked and sunken transports – thus reducing many of his formidable cavalrymen to the unfamiliar role of foot-soldiers. He had accordingly despatched an urgent message to his allies in

Selinus asking them to send all their available cavalry. Unfortunately for the Carthaginian Suffete the returning messenger from Selinus was intercepted by the Greeks, who were roaming the countryside round about almost unchallenged. This was an almost miraculous stroke of fortune, for the message even revealed on what day the cavalry from Selinus were due to appear – obviously so that the Carthaginian lookouts would sight them as they came over the hills to the south and have the gates of their fortified camp open and ready for them. Now Selinus, although an ally of Carthage, was a Greek city, and its soldiers and cavalrymen, therefore, bore the same uniforms, armour, and horse-trappings as any of the other Sicilian Greeks. Here lay the seed of Gelon's brilliant idea, and here lay the ultimate downfall of Hamilcar. Prior to this all-important secret falling into his hands Gelon had already established himself in a formidable position, setting up his camp on the east bank of the River Himeras opposite the city, on whose landward side he had dug a long ditch and erected a stockade. There was thus no chance of his being outflanked by any Carthaginian move from the west, and in any case the current superiority of his cavalry throughout the country round about meant that the Carthaginians were almost as much besieged as the Greeks in Himera. Although their transports could come and go unthreatened by any Greek warships, bringing provisions from the fertile lands around Panormus, they were largely denied access to the country immediately surrounding Himera.

Prior to the message from Selinus falling into his hands Gelon had been contemplating making a raid on the enemy's ships, during the confusion of which he would loose his major frontal attack on their encampment. But now he hazarded his fortune on a far better idea. On the appointed day, when the Carthaginians would be expecting the cavalry from Selinus, he would anticipate them, sending out his finest squadron from Syracuse to make a detour into the hills while it was dark and then show themselves at daylight and make their way down to Hamilcar's camp, posing as the expected reinforcements. As soon as they had been admitted through the palisade they would declare their true nature, wreak as much destruction as possible, and above all, if they could find him, kill Hamilcar. Gelon had scouts posted on the hills overlooking the town to give the signal the moment that they had seen their cavalry admitted. Gelon with all his troops would unleash an assault on the Carthaginian position while Theron's troops inside Himera would also burst out in a head-on attack on the enemy. To execute this brilliant stratagem everything depended on timing and perfect discipline. The fact that it succeeded suggests, as comment-ators have pointed out, that the autocratic rulers of the Greek city-states in Sicily possessed a marked advantage over the divided counsels that were part and parcel of alliances in Greece itself.

Hamilcar had intended on that day to make a great sacrifice to the Greek sea-god Poseidon, not only to ensure victory but most probably to show his new helpers from Selinus how much he welcomed them and thanked one of their most important gods for their assistance. A huge altar had been prepared, the fire had been lit and the slaughtered animals were sending up their tribute of burning flesh to Poseidon when the Syracusan cavalry were welcomed into the camp as the eagerly awaited reinforcements from Selinus. No sooner were they through the gate than they set about firing tents, ships, and anything that would burn to add to the general confusion. Within minutes the troops of Theron had struck from the east while the troops out of Himera poured over the frontal defences of the camp. The Suffete Hamilcar dressed in priestly robes and officiating over the great offering to Poseidon was a figure that could hardly escape notice. He was cut down in front of the blazing sacrificial altar and his body hurled on to it to join the previous victims. Despite the totally unexpected nature of the attack the battle was not won without considerable hand-to-hand fighting and there was even a moment when some of the Greeks, thinking victory was theirs, broke ranks and began looting. A counter-attack of hardy Spanish troops, which for a moment threatened the Greek position, was staved off by Theron, who ordered the troops with him to fire all the tents on the landward side, thus creating a flaming, smoking barrier between the Greeks on the one side and the enemy on the other. The news of Hamilcar's death must have served to complete the demoralisation of his army and, in their ensuing flight, hundreds of them were slaughtered. Gelon had given orders for no quarter to be given. A large number of survivors, however, managed to make their escape to a hill position (most probably Mount Calogero about five miles west of Himera) where they proceeded to dig themselves in. Gelon had the hill surrounded, but made no move to attempt any assault on the Carthaginian position. He knew something that these foreigners to Sicily could hardly be aware of: Calogero is waterless. In August, under the 'lion sun' of Sicily, men who had been fighting and then running and climbing could hardly hold out for long. Thirst drove them to surrender, and this time their lives were spared. Something like half of Hamilcar's army now became Greek slaves: they would work for the rest of their lives enriching with their labour the cities of their Sicilian masters.

As for the fleet, one can do no more than presume, since accurate accounts are not available, that all the beached ships behind their protective palisade were destroyed. The squadron of twenty triremes that had been cruising offshore put in hastily and took off all the survivors from the army that they could carry – too many as it turned out. On their way homewards they too ran into a storm and, according to Diodorus, all but a single vessel were lost. One thing is certain: the Sicilian expedition was such a disaster that Carthage, terrified that the triumphant Greeks might swoop down and sack their great city by the sea, sent ambassadors to Gelon to sue for peace. He could afford to dictate his own terms and exacted a large indemnity of 2000 talents, while Theron's beautiful daughter, Damarete, the wife of Gelon of Syracuse, was presented with a golden crown worth 100 talents. One of the most beautiful of all Greek coins, the Damaretia, which shows a winged Victory, a chariot and, below, a submissive lion (in the coinage language of the time, almost certainly symbolic of Carthage), was minted from the Carthaginian indemnity. On the obverse, familiar from thousands of reproductions, is a female head surrounded by dolphins, usually identified with the fountain-nymph Arethusa of Syracuse – and possibly a portrait of Damarete herself.

The battle of Himera, which for many years to come eliminated the Eastern and African threat to Sicily and the West, was rightly recognised at the time for what it was – a brilliant victory that rivalled that of Salamis. It was hardly surprising that popular tradition, even within the memory of those who had been living at the time, should maintain that these two great victories had taken place on the same day. Victory in the West together with victory at home in Greece showed, as it were, a divine blessing spread over the Greek cause. Aristotle, as Burn points out, was sceptical about such a temporal coincidence. It is indeed very unlikely, for the battle of Salamis was fought on or about 20 September 480. This was late in the year for warfare in those times, but necessitated by Xerxes' protracted progress through Greece, the delay occasioned by Thermopylae, the fleet losses by storm, and by the Greek action at Artemisium. It is very unlikely that the Carthaginian landing in Panormus Bay, followed by the action at Himera, occurred at such a late date. Hamilcar, in his concerted action with Xerxes against the Greeks, would hardly have waited until September (when the weather in the central Mediterranean usually breaks) to move his entirely shipborne army from north Africa across to Sicily. There was very little delay – and no opposition – between his initial landing and his investment of Himera. He suffered a grave misfortune in encountering a *mistral* while the fleet was on passage, but this, while it occasioned the loss of a great many transports, did not delay him for days, let alone weeks. It seems probable, therefore, that the Carthaginian armada arrived off Sicily in August. (July would have been a better month to make a seaborne assault, but the administrative difficulties of mustering a great army of allies from various quarters of the Mediterranean in those days of primitive communications could well account for this.) In conclusion it seems safer to rely upon that native Sicilian historian, Diodorus, who states categorically that the battle at Himera took place on the same day as Thermopylae – that is, 20 August, rather than 20 September, Salamis. It was somewhat natural that tradition should later equate the two decisive Greek victories, but it is far more likely that Gelon was triumphant in Sicily on or about the day that Leonidas and the Three Hundred were dying in the rocky pass in distant Greece.

20

THE ADVANCE

THREE DAYS AFTER THE FALL of Thermopylae the main body of Xerxes' army was moving south and, now that there was no opposition, they had the choice of a number of routes. Some probably passed through the ravine of the Asopus river, while the transport and baggage-wagons will have followed the coastal road through Locris. A squadron of cavalry and crack troops had already gone on ahead to clear the way through to Athens. There would be no resistance. With the collapse of the Greek defence at Thermopylae and the withdrawal of their fleet from Artemisium everything was clear for the Persian advance by land and sea. Xerxes was naturally anxious to confirm that the way was open and, hearing that some Greek deserters had arrived in his camp, had them sent for and interviewed by an interpreter. The men were from Arcadia and 'having nothing to live on, wanted employment'. These would-be mercenaries present an interesting problem, for why would Arcadians come all the way from southern Greece merely to seek employment when they could certainly have found this among their fellow Greeks at the defence-line of the Isthmus? It seems more than likely that, even if they were actively pro-Persian, they would not have journeyed so far to bear arms for Xerxes' cause. If they were violently anti-Spartan (like Argos), all they had to do was stay in Arcadia and join the Persians when they occupied the Peloponnese. The answer must surely be that these renegades came from the 2120 Arcadians who had joined up with Leonidas as he marched north to the Isthmus. They had fought in the first two days at Thermopylae and had left with the other allies when Leonidas had prepared for his last stand. They had seen the unbelievable manpower of the Persian army and they knew that even a Spartan king and those lords of the Peloponnese, the Spartiate warrior-caste, were not invincible. It was hardly surprising that they should wish to join what they must surely have seen as the inevitable victors. It must also be remembered that at this period in Greek history there was little or no ethnic patriotism (even though Thermopylae may have helped to promote it). A man belonged to his city-state, his small land area, his 'clan' almost, long before he had any concept of 'Hellas' or of all mainland Greeks forming a nation. It was not for over a hundred years, when Alexander the Great had united Greece by force and established his vast empire, that this sense of nationhood was achieved.

Xerxes asked these Arcadians what the other Greeks were doing at the moment, wanting very naturally to find out whether the Athenians were busily fortifying their city or whether all the Greeks had withdrawn to hold the line at the Isthmus. Now the Arcadians, if they had indeed come up from the south or were, as seems almost indisputable, deserters from the remnants of Leonidas' army, would have known what every Greek knew. Quite apart from the Carneian festival on 20 August, at the second full moon of the month, it was also the year for the Olympic games which were held at the time of the same full moon. Although, in view of the invasion, there were many Greeks who could not attend, the fact remained that even in the face of the attack upon their homeland the games were still being held (something else that sounds unbelievable to a modern, but in no way surprises Herodotus). '. . . [Xerxes] was told in reply that the Greeks were celebrating the Olympic festival, where they were watching athletic contests and chariot-races.' The king, imagining that for the Greeks to indulge in athletics when his army was threatening to engulf their country, naturally jumped to the conclusion that these Greeks (he knew their mercenary nature) must only be doing so because there were prizes of immense value to be won. He was astounded to hear that it was not for gold or silver that they were competing but for 'the wreath of olives which it is our custom to give'. The son of Artabanus (Xerxes' uncle who had been sent home for giving him sage advice about the dangers attendant on the expedition) was so astonished when the interpreter repeated these words that he exclaimed in a loud voice to the King's brother-in-law: 'Good heavens, Mardonius, what kind of men are these that you have brought us to fight against – men who compete with one another for no material reward, but only for honour!' It is reasonable to suspect that the young man was immediately marked down as being defeatist like his uncle and unsuitable for promotion. . . .

After what Herodotus calls 'the disaster at Thermopylae' (with his pro-Athenian bias he was not willing to see that the Spartan stand at Thermopylae had made Artemisium possible), the march of the Persian army was now facilitated by the Thessalians. The Phocians, who had, however inefficiently, fought for the Greek cause, were not to be persuaded by the Thessalians' offer to protect them against the wrath of the Great King if they were given a large sum of money. The Thessalians, in any case, hated the people of Phocis for having quite recently – and most successfully – rebelled against them, and their own pro-Persian attitude was more than offended by the Phocians' sharp reply that, whatever other people did, the men of Phocis 'would on no account be traitors to Greece'. Encouraged by the active collaboration of the people of Thessaly, Xerxes determined to make an example of Phocis, its fertile land, and all its people. Small states which dared to make a stand against his inexorable advance should be taught so savage a lesson that all the others would quickly learn that it was better to collaborate than to try for independence. (Once again, as throughout so much of this distant war, the twentieth-century reader is likely to be reminded of the actions of the Germans in the Second World War and of the Russians in Eastern Europe subsequently.) In the words of Herodotus: 'All Phocis was overrun; the Thessalians did not let the Persians miss a bit of it, and everywhere they went there was devastation by fire and sword, and towns and temples were burned.' In the gracious valley of the Cephisus no village or township was spared and, as in all wars, 'some women were raped successively by so many of the soldiers that they died'. Nevertheless, most of the population managed to escape, either by taking to the hills in the area of Parnassus or fleeing westward to Amphissa on the far side of the great massif. The smoke of the burning towns and farms and temples could be seen for miles away, and the pro-Persian inhabitants of Orchomenus could congratulate themselves on their political foresight. The news of the devastation was spread far and wide by the fleeing refugees and it will not have been long before the inhabitants of even the remotest hamlets in Attica will have learned the fate that lay in store for them.

In Athens itself, the news of the fall of Thermopylae and the withdrawal of the fleet from Artemisium will have been received quite quickly; either by a series of couriers, a fast cutter, or by signal-fires. Despite Themistocles' earlier arrangements for the evacuation of the greater part of the population it is clear that, as so often happens, there were many who had been unwilling to comprehend that their land and even their city would ever be seriously threatened by the invaders. Few of them were in a position to know how small was the holding force that had gone north to Thermopylae. Now they learned the horrifying truth that an army led by Spartans had been defeated, and that a Spartan king had perished. This was the writing on the wall with a vengeance: even the Athenians, proud as they were after their victory at Marathon, conceded in their hearts that the Spartans were the most formidable soldiers known to man. A shudder ran round the community that had stayed behind. Where, for instance, was the major force from the Peloponnese that should have come up to reinforce Leonidas? 'The Athenians', as Plutarch put it, 'pressed them [the Peloponnesians] to make a stand in Boeotia and protect Attica, just as they themselves had gone out by sea to fight in defence of the rest of Greece at Artemisium, but nobody would listen to them; instead, the remainder of the allies refused to budge from the Peloponnese.' In this decision the Greeks from the south were, for once, quite right: no amount of men that they could muster would have been able to stem the Persian advance, once their army had begun to swarm all over the land to the north.

Panic set in. Every available craft was commandeered and, no doubt, there was a good deal of black-marketeering being done by boat-owners as farmers and prosperous citizens, who had hitherto neglected Themistocles' previous warnings and arrangements, now sought to make their getaway. Both Plutarch and Aelius Aristides describe the heart-rending scenes as husbands and wives were parted, most of the women and children joining their predecessors in Troezen, old men being left behind, and pet dogs howling and running to and fro as their masters embarked. The fleet had rounded Sunium and made up for Salamis Sound where they took aboard all the refugees that they could. No doubt it was the sight of their fleet, upon which they had staked everything, retreating to Salamis, that completed the desperation of the remaining Athenians. Here was tangible evidence indeed that everything to the north was lost and that soon it would be the turn of their beloved city. Apart from Troezen, whither most of the more provident citizens had sent their wives and children long ago in June, and which now received a further influx of refugees, Salamis took many of these late-comers. Even Athens' former mortal enemy, Aegina, opened its homes and hearths to this sudden, last-minute influx of Athenians. Aegina's action is remarkable in showing that, at long last, deep-rooted enmities were forgotten in the face of the imminent destruction of everything that the Greek-speaking peoples, however much their states had been at variance, now faced together.

The death of a Spartan king, far from his home, fighting on behalf of all Greeks, may have symbolised this new concept of unity. It had little effect upon the general view of the Peloponnesians that, since Attica and Athens itself were clearly doomed, the original plan of holding the line at the Isthmus was the right one. Under the command of Cleombrotus, the younger brother of Leonidas, some 30,000 Peloponnesians manned a defensive line across the Isthmus, a little south of the slipway used for the land-transport of vessels between the Aegean and the Gulf of Corinth. While all this frenzied activity was taking place on the Greek side the army of Xerxes continued its inexorable advance and began to enter Boeotia, at which point the looting and the vandalising that had characterised their progress through Phocian territory was ordered to cease. The Boeotians, through the good offices of Alexander of Macedon, had already negotiated their surrender and their willingness to act in concert with their old enemies in Thessaly. They, too, had come out in favour of the Persian cause.

From Boeotia part of the Persian army turned westwards and moved towards Delphi. It is unlikely that there can ever have been any intention of plundering and sacking that rich shrine – that 'Navel of the Earth' – for Delphi, always remembering the clemency displayed to Delos in the expedition of Darius, had undoubtedly shown a pro-Persian bias through its 'inspired' utterances, both before and during the campaign of Xerxes. The question is worth asking – was Delphi and its priesthood Machiavellian in its attitude towards the Greco-Persian conflict, or was it no more than concerned with its own survival as the Fountain of Wisdom? There is no proof, but it seems possible that Delphi had taken Persian gold in return for giving pessimistic utterances to Greek cities; above all, to Syracuse, to Athens, to Argos, to Crete, and to Sparta. Delphi was primarily a great religious centre for all of the Greek-speaking world but, in the course of being established as such, it had long been involved in the field of politics. (In very similar fashion, at various periods in its history, the Papacy, in order to survive, has been drawn into making accommodations with temporal powers.)

Delphi was spared. Although the inhabitants of Delphi were themselves of Phocian stock they had, over the years, tended to dissociate themselves from their rural brothers. They had certainly made no efforts during the invasion to help them in any way, but had preserved a strict neutrality. Xerxes, therefore, had no reason to subject the territory of Apollo to the same treatment that had been handed out to the unhappy people of the devastated land of Phocis. According to Greek authorities the Great King sent 4000 men to seize the shrine and carry off the immense wealth of treasures that had accumulated there over the years. Now, with the exception of the Prophet of the Oracle, Aceratus, and sixty men (the latter presumably staying to guard the treasures against any local vandals) all the inhabitants of Delphi, men, women and children, had fled the area, some taking to the heights of Parnassus, others going to Amphissa, and yet others proceeding by boats from the Gulf of Itea across to Achaea. The shrine, then, and all its temples and buildings were, in effect, left undefended. If it was Xerxes' intention to loot this rich and most sacred place in Greece, one can but wonder at his strange failure to do so. The answer, as legend had it, was that Apollo, by miraculous intervention, drove away the advancing column. What must strike a modern commentator on the events as singular, to say the least, is that none of the treasures of Delphi had been removed to safe-keeping; neither taken over to Achaea nor hidden in the mountain caves (especially the large and hard-to-find Corycian Cave – used by refugees in the Second World War) whither a number of Delphians had fled for safety. The story as promulgated to all later Greeks was that Apollo had personally assured the Priest of the Oracle and all the people of Delphi that he could, and would, take care of his own. Thus arose the very convenient tale of heavenly thunder, vast rocks being torn from the slopes of Parnassus and hurled at the invaders, and a great voice shouting from the innermost sanctuary itself, while two giant warriors suddenly emerged and pursued the Persian column headlong back to Boeotia from the sacred precincts.

One does not need to be cynical to doubt these stories. What is necessary, however, is to try to understand why – if such was the will of Xerxes – Delphi was not seized and looted. There are two comparatively simple answers to this question: first, that Delphi had all along collaborated with Persia; and, secondly, that after the ultimate Greek victory it was more than necessary for the Delphic priesthood to establish Greek faith in this most enduring of all their oracular shrines. If people asked later why Xerxes did not destroy, burn and loot Delphi as he had done already with numerous sacred places in Phocis, and as he was to do in Athens itself, the only answer that could be given was a miraculous one. Indeed, to simple people the fact that unimportant villages on Parnassus and the town of Daulis nearby had been set afire and destroyed – while Delphi had been spared – could only suggest divine intervention. It is just possible (although there is no evidence) that there was a secret agreement between Xerxes and Delphi, but this seems unlikely and, furthermore, unnecessary. On the verge of triumph, as it seemed, Xerxes would have had to be as blinded with *hubris* as Herodotus often tends to picture him to contemplate so gross a folly as to destroy the shrine. Delphi, whether bought with Persian gold or not, had served his cause well and if, as a Zoroastrian, he did not find it difficult to equate Apollo with Ahuramazda, the Principle of Light, he would hardly have treated this major place of worship with such sacrilegious contempt. Delos and Delphi between them might well become, under the Persian domination of Greece, two great centres from which the truth as revealed by Zoroaster might be disseminated among the pagan Greeks.

21

INTO ATTICA

BY THE END OF AUGUST the main body of the Persian army was
into Attica. The advance guard was already on the outskirts of
abandoned Athens and the fleet had rounded up into Phaleron Bay.
Behind them both army and fleet left a trail of devastation. It was
natural enough that the Great King and his advisers should take
the ruthless path of destroying the towns, villages, and temples of
their enemies, for such was the normal way of conquest in the face
of determined hostility. In any case, certain victory beckoned, and
they never for a moment had reckoned that their troops would
have to spend many months in a ruined land. Their destruction of
the crops was an act of stupidity for, even if the conquest of all of
Greece had gone ahead according to plan, it would still have been
necessary to maintain an army of occupation during the months
that were to come. However, their flank to the east on Euboea was
secured, most of the inhabitants having taken to the hills, and it is
significant that Xerxes did not even bother to divert troops to
occupy the island. Presumably such raids as were carried out by his
fleet as they moved down the channel were sufficient to have
neutralised the towns and fishing villages in that area, while Carystus
in its bay to the south remained friendly and provided a useful
guard-post over the Euboea–Andros passage into the Aegean.

In Athens, meanwhile, the evacuation continued apace, the panic
departure of the last citizens being speeded by the news that the
sacred snake, reputed to guard the Acropolis, had not been eating
the ration of honey-cake which was ritually put out for it. The
snake, therefore, was presumed to have left the sanctuary – assuredly a sign of doom. It is possible, as Plutarch suggests, that Themistocles (he was quite wily enough) had a hand in promulgating this
story so as to speed the departure of the last inhabitants. Another
tale has it that in order to provide money for some of the penniless

he gave it out that the ornament of the Gorgon's head which was set into the breastplate of the statue of Athene had been stolen. It may be presumed that this was of gold, and it is just possible that in the general panic some vandal had indeed managed to remove it, to be converted in due course into ready cash. In any case this missing adornment gave Themistocles the pretext to have the bags and baggage of the evacuees searched, thus revealing, as might well be expected, that some of the citizens had far more money and valuables on them than they either needed or, in some cases, could have acquired honestly. These were put into the public fund which had already been opened to provide the commanders of the fleet with enough money to pay their troops and oarsmen. In any case, there is no further reference to this doubtless archaic Gorgon-ornament in subsequent history.

It was three months after he had crossed the Hellespont and had first set foot in Europe that Xerxes gazed on the city which had defied him, lying empty and abandoned before his conquering army. Although, as has been said, his progress should – and possibly could – have been somewhat faster, it was no mean feat to have reached the capital of his enemies in such a time. He stood where no other Persian monarch had ever stood before and beheld the key to Europe before him. Syracuse in distant Sicily may have been in one sense a richer city, but Athens metaphorically represented the capital of the West and of all the rich lands that fringed the Mediterranean basin. From his far-travelled Phoenician advisers he knew the basic geography of this sea even as far as the Straits of Gibraltar and, indeed, beyond that – for had not their ancestors, at the behest of the Pharaoh Necho, well over a century earlier, circumnavigated all of Africa? He knew of Spain and its trading posts and metal mines, of the French littoral and the great port at Massilia, of the Balearics, the islands of Sardinia and Corsica, of southern Italy, and of the wealth of Etruria to the north. . . . All, with the help of his Carthaginian allies, should ultimately come under the control of the East. The Great King must have envisaged all this in terms of a vast expansion of the Persian Empire – something that would make even the achievements of Cyrus and Darius appear comparatively minor. Like all great conquerors, what he was, in effect, dreaming of was a change in world-history quite beyond his immediate comprehension. At this far remove in time it is just possible to envisage what a Persian–Carthaginian conquest of all the Mediterranean lands might have brought about – though not what would have ultimately succeeded it. Such speculation is perhaps as fruitless as changing the direction of some famous chess-game with the benefit of hindsight. Xerxes, in any case, had the next immediate move upon his hands – the capture of the Acropolis of Athens. Not until the high point of the city and its shrine were in his hands could he send the couriers back to Susa with the news of his triumph.

The defenders of the Acropolis were a curious mixture: the stewards, or treasurers, of the sanctuary and, in the words of Herodotus, 'a number of poor men who lacked the means to get themselves to Salamis'. (From one's knowledge of later wars one may feel assured that the rich had removed their families to safety a long time ago.) Another reason given for some of these poorer and simpler members of society staying behind in the last of their sacred and ancient places was that they believed the words of the Delphic oracle – 'the wooden wall will not be taken' – to refer to the out-of-date wooden palisade that surrounded the Acropolis. Certainly, it required some sophistication of thinking to equate the wooden wall with the new Athenian navy, even though this was the interpretation that Themistocles had cared to place upon it. There can be no doubt about the courage of these men who stayed behind on the Acropolis but, unlike Thermopylae, their defence had no tactical, let alone strategic, significance. The Acropolis could be bypassed or starved out; this small precipitous rock had no relevance to the war as such; its value to those who defended it, and to Xerxes who ordered his troops to attack it, was purely symbolic.

The wooden wall which protected part of the Acropolis was on the western side, and it did not take the Persians long to site themselves on the Areopagus rock facing it and open fire on the defences with 'arrows with burning tow attached to them'. This 'Wild West' technique was admirably successful, and it was not long before these inadequate defences were set alight and shown to be as value-less as most oracles – if, of course, the defenders had read the Delphic utterance correctly! Even so, the steepness of the approach proved a deterrent, and Xerxes despatched a group of pro-Persian Athenians to reason with the defenders. These were members of the Peisistratid family who had never given up hope of a return to an aristocratic government of Athens – which meant, of course, by themselves. These collaborators were suitably rebuffed, so an attack was ordered against the smouldering wall. The defence had been prepared for this and had stacked up boulders, and possibly drums from unfinished columns, which they rolled down against the Persians as they toiled up the harsh slope. This was warfare at its most primitive, something for which the Acropolis of Athens, as well as those high points of other cities, had been carefully chosen in ancient days. The Persians were beaten back, 'and for a long time Xerxes was baffled by his inability to capture the defenders'.

Quite how long a time the defence of the Acropolis caused Xerxes to be delayed is something that has given rise to much debate, principally because Herodotus ceases his time-count upon the occupation of Athens itself and does not resume it until after the battle of Salamis. Eager to get on with the story-telling aspect of his history, he does not bother too much with the missing two or three weeks between Xerxes' arrival at the city and the fateful battle. It cannot be believed, however, that the defence of the Acropolis, gallant though it was, held up the attackers for more than a few days at the most. The rest of the time, as will be seen, was largely spent by both sides in watching each other like wary boxers circling in a ring, waiting for one party or the other to declare his intentions or make some fatal error.

The fall of the Acropolis, which one may guess (but no more) as having occurred early in the first week of September 480, was swift and sudden. As well as being mountain-men the Persians were long skilled in siege warfare and attacks on supposedly impregnable citadels. Trained soldiers and their commanders made a careful reconnaissance of the rock, looking for a place so apparently unscalable that the limited number of defenders would necessarily have neglected it. Finally they found it 'in the front part of the Acropolis, but behind the approach to the gates – a point which was left unguarded because it was not believed that any man could climb it'. A special assault group finally made it silently in the dark of the night, coming out on to the Acropolis near the shrine of Aglaurus, and made their way straight for the gates. Once these were opened the waiting Persians burst in and the slaughter of the

Athenians and the plundering and firing of the Acropolis began. Some of the defenders, realising all was lost, threw themselves down to death from the walls, while others made for the sanctuary of Athene. But Athene, guardian and patroness of these mercurial and intractable people of the city that bore her name, was not to be accorded the respect shown to Apollo, Lord of Light. All the people on the Acropolis, including those in the sanctuary, were slaughtered, the temple was stripped of its treasures, and then the whole area was set on fire. Xerxes was at last absolute master of Athens.

He wasted no time in sending the great good news by courier to Artabanus in Susa. His triumph, for the moment at least, must have seemed almost complete and the king's pleasure was surely increased by being able to tell his uncle Artabanus that he, Xerxes, had confounded the latter's pessimism. What had the old man said: 'Your two worst enemies will be the land and the sea'? Well, here the Great King stood, watching the Acropolis go up in flames, having reached Athens in three months, having defeated the so-called unconquerable Spartans at Thermopylae, and having driven the fleet of Athens before him down the Euripus Channel. Artabanus had cautioned him about there being no harbours on all the coast? Yet, here in Phaleron Bay, the principal naval base of the Athenians, his fleet was safely secured. What Xerxes perhaps forgot was the conclusion of the old man's speech all those months ago, when they had stood together at Abydos: 'Remember, I beg you, the truth of the old saying, that the end is not always to be seen in the beginning.' Westwards in Salamis, however, the Greeks saw that great fire in the sky and felt their hearts sink. There would be much debate between them before they could bring themselves to face these conquerors of Athens, the new rulers of Attica and of all northern Greece.

It is significant that the next day Xerxes seems to have been worried by the fact that he had permitted this sacking and desecration of Athens' temple. Unlike Darius, who was sagely tolerant towards other religions in his great empire, Xerxes had a touch of the fanatic in his nature, as he had shown in his treatment of the polytheism of Egypt. Nevertheless, although he placed his faith firmly in Ahuramazda and the teachings of Zoroaster, he seems to have felt uneasy at the desecration of so ancient a shrine. He was in Europe now, another part of the world altogether from Asia

Minor and the East with which he was familiar. . . . It might just be possible that in these foreign lands the local gods possessed some kind of power? It would be unwise to give any offence at this crucial stage in his great campaign.

'[So] on the following day he summoned to his presence the Athenian exiles who were serving with the Persian forces, and ordered them to go up into the Acropolis and offer sacrifice there according to Athenian usage. . . . The Athenian exiles did as they were bidden.' Herodotus goes on:

> I mention these details for a particular reason: on the Acropolis there is a spot which is sacred to Erechtheus – the 'earth-born', and within it is an olive tree and a spring of salt water. According to the local legend they were put there by Poseidon and Athene, when they contended the possession of the land, as tokens of their claims to it. Now this olive was destroyed by fire together with the rest of the sanctuary; nevertheless on the very next day, when the Athenians, who were ordered by the king to offer the sacrifice, went up to that sacred place, they saw that a new shoot eighteen inches long had sprung from the stump. They told the king of this.

(This is a very pleasant instance of the use of hindsight in symbolism while, as Burn has pointed out, the story contains some of the earliest description of the topography of the Acropolis as well as its legends.)

The destruction of the Acropolis naturally caused consternation at Salamis and some of the commanders (not the Athenians, one feels sure) 'hoisted sail for immediate flight'. During the days that followed there seems to have been incessant debate, and conference after conference between the Greek admirals. Eurybiades, nominally commander-in-chief, who had shown so little wish to engage the Persians earlier from the Artemisium base, was naturally in favour of withdrawal to the Isthmus where the Peloponnesian army was concentrated. Plutarch tells an anecdote which shows how high passions were running:

> Themistocles, however, opposed this plan and it was then that he uttered a remark which became famous. Eurybiades had said

to him: 'You know, Themistocles, at the games they thrash anybody who starts before the signal?' To this Themistocles replied,
'Yes, but they do not crown anybody who gets left at the post.'
At this point Eurybiades lifted up his staff of office as if to strike
him. Themistocles, maintaining his self-possession, said: 'You
can hit me if you like, but still you must listen to me.'

Eurybiades conceded that this was true and the debate continued,
with Themistocles naturally doing all that he could to preserve the
unity of the fleet in the very place where they were already –
Salamis. One commander, growing irritated by Themistocles'
argument, and eager no doubt to see the old original plan of the
defence of the Isthmus put into action, sarcastically pointed out
that Themistocles had no right to speak at all. He was a man without a city. (It is possible that he waved with the back of his hand
towards the smoke that still lifted from the Acropolis.) Themistocles,
therefore, was in no position to tell men who still belonged to a
city and a state what they should do about the conduct of the war.
The latter's reply was characteristically Churchillian in its fire and
vigour:

> It is quite true that we have given up our houses and our city
> walls, because we did not choose to become enslaved for the
> sake of things that have no life or soul. But what we still possess
> is the greatest city in all Greece, our 200 ships of war, which are
> ready to defend you, if you are still willing to be saved by them.
> But if you run away and betray us, as you did once before, the
> Greeks will soon hear the news that the Athenians have found
> for ourselves as free a city and as fine a country as the one they
> have sacrificed.'

There could be no doubting the menace behind the words.
Without the Athenian fleet there could be no possible means of
holding the Isthmus or any part of the Peloponnese. Once the
Athenian fleet was withdrawn, not only the disciplined core of the
Greek navy collapsed but also all co-ordinating authority. Herodotus
gives an interesting detail, which is not in Plutarch's account of
this meeting, that Themistocles even went so far as to name the
place to which the Athenians would withdraw. This was Siris in

the Gulf of Taranto, which Themistocles (somewhat dubiously) claimed had long belonged to Athens. It hardly mattered – he might as well have named ruined Sybaris. Thither, he said, the Athenians with their fleet would withdraw (having presumably collected the women and children from Salamis and Troezen). The scarcely exploited richness of Italy was well enough known to all Greeks, and the Athenian fleet would have encountered practically no opposition in making a landing and establishing a new city in many a suitable place. Vast areas of the Mediterranean were at that time as open to colonisation by the sea-borne Greeks as were America and other lands to the Europeans of later centuries.

Even among the vociferous and volatile Greeks, a great silence must have followed these words.

22

SPARRING FOR POSITION

THE DEBATE WAS CARRIED ON ALL NIGHT, but there can be no doubt that from that moment it was, in effect, concluded. Eurybiades and his Peloponnesians knew when they were beaten, and in any case Aegina and Megara (both of whom would have been thrown to the wolves if the fleet had withdrawn) came out in favour of staying at Salamis and fighting it out as Themistocles had suggested. Since Aegina was providing thirty triremes and Megara twenty they, combined with the Athenians, formed about three-quarters of the whole fleet. As Themistocles – despite Athenian opposition – had cannily recognised months before, the concession to the Peloponnesians that the commander-in-chief of the fleet should be a Spartan mattered little. In the long run, what would matter was who had the commanding number of ships. He had already pointed out to Eurybiades and the other commanders the disadvantages of fighting off the Isthmus, because this would involve a battle in open waters where the greater numbers and the better manœuvrability of the Persian ships would give them an immense advantage over the Greeks. He himself had always known that Salamis was the key. Themistocles was not only a brilliant diplomat, wily politician, admirable strategist, but also a master-tactician. There have been few men like him in history. Herodotus now records the conclusion of his speech: words which sound so authentic that, although it cannot be a direct quotation, they read as if they had stayed engraved in the memory of someone who was there:

Now for my plan: it will bring, if you adopt it, the following advantages; first, we shall be fighting in narrow waters, and there, with our inferior numbers, we shall win, provided things go as we may reasonably expect. Fighting in a confined space favours us but the open sea favours the enemy. Secondly, Salamis, where we have put our women and children, will be preserved and thirdly – for you the most important point of all – you will be fighting in defence of the Peloponnese by remaining here just as much as by withdrawing to the Isthmus – nor, if you have the sense to follow my advice, will you draw the Persian army to the Peloponnese. If we beat them at sea, as I expect we shall, they will not advance to attack you on the Isthmus, or come any further than Attica; they will retreat in disorder, and we shall gain by the preservation of Megara, Aegina, and Salamis – where an oracle has already foretold our victory. Let a man lay his plans with due regard to common sense, and he will usually succeed.

If there was much debate going on among the Greek allies as to the future conduct of the war, the same can equally be said of the councils of their enemy. There was one salient difference, however; the Greeks seem to have reached their decision as to how to act within a night or two of the burning of the Acropolis. The persuasive brilliance of Themistocles, coupled with the adherence to his views of Aegina and Megara, and also of Adeimantus, the Corinthian leader (much maligned by Herodotus), and the final acquiescence of Eurybiades had seemingly produced a united front – something rare enough among allies. Xerxes and his advisers were not faced with such a simple choice as the Greeks: to defend Salamis or withdraw to the Isthmus. The Greeks, for one thing, were in their home waters, every cable of distance and every fathom of depth of which they knew as natives of this sea. The Persians (as old Artabanus had warned) were far from home and they were faced with problems of logistics that did not affect the Greeks to anything like a similar degree. For one thing the army was largely dependent upon sea-borne supplies (always hazardous even in modern wars), and for another there was the time factor: they were into the month of September. If August storms had caused such havoc among the fleet, what could be expected in a few weeks' time when, as all seamen knew, the Mediterranean weather almost invariably broke in violent equinoctial gales? It was true that the army could advance without opposition until they reached the Isthmian line defended by the Peloponnesians, but they would still need to be supplied – and how could that be achieved with the Greek fleet gathered *en masse* at Salamis? It might have been possible, as Demaratus had suggested after Thermopylae, if Xerxes could have divided his fleet, sending one part down to harass the Peloponnese while keeping the other to engage the Greeks at sea but, as his brother Achaemenes had pointed out to him at the time, his fleet was no longer large enough to submit to such a division. Although it might not seem so at a superficial glance, yet Xerxes was even more between the Devil and the Deep than his opponents. He had left devastated and conquered (therefore unfriendly) territory behind him, and to the north of that were lands that had happily medised – but how far, if things went against him, could he trust such collaborators? And then, if it came to that, how far could the Ionian ships in the fleet really be relied upon if things looked black? They were, after all, Greeks by blood, and their subservience to Persia had only been achieved by siege and fire and the sword. (Few of the Ionians or the Aegean islanders did in fact desert Xerxes, most of the latter abstaining out of a terrified neutrality.)

Neither Xerxes nor his advisers were fools, and he had among his naval staff some of the greatest mariners of antiquity – Phoenicians who had tangled with the Greeks often enough and who had formed the backbone of the Pharaohs' fleet long before Egypt had come under the dominance of Persia. They would have been among the first to point out that they could not maintain a supply line to the army if it was encamped in the Isthmus, so long as the powerful Greek fleet could strike out from Salamis. To the Persians, then, as to the Greeks, the island of Salamis represented the key to the whole campaign. In capturing deserted Athens, even with the burning of the Acropolis (symbolic and little more), they had set the Great King's seal upon all of northern Greece. But they remembered Thermopylae and they had certainly not forgotten Artemisium. South of them lay Sparta and the indomitable warriors who had inflicted such grave losses on the finest troops of the Persian army. Just to the west of them lay those ships from which 'they had been happy to make all speed back to their moorings' after their last encounter.

Athens had been no more than a husk, but Salamis represented the kernel of Athenian government and of Greek resistance. They had learned by now that their faster triremes, especially given their numerical superiority, would be capable of enfolding the Greeks in a half-moon battle-line in the open sea and gradually constricting the enemy until they became enmeshed with one another like fish in a seine net. They had learned to their cost, however, that in constricted waters the heavier Greek ships with their immaculate discipline were a match for them. The limited area of Salamis, therefore, was clearly a trap. Was it possible to attack the island and destroy the Greek headquarters, thus cutting off the head from the whole Greek body, without risking a fleet engagement? Herodotus to the contrary (who maintains that the operation was conceived *after* Xerxes had decided on withdrawal), it seems probable that some later and generally considered inferior sources were correct: Xerxes decided to run a mole out from the mainland near modern Perama to what in those days was an islet and which is now a half-submerged reef. The ancient sea-level of the Mediterranean was lower than it is today. For a king who had bridged the Hellespont and who had cut a channel through the land behind Mount Athos, the idea of bridging an area less than a mile in width did not seem at all impracticable.

The first part of the construction would, it seemed, be easy enough, for Xerxes had almost unlimited manpower at his disposal, and the men were set to work building out a stone causeway on a substratum of rocks to the nearby islet. At the same time Phoenician merchantmen were brought along close to the shore of the mainland, where the Greeks could not get at them. The next part of the operation would entail lashing the merchantships together (somewhat as had been done at the Hellespont) and bridging the channel between the islet and what is now St George's Island. This would have been by far the most difficult part of the operation, for it would have laid the vessels open to attacks by individual or concerted forces of Greek triremes, and in any case, St George's Island (largest of what were then called the Pharmakoussae) was strongly held by the Greeks. It was unlikely that they would tamely permit this floating bridge to reach the shore. If, however, this could have been achieved, the crossing between the island and the coast of Salamis itself was only a few metres of comparatively shallow water. Clearly the Persians must have intended to protect the ship-bridge across the channel by keeping off the Greeks with heavy archery fire – and their army, as we know, had an abundance of archers. Curiously enough, in the end it was the Greeks who made successful use of this military arm, which they usually tended to neglect. We have it on one authority that the major part of these archers were from Crete (Cretan archers had long been renowned for their skill), who must of necessity have been mercenaries since their great island was not involved in the war. In any case their continuous harassment of the Persian workforce soon made it clear that the project, which in theory had looked so easy, was impracticable. It is very doubtful if even the mole out to the nearby islet was ever completed, and certainly the bridge of boats can never have got under way for it would have proved a navigational hazard in the subsequent battle and would certainly have been recorded as such by Herodotus and others.

It was clear that the Persians, like the Greeks, were now faced with only one solution – a sea battle. Xerxes' naval commanders were, therefore, summoned to a conference: the kings of Sidon, of Tyre, of Arvad (all Phoenicians), and then the others (mostly Greek) in order of their seniority. Xerxes himself presided over the meeting but left the conduct of the proceedings and the consultation with these experienced seamen to his son-in-law Mardonius. It seems as if the Great King, already foiled in his attempt to bridge the narrows of Salamis, may have made up his mind that there was nothing left for it but to engage the Greeks at sea; at the same time (an indication of an indecision hitherto unknown) it was as if he wished to be reassured. It may be that his naval advisers sensed this or, equally, it may be they thought that even with their whittled-down fleet (approximately 400 against some 300 Greek triremes) they had sufficient superiority. Furthermore, one may hazard a guess that in those days, as so often subsequently, there was a rivalry between navy and army commanders. Here was the mighty army of the Great King sitting impotent ashore and unable to move without a decisive action by the fleet. It was true that the soldiers (at great cost) had won at Thermopylae and had burned an abandoned Athens – but the fleet commanders could hardly feel that Artemisium had been a victory. All, with one exceptional dissentient, were unanimous in giving battle to the Greeks.

The lone voice opposing a naval action was that of an exceptional woman, Queen Artemisia of Halicarnassus in Caria. Her mother had been a Cretan, her father a Greek Carian. She was a widow and on her husband's death had become the sovereign of her city. Although she had a grown-up son, she had still decided that she herself would sail in command of her fleet, which consisted of five triremes from Halicarnassus together with contingents from the off-lying Aegean islands of Cos, Nisyros and Calymnos. 'Her own spirit of adventure and manly courage', comments Herodotus, 'were her only incentives.' She had distinguished herself at Artemisium and her naval contingent, though small, was considered the most efficient in the Persian fleet after that of the Sidonians. The words of this remarkable Amazon, coupled with the fact that she alone stood out against a naval engagement, made Mardonius listen to her with close attention. The speech which Herodotus puts into her mouth is vivid and bears the ring of authenticity. (Since Herodotus was himself a native of Halicarnassus, it may well be that he heard as a young man some more or less authentic account of what this great queen had said at the conference – words handed down from her own report after she had returned to her city on the conclusion of the war.)

She began by pointing out that their recent experience at sea had shown that the Greeks were superior in naval tactics. It would be foolish to rush into a naval action at this moment, especially in a place that was of the Greeks' own contriving. Her grasp of the whole situation was so extensive that the kernel of her speech deserves quoting:

Have you not taken Athens, the main objective of the war? Is not the rest of Greece in your power? There is no one now to resist you. . . . Let me tell you how I think things will now go with the enemy; if only you are not in too great a hurry to fight at sea – if you keep the fleet on the coast where it is now – then, whether you stay here or advance into the Peloponnese, you will easily accomplish your purpose. The Greeks will not be able to hold out against you for long; you will soon cause their forces to disperse – they will soon break up and go home. I hear they have no supplies in the island where they now are; and the Peloponnesian contingents, at least, are not likely to be very easy in their minds if you march with the army towards their country – they will hardly like the idea of fighting in defence of Athens.

She then launched into a diatribe against the quality of some of Xerxes' other naval contingents, including in her venom the Egyptian fleet (which had in fact distinguished itself), but she was clearly one of those passionate women who, although the bulk of their advice is sound, cannot resist dragging in personal jealousies and animosities. When Mardonius reported her words to Xerxes there can be no doubt that the king considered them very carefully. Artemisia was clearly a woman who commanded admiration (though obviously envy and hatred among those for whom she expressed contempt). However, she was in a minority of one, and the king was unlikely to reject the advice of all his other senior naval commanders. He gave orders for the fleet, or at any rate some advance squadrons, to move up from Phaleron and begin to close in on the Salamis Channel.

Despite Herodotus, who implies that Xerxes, while admiring Artemisia's plain speaking, paid no attention to it but followed the advice of the majority, the evidence lies all against this. For instance, he did not give orders for the whole fleet to go to battle stations and come out *en masse* for a major action against the Greeks at Salamis. On the contrary, he tried to lure the latter out by dangling this bait which, if the Greeks had proved unwise, might have led to a major engagement in the Saronic Gulf where (as Artemisia had foreseen) the superior numbers and the greater mobility of the Persians would have given them the advantage. The Greek fleet was like an octopus in its rocky lair, which needed the flicker of a white cloth, with its concealed barb, to induce it to strike. . . .

At the same time it seems that Xerxes ordered an army corps of about 30,000 men to march by the coast road past Eleusis towards Megara as if they were on their way to the Isthmus – something which would clearly cause panic and dissension among the Greeks at Salamis. The Peloponnesians would fear for the security of the Isthmian line and would provoke once again the old argument (still perhaps tacitly accepted by Eurybiades) that the Salamis strategy was wrong. Xerxes, in fact, does not seem to have rejected the sage advice of Artemisia but to have decided, rather than to accept it whole-heartedly, to adopt a compromise. He would make a feint of threatening the Peloponnese while at the same time trying to provoke a sea-battle in open waters. (A *Supremo* may inwardly accept that the advice of one of his admirals or generals is correct, but he is also constrained by his dominant authority and by the fact that he cannot entirely ignore the opinions of all the others.) Compromise rarely succeeds in warfare. Caesar knew this when he said at the crossing of the Rubicon: 'The die is cast.' Xerxes would have done better to accept the advice of the Halicarnassian queen, and not try to hedge his bets.

EVE OF BATTLE

THE MOVEMENT OF A LARGE BODY of Persian troops towards Megara on the route to the Isthmus of Corinth led to consternation, and the usual division of opinion, among the Greeks assembled at Salamis. It is clear that the Persians made every effort to ensure that the whole operation should be as noisy and ostentatious as possible – something that would hardly be likely if they had intended a serious attack on the Isthmian line. This was an exercise to set the Greeks at odds with one another, and to divert them from their concordance to stand together at Salamis.

An unusual story in Herodotus seems unwittingly to confirm this. An Athenian exile named Dicaeus was out in the plain to the north of Eleusis along with the exiled Spartan king Demaratus at the time when the Persian troops had been ordered on the road that leads past Eleusis. The two men were most probably alone together so that they could talk freely and discuss their situation in the light of current circumstances. Herodotus specifically states that Dicaeus used to retell the story in later years and would tell any sceptics to consult Demaratus if they wanted confirmation of it. 'They saw a cloud of dust, such as might have been raised by an army of thirty thousand men on the march, coming from the direction of Eleusis, and were wondering what troops they could be, when they suddenly heard the sound of voices. Dicaeus thought he recognised the *Iacchus* song, which is sung at the Dionysiac mysteries. . . .' This is the first indication that we get in Herodotus of any date after the occupation of Athens; for the sacred rites at Eleusis were held at the time of the full moon of what is now the month of September. This puts the date on which Dicaeus fancied for the moment that he witnessed something to do with the Eleusinian mysteries taking place (he was possibly an initiate himself) at about the time of the full moon of 17 September. Demaratus, who, as a Spartan, knew little or nothing about the rites of Eleusis, is said to have asked his companion the reason for the noise. Dicaeus – realising that, in view of the devastated state of Attica, it could not be the normal annual procession – told him that the sound and the dust cloud could only have some mystic significance. Coming as it did from the direction of Eleusis, he concluded that it must necessarily betoken something of ill-omen towards these foreign invaders of the sacred soil. He came to the conclusion that the singing was of some divine nature (not the voices of distant troops, who were out of sight, singing in a foreign mode and tongue) and that it could only mean that some unearthly power was about to save the Athenians and their allies. Pointing to the dust cloud, which seemed to provide a strange omen on that autumn day, he said to Demaratus that the direction in which it moved would show where the Great King would be worsted – whether by land or by sea. The Spartan told him that when they got back among the Persians he had better keep his mouth shut or he would certainly lose his head. While Demaratus was speaking the dust cloud rose high in the air and drifted towards Salamis. . . .

The folly of Eurybiades, as the Peloponnesians saw it, in agreeing to the plan of this stateless Athenian Themistocles, immediately provoked another violent debate.

> The smothered feeling broke out into open resentment, and another meeting was held. All the old ground was gone over again, one side urging that it was useless to stay and fight for a country which was already in enemy hands, and that the fleet should sail and risk an action in defence of the Peloponnese [just what Xerxes hoped], while the Athenians, Aeginetans, and Megarians still maintained that they should stay and fight at Salamis.

Themistocles acted promptly. He left the meeting and sent for an Asiatic Greek slave, Sicinnus, who had been the guardian of his children. It is interesting that Herodotus says 'he slipped away', but this seems somewhat dubious since the absence of the principal figure in the discussion could hardly have gone unremarked. It is more probable that, having made his position clear, he left the others to shout and wrangle (in a manner not uncommon among modern Greeks). His choice of Sicinnus is interesting for it reveals that trust in the devoted family slave to be found also in Greek tragedy, and going back as far as Eumaeus, the swineherd of Odysseus. As Herodotus tells the story, it would seem that this action of Themistocles was unpremeditated and done on the spur of the moment, but from the use that he made of Sicinnus one feels it was something which he had long conceived in the event of a breakdown in the Greek resolve to stay at Salamis. Furthermore, the fact that Sicinnus was ordered to take a small boat and cross over to the Persian lines under cover of darkness suggests that Themistocles must have had some supporters who agreed with him on this last desperate ploy. A man in a boat could hardly have got away unnoticed at that crisis in Greek affairs without some considerable authority being exercised over those on guard at the various landing-stages.

The message that Sicinnus was told to relay was, on the surface, simple enough. In fact, a number of modern scholars, thinking in terms of the complex twentieth century, have been unable to credit that the Great King could ever have believed it. (This is the mistake of hindsight and over-sophistication.) Since the versions given both by Herodotus and by Aeschylus, who fought in the battle, are so similar they seem more than worthy of credence. Herodotus writes:

> . . . Sicinnus made his way to the Persian commanders and said: 'I am the bearer of a secret communication from the Athenian commander, who is a well-wisher to your king and hopes for a Persian victory. He has told me to report to you that the Greeks are afraid and are planning to slip away. Only prevent them from slipping through your fingers, and you have at this moment an opportunity of unparalleled success. They are at daggers drawn with each other, and will offer no opposition – on the contrary, you will see the pro-Persians amongst them fighting the rest.'

There can be no doubt that Sicinnus did not have an audience with the king, but with some senior officers – possibly no more than the trierarchs of one or more of the Persian triremes. It seems surprising that he was not detained for further questioning, but it is possible that he may never even have left his boat for, 'his message delivered, Sicinnus lost no time in getting away'. One can hazard the guess that this message was delivered in the early hours of 19 September, and purported to be the conclusions of the Greeks' last council of war from which Themistocles had recently with-drawn. Quite apart from the account given by Herodotus the story of Sicinnus is borne out by Aeschylus in his play *The Persians*. It seems also confirmed by the fact that, after the war was over, Themistocles freed his former slave and had him made a citizen of Thespiae at a time 'when the Thespians were enrolling additional citizens, and made him a rich man'. Themistocles – despite his many virtues – was not noted for his generosity, so one may reasonably conclude that Sicinnus performed a service that was almost 'beyond the call of duty'.

Xerxes, it would seem, swallowed the tale. On the surface this is almost impossible to believe: the king and his advisers had never previously shown themselves at all ingenuous about the duplicity and cunning nature of the Greeks. On the other hand, they cannot have been ignorant of the fact that there was deep dissension among the Greeks at Salamis (they hardly needed Queen Artemisia to remind them of that) and it must have been clear to all that Xerxes' manœuvre in sending an army corps to march blatantly along the coast road in the direction of Megara would bring the division among the Peloponnesians and the Athenians to a head. The message that now reached them from this slave sent by Themistocles seemed to confirm this. Green comments that 'Xerxes' experience during this campaign, not least in Phocis and Boeotia, might well have convinced him that any Greek state's resentment against Persia ran a very poor second to the implacable hatred it reserved for its own neighbours: why should Athens be any exception to this rule?' And then there was the example of the Arcadians who had come over to join the Persian army after the defeat of the Spartans at Thermopylae. If Greeks from remote Arcadia were willing to defect, was it not possible that even the Athenians, despite their deep hostility to Persia, had now – having seen their city and their shrines go up in flames – abandoned hope and decided to throw their hand in with the all-conquering monarch? Spies must have been rife in those days, and word may even have reached the king that Themistocles had already threatened to pull out the Athenian fleet and found a new colony in southern Italy. In con-clusion one must take into account the nature of the Great King himself.

Xerxes had not yet achieved the kind of overwhelming triumph that his nature craved. Thermopylae had been a dearly bought victory and the price paid for it in Persian dead had necessitated a cover-up before the men from the fleet could be invited over to inspect the scene. Furthermore, what was the destruction of a handful of men in a little rocky pass? This was not the way major battles were fought in the East, where the monarch sat and surveyed the whole field from some suitable place and watched an enormous drama opening before his eyes – a drama of which he was the author, director and producer, and which he expected to conclude exactly as he had planned it. The capture of undefended Athens, even the assault on the Acropolis, had not provided the dénouement that was called for by the years of preparations: by the massive works of bridging the Hellespont and turning Mount Athos into an island. The epic nature of the whole expedition required a grand finale and now it seemed that the opportunity presented itself.

Although Xerxes was hardly the Oriental hubristic tyrant that Greek writers depicted, yet certainly there was enough arrogance in his nature to wish for a climactic battle to round off the campaign. The Greeks, furthermore, had not taken the bait of his advanced ships – proof, perhaps, that they were afraid? If this was so, then the likelihood of their trying to slip away under cover of darkness seemed plausible. Quite apart from the fact that it was now the third week of September, and the weather might be expected to break at any moment, there were other practical reasons why Xerxes would have wished to conclude the Greek campaign as swiftly as possible. Admirably organised though it was, the Persian Empire was held together by the military might of the army, the ability of his generals, councillors and advisers, and the presence of the Great King himself. Ionia, despite – or perhaps because of – the absence of its ships and commanders, was restless; Egypt, where the influence of the priests was still strong, had not forgotten the harrowing of its religious practices, nor forgotten its harsh conquest; and the borders of empire were always being frayed by savage tribes. Furthermore, Xerxes must have known of the failure of 'Operation Europe' in the West. For, whether the battle of Himera took place in August or September, the news would certainly have reached the Persians that the great Carthaginian expedition against Sicily had ended in disaster. There was every reason for haste.

24

'SEA-BORN SALAMIS'

THROUGHOUT 19 SEPTEMBER the king's council together with the senior naval commanders debated what was the appropriate action to take. There were two ways in which the Greeks could escape from their Salamis base and it seemed clear that both would be used. The first was to slide around the promontory of Cynosura and, passing between it and the off-lying island of Psyttaleia, make their way south into the Saronic Gulf. This route, on the face of it the simplest, was hazardous because the Persian navy (by now on the *qui vive*) would be patrolling the area and it would be impossible for any large body of ships to escape detection. The moon was almost full and the nights at that time of the year, if the weather has not broken, are often cloudless. The fleeing Greeks should thus be easily visible and, in any case, in those phosphorescent waters the concurrence of many oars and the wakes of large vessels would stain the sea with silver. There was yet another factor which would have revealed the movement of triremes: the rhythmic plash of their oars as close on 200 men per vessel toiled at their thole-pins. Even if moving at a slow speed, three to four knots, the noise of a body of triremes would have been unmistakable. The other course for the Greeks to take – and one which would not be so easily detectable – was through the Bay of Eleusis, then down through the narrow Megarian Channel, and south into the Saronic Gulf. It was clear that this escape route must immediately be blocked. The Egyptian fleet, which had distinguished itself at Artemisium, was chosen for the task. Their heavily armed marines had already proved their worth and, in the narrows of the channel where the Greeks would not be able to deploy their ships, they would be met bow-to-bow by the larger Egyptian vessels. The channel would not be a means of escape, but a trap.

There can be practically no doubt, despite the assertion of

Herodotus that 'the Greek commanders at Salamis were still at loggerheads', that the very reverse was true. The battle which was to follow could only have been the product of careful and close planning between all the Greek commanders involved. True, Themistocles deserves most of the credit for having envisaged the strategy of Salamis a long time before, but without sophisticated co-ordination between the whole fleet – not just the Athenians – the battle would have been lost. Xerxes, on the other hand, together with his council and commanders, accepted the Greek misinformation that had been fed to them and committed the gravest error: they diversified their forces. The strong and efficient Egyptian

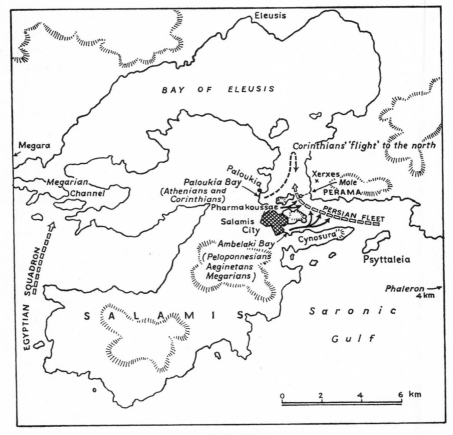

5   SALAMIS

squadron was despatched (no doubt after dusk on that day) to round Salamis and head for the Megara Channel while two of the squadrons, which had been sent out earlier as bait to tempt the Greeks, were reinforced and ordered to guard the passages either side of the island of Psyttaleia. At the same time 400 men were landed on that island, 'because it lay right in the path of the impending action, and once the fighting began, many men and damaged vessels would be carried on to it, and could be saved or destroyed according as they were friends or enemies'. Aeschylus tells how, after the evening meal, the Persians manned their ships and, once the sun was down, 'the long ships moved, each out to its appointed place'. The net, it seemed, was closed around the Greeks.

Disentangling our sources, which are confusing and which tend to have a bias implanted by later Athenian landowners (the hoplite class who had shown little initiative since Marathon) and were designed to denigrate Themistocles and the 'navy party', is not easy. Aristeides 'the Just' is purported to have returned from exile at this crucial moment and had a meeting in which it is claimed that it was he who told Themistocles that the Greeks were now surrounded and offered his services in this hour of need. Themistocles, if we are to believe the account, remarked that this was good news and just what he had hoped for (true), and asked Aristeides to go in person and tell the assembly because they would certainly believe him – while they would not believe Themistocles. The imputation is that the Greek leaders were *still* arguing the pros and cons of staying at Salamis or withdrawing to the Peloponnese. And this on the eve of the Battle of Salamis – one of the most perfectly co-ordinated and long-devised stratagems in all naval history!

What does seem perfectly true about the accounts of the night's events is that a trireme from the Persian-occupied island of Tenos, commanded by a Greek whose name is deservedly commemorated, Panaetius son of Sosimenes, slipped out of the Persian lines and joined the fleet at Salamis. Panaetius brought them the latest news: how Xerxes had divided the fleet and sent the strong Egyptian contingent to guard the narrows of Megara, while the others guarded the 'escape routes' north and south of Psyttaleia. Night actions were unthinkable in those days (and were to remain so for centuries to come) and the suggestion that any of the Persians had already slipped past Psyttaleia and closed in on the coast of Salamis is absurd. It will have been quite enough that, even with the advantage of bright moonlight, they had got into the positions allocated to them and were now resting on their oars, or paddling and back-paddling to maintain station.

Themistocles and the other commanders – not excluding the Spartan commander-in-chief Eurybiades – can only have been delighted. The most formidable contingent of the Persian fleet, the Egyptians, was far away, committed to a fruitless watch-and-ward away to the west. The bulk of the remaining ships was now divided either side of Psyttaleia Island. While the Greeks were rested in their rocky lair, waiting for dawn and the onslaught of battle, the Persians were at sea: their triremes slopping to-and-fro, the oarsmen cold and possibly wet, and getting hungry, forced every now and then to take up the stroke to maintain position, or idling over oars that kicked and thrust with the least breathing of the ocean. The bull, which had found its 'area of quietness', had only to watch and wait for the first pass of the matador.

As dawn was breaking 'they called an assembly of the marines. . . .' While the sailors manned their ships and prepared them for sea Themistocles was chosen to address the armoured men upon whom would fall the brunt of the day's fighting. Seeing that the fleet was fairly widely dispersed it can be assumed that it was only the Athenians whom he addressed, but the fact that his speech was so long remembered shows the quality of the resolve that inspired all the Greeks on that autumn morning. 'The whole burden of what he said was a comparison of all that was best in life and fortunes, and an exhortation to the men to choose the better.' Dawn, which found the rested Greeks manning their ships and preparing to give battle in the chosen narrows of the Salamis Channel, must have found the Persian commanders in more than something of a quandary. All night they had maintained watch and ward over the escape routes and had seen nothing. Perhaps all the Greeks, not just part of their fleet, had fled through the Bay of Eleusis and made for the Megara Channel?

If this was the case, there was nothing they could do about it; only hope that the Egyptian fleet would be able to stop them as they came in line ahead or individual groups through that congested strait. They had been informed by Xerxes that if they let the Greeks slip through their fingers 'each captain would lose his head'. As the exit from the Salamis Channel was the area that had been assigned to them to guard they were hardly likely to turn back towards Phaleron with the dawn and say that there was no sign of the enemy – for the Greeks might then make a sudden dash for safety round Cape Cynosura and south of Psyttaleia. No, they were committed to their stations and certainly no one was going to act on individual initiative. What must always be remembered is the primitive state of communications in those days, and the non-existence of them under night-time conditions.

The disposition of the Greek fleet had been well thought out: the main bulk lying behind St George's Island with the Athenians on the left of the line. To the north of them the Corinthians held the narrowest part leading towards the Bay of Eleusis, while the Peloponnesian contingents with Eurybiades as commander-in-chief held the right flank, generally regarded as the position of honour, 'and the ships of Megara and Aegina off the town of Salamis in Ambelaki Bay'. 'The Greek object', as Burn has pointed out, 'was to envelop in a net formed of an ordered line the head of a column coming up the straits'. The Persian fleet possibly numbered 400 ships and the Greeks about 300. This meant that if the Persians could be enticed into the narrows their numbers would be to no advantage; rather the reverse, for triremes under way probably required about fifty-foot intervals between them since, although only about fifteen feet on the beam, their oars on either side required at least a further ten feet. It is easy to see what confusion could take place if such basically unwieldy vessels could be lured into a position where they could not happily maintain their distance from one another.

The salient question that arises is why Xerxes ever gave the order for the attack to begin at all. Yet he had clearly made up his mind on that day to witness his fleet defeating the Greeks, for he had established his command-post – probably on a 200-feet-high eminence a little to the north-east of the islet and the uncompleted mole from which he had intended to bridge the sea to Salamis. Here was set that famous gold throne and here his staff and aides must already have been gathered by first light on the morning of 20 September. Such arrangements are hardly made on the spur of the moment. He had determined, then, on a set-piece battle just in the area which he knew on good advice would give the Greeks every advantage. At first glance it appears incomprehensible, but on careful reflection one can see his reasons. He had been told that the Greeks were at loggerheads with one another, that the Athenians intended to flee, and that other contingents no doubt would either withdraw from battle or would come over to his victorious side. He had effectively sealed the Megara Channel with his Egyptians, and the fact that none of the Greeks had attempted to escape round Cape Cynosura during the night seemed to confirm that either the bulk of them had fled via the Bay of Eleusis, or that those who were still at Salamis were sufficiently demoralised to offer no effective resistance. In such circumstances he might expect a true and easy triumph and afterwards watch the capture of Salamis and the effective destruction of the headquarters of Athenian resistance (Athens itself had been a hollow affair).

By the time that the orders had been given for the fleet to advance into the narrows it was too late. Once squadron after squadron had been committed and begun their advance there was no way of recalling them. The front line could not halt, nor wheel and turn, without falling foul of those that followed them, and the same thing would take place all down the serried line. What still seems puzzling is why the Persians proceeded with such complete confidence into the narrows, so certain that they had a beaten and demoralised enemy in front of them. The answer to this is to be found in Herodotus (though his biased account suggests cowardice on the part of the Corinthians). As the sun rose, the advancing ships saw to the north-west of them a squadron of Greek triremes (the fifty Corinthians), their sails hoisted, apparently fleeing up towards the Bay of Eleusis. Now, as has been seen, no trireme ever went into action with her square-sail set. So this could only indicate that part (or perhaps even the last) of the Greek ships at Salamis was making good its escape. This was encouragement indeed: proof if any were needed that the whole Greek fleet was divided and that very little resistance might be expected from whatever of their ships still remained behind at their island base. The whole operation indicates the most immaculate planning on the part of Themistocles and the other Greek commanders – particularly Adeimantus, the Corinthian commander, who made this feint of betraying his comrades in the hour of danger. We know from later records that the Corinthians under Adeimantus fought most gallant-

ly in the subsequent battle, so it is not difficult to follow what happened. After their carefully pretended flight – largely responsible
for enticing the Persians into the narrows – the Corinthians downed
masts, spars and sails, and returned in normal fashion under oars
into the fray. The Persian commanders – falling into an extension
of the trap that had caught their lord and master – pressed on
confident of victory. (It was not for nothing that that prototype
of all great Greek seamen was known as 'the wily Odysseus'. The
ingenuity of the inventor of the Trojan Horse was not lacking in
his descendants.)

At almost the same time as the apparently fleeing Corinthians
were sighted, the main body of the Greek fleet, the Athenians and
Peloponnesians, disclosed themselves from behind the bulk of St
George's Island (where they would previously have been invisible
to the ships entering the narrows) and came out in columns of line
ahead. They also turned towards the north. Although they were
under oar, it may have seemed to the leading Persians that this was
only until they had got clear of Paloukia Bay – at which time it
might be expected that they too would hoist sail and follow their
fleeing comrades. The triremes of Megara and Aegina, one can
only assume, began to make ready in Ambelaki Bay. They would
provide the closure of the net once the Persians were totally committed into the area between Salamis town and the islet on the far
side – above which Xerxes sat to watch his triumph.

Aeschylus brilliantly puts into the mouth of a Persian aboard one
of their front-line vessels what happened as darkness faded. (The
translation is by A. R. Burn.)

> Night wore on
> And still no Greeks came out in secret flight;
> But when at last the sun's bright chariot rose,
> Then we could hear them – singing; loud and strong
> Rang back the echo from the island rocks,
> And with the sound came the first chill of fear.
> Something was wrong. This was not flight; they sang
> The deep-toned hymn, Apollo, Saving Lord,
> That cheers the Hellene armies into battle.
> Then trumpets over there set all on fire;
> Then the sea foamed as oars struck all together,

197

And swiftly, there they were! The right wing first
Led on the ordered line, then all the rest
Came on, came out. . . .

So much about the battle must inevitably remain conjecture, but
what would seem to have happened – and which makes sound
nautical sense – is that the right wing referred to was composed not
only of Eurybiades' Peloponnesians but also of the Aeginetans and
Megarians who had been lurking in Ambelaki Bay. As the main
body of the Greek fleet moved down from the north, seeing the
enemy well committed into the narrows, the ships from Ambelaki
were able to strike out, roaring the Paean to Apollo, catching the
enemy broadside on as they moved confidently down channel after
what they had assumed were the fleeing Greeks. This right
wing, suddenly emerging on to their exposed port flank, must have
seemed like a bolt from heaven, accompanied as it was by the thunder of the hymn. (Similarly, in Nelson's navy, British sailors always
used to cheer as they went into action – not only for their own
morale but because it had a demoralising effect upon the enemy.)
Shortly after this devasting flank attack developed, throwing the
Persians into disarray because in their close-ordered ranks there was
little or no chance of manœuvring, the main attack at the head of
the column developed. What the Persians had seen as a demoralised
and fleeing enemy suddenly became a noose that tightened around
their advance guard. The Athenian Ameinias of Pallene is credited
with having been in the forefront and with having engaged the
flagship of the Phoenician admiral, a much larger vessel than the
low-lying Athenian trireme. The ships met head on, bronze rams
sheering past each other so that the two vessels were locked together.
In the boarding action which followed, Ariabignes, the admiral,
'a man of great courage', led the charge over his lofty ship's side
and was killed by Ameinias and his first lieutenant. The Phoenician's
death seems to have been a grave loss to the command – an instance
that in the fleet of Xerxes command was centralised, whereas
among the individualistic Greeks, once the main battle had developed, each trierarch very largely exercised his own initiative. (One
is reminded again of Nelson's 'Band of Brothers' at Trafalgar
where, as Collingwood remarked, 'We all know what we have to
do'.)

The general action which now developed most probably took place between St George's Island and that other islet out to which the Persians had begun to run their mole. Xerxes, in fact, from his vantage-point had a perfect view of what should have been a perfect victory. His humiliation was complete, as the chaos in the strait became apparent even to a landsman's eye. The advancing squadrons had had to reduce to no more than about sixteen triremes abreast, as the distance between the islet and St George's Island was then probably no more than a thousand yards. As ships backwatered, inevitably they fell foul of those coming up astern of them. The press of ships moving up in their lines from the point of Cape Cynosura cannot have known what was happening ahead, nor known for a moment that their powerful vanguard had been trapped.

> At first, the torrent of the Persian fleet
> bore up: but when the press of shipping jammed
> there in the narrows, none could help another. . . .

Aeschylus goes on to describe how the Greek triremes 'kept the outer station' and, under their disciplined handling, encircled the Persians, striking in as suited them at the floundering mass. (Anyone who has witnessed a *mattanza* or the netting and slaughtering of tunny, to be seen in a number of places in the Mediterranean to this day, will recognise the accuracy of the great poet's observation.)

> Meanwhile the enemy, as men gaff tunnies
> Or some great shoal of fish, with broken oars
> And bits of wreckage hacked and killed; and shrieks
> And cries filled the whole sea, till night came down.

Herodotus gives instances of a number of individual exploits in the general *mêlée* that followed – not excluding the dash and bravery of Queen Artemisia, his fellow Halicarnassian, whose exploits were such as supposedly to have wrung from Xerxes the cry: 'My men have turned into women, my women into men!' But the result of the action was a foregone conclusion once the Persians had put their head into the snare. They

suffered severely in the battle, the Athenians and Aeginetans accounting for a great many of their ships. Since the Greek fleet worked together as a whole, while the Persians had lost form-ation and were no longer fighting on any plan. . . . None the less they fought well that day – far better than in the actions off Euboea. Every man of them did his best for fear of Xerxes, feeling that the king's eye was on him.

There can be no doubt that this was a powerful incentive, the king's secretaries taking careful note of those who did well: two of these, both Samians, were later rewarded by the king, one being made ruler of Samos and the other being given large estates. But it was a case of 'woe betide' those who were deemed to have cut and run. Some Phoenicians who, in common, one suspects, with many other captains, had been forced to run their ships aground on the Attic coast to get clear of the general confusion were unwise enough to make their way to Xerxes. They must have been foolish men indeed to approach 'the King, King of Kings, King of the lands' at such a moment. They tried to excuse themselves for what was clearly by now a defeat by putting all the blame on the Ionian contingents, which Xerxes himself was able to see were putting up the best fight of all the elements of his navy. (In fact, on that day, it would seem that the fiercest fighting took place where Greek met Greek.) Xerxes wasted no time – he had the Phoenicians beheaded on the spot.

On the morning of that day there had been a southerly wind, and it was with this under their sterns that the Corinthians had hoisted their sails and made their feigned flight to the north. The same wind blowing on to the shores of Attica had also (as is still common enough) kicked up a nasty short sea in the Salamis Channel. This had been yet another gift from the gods, like the northerlies in the early phases of the invasion, which had favoured the Greeks. Their smaller triremes, lying lower in the water, had ridden it out with little discomfort (after all, this was the sea for which they were built), whereas most of the Persian ships, with their high freeboard, had suffered from the wind and swell, particularly since their westerly course put it broad on their beam. Now in the afternoon of confusion, when wreckage and drowned men littered the channel, the wind shifted round, as it often does in that part as the sun declines, and began to pipe up from the west. This may have helped the

Persians in what had by now become a rout; enabling some of them, perhaps, to hoist masts and spars and make their getaway. The wind also helped to clear the narrow channel of the wreckage, sending it on down towards Phaleron, where no doubt it helped in the further demoralisation of the Persian ships as they reassembled there. It helped the Greeks too in what seems to have been a somewhat sporadic pursuit. It also effectively marooned on Psyttaleia Island the picked force of Persian soldiers who had been set there to kill any shipwrecked Greeks and succour any of their own side who might reach the safety of its shores. (It is interesting to note that many of the Greeks from wrecked triremes made their escape by swimming whereas few of the enemy appear to have been able to swim.) To Psyttaleia, then, a mixed force of hoplites and marines now made their way – possibly under the command of Aristeides – and proceeded to round up the Persians. They were slaughtered to a man. It was not a day for giving any quarter.

AFTERMATH

THROUGHOUT THAT NIGHT the Greeks laboured to repair their ships, fully expecting that the following day the Persians would return to the attack. Herodotus gives us no figures for the battle casualties and it is only from the later writer Ephorus, who seems far more sound as a naval historian than Herodotus, that we gain any figures for the respective losses – figures which seem, in view of Xerxes' subsequent actions, to make good sense. The Greeks, he says, lost 40 triremes (though there is no mention of how many were badly damaged) while the Persians lost 200, not excluding those that were captured (again no figures). If this was indeed the case, then even if the Egyptian fleet had returned from its fruitless guard over the Megara Channel the Persian fleet would still have had little more than parity of numbers.

There can be no doubt that when the ships reassembled at Phaleron their morale was completely shattered. They had been tricked into fighting in the wrong place and at the wrong time (that southerly wind), and the discipline and ability of the Greeks had proved totally superior to their own. They had been disgraced under the eye of the Great King, and the Phoenicians, who had hitherto regarded themselves as the greatest sailors in the world, had suffered such a severe mauling that it would be years before they would ever again challenge the Greeks at sea. Ephorus says that, infuriated by the execution of those captains who had so unwisely made their way into Xerxes' presence, the Phoenicians now deserted and made their own way home. This may or may not be true, but in any case, since they had been in the vanguard and had been the principal victims of the Greek trap, it is doubtful if there were many of their ships in a seaworthy condition.

The Greeks, for their part, licking their wounds and making good what essential repairs they could, did not realise the extent of their victory. The Grand Army was still encamped on the shores opposite Salamis, and with the dawn of 21 September Xerxes had his men set to work again on the mole. There seemed every evidence that his intention still was, with all the manpower at his disposal, to cross over to Salamis and annihilate the last of the resistance. Meanwhile, from what could be made out of the Persian squadrons at Phaleron, renewed signs of activity (possibly the sending out of further patrols off Psyttaleia) suggested that in a day or so they might expect a further attack – and next time there could be no possibility of the Persians falling into that beautiful seine-net trap. They would probably (as had been Artemisia's advice to Xerxes) surround the island, guard all the escape routes, and quietly starve out the Greeks. Meanwhile their army marching on the Isthmian line and with its vast weight of numbers – as they had seen at Thermopylae – might overwhelm the Peloponnesian resistance.

Xerxes, however, saw things quite differently. He knew, which the Greeks did not, that his fleet was shattered and demoralised. He knew also – something of which the Greeks must also have been aware – that the weather might break at any minute, and no trireme could keep the sea once the season of gales started. Furthermore he knew that his great achievement, the bridge across the Helles-pont, which had enabled his forces to enter Europe, was now his Achilles' heel. The Greeks, conscious of their triumph – which, as yet, they were not – might move swiftly and destroy it. Failing that, the onset of heavy weather from the north, which was to be expected in the near future, might wreck it, as had happened to its predecessor. As has been seen, there were problems on the boun-daries of the Empire and Ionia was insecure. The latter gave rise to a further anxiety in the king's mind. Suppose the Greeks, instead of destroying the bridges, moved against Ionia? The news that the Persians had suffered a severe naval reverse at Salamis would soon be on its way to Susa, for 'there is nothing in the world that travels faster than Persian couriers'. If the victorious Greek fleet were to appear off Ionia and the eastern islands, the whole province might rise. It had happened before, and Xerxes was under no illusion that the Ionians preferred Persian dominion to being free and independent. There could be no doubt about it but that the place of the Great King was back in Susa, his hands upon the reins of Empire. Meanwhile, though, it was unthinkable after the success of the land campaign in northern Greece that the whole of the Grand Army should withdraw, as if in defeat. His conquests, which had been widely acclaimed by his people and which must have terrified nations like Egypt, must be seen to be firmly established.

The Persians, as has been said, were not seamen. They had acquired their navy through the conquest of seagoing people such as the Phoenicians, Ionians, and Egyptians. They were soldiers first and foremost. So far, the record of their army in northern Greece, the annihilation of the famous warrior-caste of Spartans at Thermopylae, and their occupation and destruction of Athens 'including its sacred high place, the Acropolis' was all evidence of victory. The defeat at Salamis could be ascribed to the failure and inefficiency of their foreign fleet. But, as Hignett puts it, 'the ignominious retirement of its army from Europe without any further attempt to force a battle on land with the main Greek army would have meant a loss of face that would have fatally compromised the prestige of the ruling race'. Empires, inevitably, depend a great deal upon 'face' for without it their subject peoples are quick to realise that the master is not invincible. (In the history of the twentieth century, Ireland played a similar part in revealing the weakness of the British Lion.) Xerxes was not slow to realise what the withdrawal of the whole army would mean. He himself must return to the seat of power, but a large force must be left behind to hold the occupied territory, and the obvious choice for the leader of this army was Mardonius, his cousin, who had always been a prime advocate of the great invasion. Meanwhile the demoralised fleet could no longer serve any useful purpose and must be despatched as swiftly as possible.

On the morning of 22 September, the Greeks, seeing all the army still encamped against them and work proceeding on the mole, must have expected that this was the day that the blow would fall. The Persians, like themselves, had had a full twenty-four hours to make good their battle-damage, rest their men, and replace such marines and oarsmen as had been killed or wounded in the battle. With their almost inexhaustible manpower this was something that was far easier for them than for the beleaguered Greeks on their island base. Then, of a sudden, the astonishing news came through from their scouts – Phaleron roadstead was empty. The Persian navy had withdrawn! An immediate pursuit was ordered; the fleet heading in the direction of the island of Andros. Whether the Persians were heading north to protect the bridges (the most likely supposition) or making for Ionia, their natural route would be through the Andros–Euboea channel. Even rowing with the exhilaration of victory in their veins, however, the Greeks were never able to come up with the Persians: a night's start, coupled with the daylight hours during which the Greeks had been occupied in manning their fleet, had given the enemy too great a lead. Disappointed in their hope of coming up with a fleeing, demoralised fleet, the Greeks decided to rest in Andros roads. The island had been pro-Persian, like most of the Cyclades, and it was natural enough that the victors should strive to exact an indemnity. There was good enough reason for their action and for the financial pressure put on this and other islands. It was not only a matter of a justifiable penalty for having sided with the enemy, but also money was badly needed to pay the fleet, and such things of value as had been left on the Acropolis had, of course, disappeared with the Persians. To Themistocles' harsh statement, when the Andrians refused to pay, that he had two powerful gods with him that would force them to do so – Persuasion and Necessity – the Andrians replied with dry wit that they had two gods also, Poverty and Inability. Unwilling to attempt a prolonged siege of their city (remembering perhaps the fate of Miltiades under somewhat similar circumstances) Themistocles gave up, although there can be little doubt that the island was scoured for grain and fresh food and any valuables in outlying hamlets.

Meanwhile a council of war was held with Eurybiades presiding, the issue naturally being – what were they to do next? Some, including possibly Themistocles, were for pressing on north and destroying the bridges, but others, Eurybiades among them, were against this. It was the latter who carried the day. They were wise in any case, for to head north in the last week of September was to court disaster when the weather – as it must do in the very near future – finally broke. It was also a wise Spartan principle of war, as applicable at sea as on land, not to pursue a beaten enemy. This was not so much based on chivalric grounds as on the fact that desperate men may suddenly turn and rend their pursuers and nullify their previous defeat. On one point all were unanimously agreed: the most important thing was to speed the departure of

Xerxes out of Greece. The latter, for the reasons we have seen, did not need any persuasion. The story told by Herodotus that Themistocles once again sent Sicinnus to Xerxes with the message that he had better hurry home because the Greek fleet was sailing to destroy the bridges is deeply suspect. Xerxes and his staff had been badly duped once, but it is unthinkable that they should have been taken in for a second time – and by the same man. Plutarch has a slight variant on this tale – that Themistocles sent a Persian prisoner of war with a similar message. This is slightly more credible. It is just possible that the retreat of the main body of the army was hastened by such means – but unlikely, and indeed unnecessary. Neither Xerxes nor his staff needed any reminder of the time of the year and, with Mardonius left behind with a strong, hand-picked force – mostly of Persian troops – Xerxes could happily leave Attica behind and make his way, with no exaggerated semblance of haste, to cross once more into Asia.

Having decided against any attempt to break the Hellespontine bridges, but to stay nearer home, the Greek fleet proceeded to exact what indemnities they could from the surrounding Cyclades, as well as pro-Persian Carystus in southern Euboea. The rich island of Paros paid up without demur while Carystus (perhaps because it had been so useful to the Persians at one juncture) had its lands ransacked even though it had already paid the required amount. Themistocles, on the authority of Plutarch, is also said to have lined his own pockets by removing from office pro-Persians in various islands and putting back in their place – for a sum – the anti-Persians whom they had exiled. The story may well be true. Greeks today as then may well be patriotic and extremely brave, but it is almost unthinkable for them to forget the cash nexus. (As any one who has lived in that beautiful but harsh land knows, a man who can make even a moderate living out of its soil could become a millionaire in other softer countries.)

An abortive siege of Andros was called off when the news reached the fleet that the Great King had withdrawn and that his hosts no longer glowered across the strait at Salamis. Attica was cleared of the enemy and, though they did not know it as yet, Mardonius and his picked army-force had decided to winter in Thessaly. In that delirious moment the Greeks may have thought that the war was finally over. They were to learn differently with the spring, but in the meantime it was all-important to get on with the autumn sowing, for they had already lost one crop. Themistocles was undoubtedly the hero of the hour and in his certainty declared that the Persians were gone for good and all. He was wise enough, however, to point out that they must all set to work at once on the land itself and on rebuilding Athens. Soon the winter would be down, and Athens is no place in which to be roofless when the snows are on the mountains. At the same time, not unmindful of what certainly seemed like divine help in their survival, three captured triremes were consecrated, one at the Isthmus (which Herodotus himself saw still there some forty years later), one on Sunium, and one on Salamis. More enduring monuments were a bronze Zeus at Olympia, and at Delphi (willingly forgetful of the oracle's pessimistic predictions) an eighteen-feet-high figure of a young man holding the prow of a ship in his hand – a symbol of the fighting men of Greece offering to Apollo evidence of their triumph. On the all-important peninsula of Cynosura a marble column was erected, a reminder to later seafarers that it was off here in the narrow strait of Salamis that Greek seamen had defeated the armada of the Great King.

While the Peloponnesians happily returned to their homes – for, although their territories had not been devastated, they too had their lands to cultivate – Xerxes continued on his march north. The number of men left behind under the command of Mardonius is quoted by Herodotus as 300,000 but, if one accepts as with all his previous figures that he is misreading the Persian chiliad (1000) for myriad (10,000), this comes down to the more reasonable number of 30,000 – ample to garrison northern Greece and ample, too, for a further attack on the south in the following spring. The Spartans, before leaving for their homeland by the Eurotas, are said to have sent a messenger after what they presumed was the defeated monarch, demanding satisfaction for the death of their king, Leonidas. If they imagined that Xerxes would make some formal apology or offer some token indicating that he was beaten, they were sadly mistaken. Xerxes burst into laughter at this effrontery, was silent a while, and then pointed to his cousin: 'You will get your repayment indeed – from Mardonius here.'

WINTER

Despite the triumphant success of Salamis the winter of 480 was not a happy one for the Greeks. The allied fleet dispersed, the commanders making their way down to the headquarters at the Isthmus where awards were to be made for distinguished conduct during the campaign. The semblance of unity, which had only just held them together during the recent months, was swiftly dissipated. Indeed, during that meeting, one may detect all the seeds of the Greek destructiveness which was to rend their city-states in the years to come. Envy and distrust of one another were dominant at what should in theory have been a happy occasion but which, knowing the Greeks, was exactly what one might have expected. Herodotus and Plutarch both tell the story that, in a secret ballot as to who should receive the crown for the most outstanding individual contribution to the victory, with a second crown for the runner-up, each commander put his own name at the top, but most put Themistocles second. This seems an unlikely tale if the voting was in secret – and the Greeks would hardly have made public declarations. The fact remains that the result was inconclusive, and the crown was never awarded. This must have been galling indeed for Themistocles, who clearly deserved the honour, but highly satisfying to men like Aristeides and others of the hoplite party. The prize for valour was awarded to the Aeginetans: a fair enough choice, perhaps, though not one likely to be appreciated by the Athenians. Nevertheless, Herodotus concludes that 'Themistocles' name was on everyone's lips, and he acquired the reputation of being by far the most able man in the country'. This may well have been so, but it was certain to lead to unpopularity, for his many enemies in Athens could hardly bear to see this upstart being declared their superior in intelligence and ability. It would probably have been even worse for him if he had indeed received the 'poisoned crown'.

The Spartans now saw the chance of making some political capital out of the situation. They had, in any case, every reason to be grateful to Themistocles. He had initiated the policy of sea-warfare, thus preserving the great bulk of their army and, by conducting the campaign off Attica, he had preserved the Peloponnese from Persian invasion. For the same reasons it is not too difficult to understand why many Athenians disliked him. The fact that the Spartans now invited him down to their city as a guest of honour was to give many Athenians a real reason to distrust him. At this winter prize-giving the Spartans awarded their own admiral Eurybiades with a crown of olive, something which he undoubtedly deserved – though largely for going along with the strategy evolved by Themistocles. But they also decorated the latter with a similar crown 'for his ability and skill'. For the proud and xenophobiac Spartans to accord such an honour to a foreigner and to a citizen of Athens, whose new naval power was already causing them uneasiness, was something extraordinary in itself, nor did they stop at this. Before Themistocles left their unwalled city by the Eurotas they made him a gift of the finest chariot in Sparta. Having praised him to the skies, after what can only be termed a 'state visit', they accorded him a royal bodyguard of 300 Spartiate horsemen as far as their frontier with Tegea – the first and only non-Spartan in history ever to be shown such an honour.

It was hardly surprising that his detractors in Athens seized the opportunity to attack him for accepting these honours from that harsh warrior-caste down in the Peloponnese. (Already one senses in the air that terrible future war between Athens and Sparta which was to break the 'Bulwark of Hellas, glorious Athens, city of god-like men'.) Herodotus gives us one revealing story:

Back in Athens he came in for a deal of abuse from a certain Timodemus of Aphidna, whose hatred of Themistocles was his only claim to distinction. Mad with jealousy, he reviled him for going to Sparta, and maintained that he had earned his honours there not by his own merit but merely by the fame of Athens. The continual repetition of this taunt at last drew from Themistocles a reply: 'I'll tell you what,' he said; 'I should never have been honoured as I was if I had been born a Belbinite – and you wouldn't, Athenian though you are!' (Belbina was an unimportant islet off Cape Sunium.)

There can be little doubt that Themistocles was arrogant in his time of triumph and this spelled his certain downfall. Throughout that winter his enemies were actively campaigning against him and circulating stories to his discredit. The landowning aristocracy had good reasons for mistrusting any extension of Themistocles' naval strategy. Mardonius and his forces were to the north and the next attack, it was quite clear, would not come by sea but on land. For this reason, above all, it was essential to secure the participation of the powerful Spartan army and it might be conjectured that the reason why the Spartans had fêted Themistocles was that they wished his naval policy to be pursued, thus preserving the Peloponnese and their own army from being the object of the forthcoming offensive. One thing is certain: in the elections in the spring of 479 Themistocles, if he gained any place at all in the command, was relegated to some insignificant role. Two men whom he had previously contrived to have sent into political exile received the principal generalships for the campaign of that year. Aristeides, predictably, was put in command of the land forces, and Xanthippus of the navy. There could hardly have been a more bitter blow to the victor of Salamis and the man who had worked so hard to create the new navy of Athens – the ships which were ultimately to give her her empire. There is no record of any comment by Themistocles who, indeed, seems to have taken no further active part in the war. His sentiments, one suspects, may have been akin to those expressed by Winston Churchill centuries later: '. . . at the onset of this mighty battle, I acquired the chief power in the State, which henceforth I wielded in ever-growing measure . . . at the end of which time, all our enemies having surrendered unconditionally or being about to do so, I was immediately dismissed by the British electorate from all further conduct of their affairs.' In the whole of the rest of Herodotus' history of this great war there is only one other brief and unimportant reference to Themistocles.

Xerxes' winter march to the north is represented by Herodotus and Aeschylus as something as disastrous and demoralised as the retreat of Napoleon from Moscow. Crossing the frozen Strymon river a number of the troops are said to have fallen through the thin ice and drowned. It is possible that some, impatient of delay, did essay the ice and drown, but a point to remember is that the river had been bridged before the campaign had started and the whole army had passed over without incident. Then again a grim picture is painted of food shortage, of troops starving and dying of dysentery, but once again one suspects that many of these lurid details were added in later years like colourful touches (in the fashion of Delacroix) to remind all who came after – and particularly the Persians – of the folly of attempting to invade Greece.

The time taken by Xerxes to reach the Hellespont, forty-five days, or half that of the advance, is made to suggest a panic-stricken rout. On the contrary, since there was no opposition to deal with at any point – no Thermopylae, for instance – and since the fleet had been able to make its way up to the Hellespont to receive the army, with no Greek fleet interposing, it sounds like a reasonable speed for withdrawal. The bridges of boats, as might have been expected, had been broken by the onset of winter's gales. Nevertheless the army passed over into Asia without any significant incidents being recorded – and there can be no doubt that Greek writers would have made much of it if there had been any disaster at sea. The northern lands through which the march took place, Thessaly, Macedonia and Thrace, did not shift from their loyalty to the Great King – something they might possibly have done if the army's retreat had been the Napoleonic disaster that the Greeks later made it out to be. Men who had fallen ill on the march were left behind in friendly Greek cities to be taken care of, and the strong garrisons such as Eion, Doriscus, and other places, guaranteed that the Persian hold over the country was as secure as ever.

The only exception to the rule occurred in December that year when some of the towns in the Chalcidice area, mostly notably Potidaea, revolted against the Persian rule. Potidaea was the most well-placed to do so, being situated astride the neck of the Pallene peninsula and virtually unassailable except by sea – and Mardonius had no fleet. Other towns of Pallene also joined in the revolt. Olynthus to the north, standing at the head of the Gulf of Torone, was unwise enough to join them, but the town did not have the strongly defensive position of Potidaea. The revolt began at about the time that Artabazus, a remarkably fine soldier, in company with

6000 of the handpicked Persian corps, had just turned back after escorting the Great King as far as his crossing of the Hellespont. Having laid siege to Potidaea, which he could see would prove a tough nut to crack, he decided to make an example of Olynthus: a far easier proposition. The city was besieged and taken, and the inhabitants driven out and slaughtered. Artabazus, wisely, instead of garrisoning it with Persian troops, and knowing the hatred so often felt by one Greek township for another, offered the governorship of Olynthus to a man from nearby Torone, whose citizens were only too delighted to enlarge their sphere of influence.

It was always the same with the Greeks, Artabazus must have reflected; by playing upon their mutual rivalries and hatreds, as well as by the transference of a little gold, you could usually get your way without a protracted siege. Potidaea was another matter, but he soon managed to get in touch with Timoxenus, the governor of the troops from nearby Scione. The two managed to communicate by a method that was probably not unusual in ancient siege warfare – that of writing a message and binding it around an arrow-shaft. What exact arrangements were being made for the betrayal of Potidaea we do not know, for the spy-link was discovered through the Persian arrow on one occasion failing to fall in the right place. It 'struck a Potidaean in the shoulder. As usually happens in war, a crowd collected round the wounded man. . . .' (A nice touch of realism!) The message was found and taken to the commanders. The astonishing thing is that Timoxenus was not accused of treachery and summarily executed, but 'in order to spare the people of Scione from being branded as traitors for ever after' no action was taken. Knowing the nature of the Greeks, this seems almost unbelievable. It suggests that either others were in the plot, or that Timoxenus was so popular with his own men that his execution would have caused them to withdraw – and Potidaea needed all the troops possible to man its walls.

Artabazus now settled down to a protracted three-month siege. Soon the spring would be upon them and he would have to march to join Mardonius for the campaign. He must have been on the point of withdrawing, when a sudden and unexpected natural phenomenon occurred. Owing, very likely, to an underwater earth-tremor the sea-level of the almost tideless Aegean suddenly dropped, leaving a shallow passage across which troops could wade to attack the exposed end of the city-wall. Artabazus acted promptly and sent an advance force to cross the channel with the idea of taking the city from the rear. Unfortunately for the Persians (as happens on occasions in Malta and southern Sicily with a somewhat similar phenomenon known as the *marrobio*) the sea suddenly came flooding back. Those of the troops who were not drowned were killed by the Potidaeans who came rushing out in small boats. Later – and with good reason – they ascribed this victory to the sea-god Poseidon, also known as the Earth-Shaker. They attributed the Persian disaster to the fact that they had desecrated Poseidon's shrine and statue which had formerly stood outside the walls. Artabazus lifted the siege and marched to join Mardonius. Potidaea had been an irritant, but neither it nor the Pallene peninsula represented any real threat to communications.

Mardonius, although his troops had wintered well in Thessaly, was not without his problems. It was true that he was in the position of ruler or satrap of the whole of northern Greece from the Hellespont down to Athens, but the 'Greek problem' was far from solved. The whole of the Peloponnese was still untouched and there lay the military core – even discounting the hoplites of Athens – which must be smashed before all these Greeks could be added to the Persian Empire. It was true also that the attack of Persia's Carthaginian allies on Sicily had been repulsed, but Sicily and then the rest of the western Mediterranean could be won, once Greece itself had been conquered. The question was – how to achieve it? Beyond him lay the stark, mountainous land, with its limited agricultural plains, the narrow isthmus of Corinth, fringed on both sides by the 'bitter water', and then the little-known Peloponnese, largely dominated by these Spartans, a small handful of whom had dared to challenge the whole of the Great King's army. Nothing suggested an easy campaign. Mardonius was more than a simple general; he was a strategist and a diplomat. Throughout the winter Persian agents had been as active as before, down in the Peloponnese, doing their best to ensure that the cities which had long had good reason to be hostile to Sparta would not help their old adversaries any more than they had in the previous year. There can be little doubt that money and promises were exchanged, but the situation had changed considerably since Xerxes and the whole army had trampled over northern Greece and Attica. Even the Argives, who are said to have promised that they would prevent the Spartans marching north (an improbable thought), must have hesitated. Salamis must have been in the minds of even these land-bound peoples; they knew that the Athenians' fleet – repaired over the winter – was still in being, so too that of Aegina, Corinth, Megara, and even Sparta. They knew also that the demoralised Persian fleet was far away and that any action which would follow must almost certainly be a military one. Mardonius might well ravage Attica again, but would he be able to storm the Isthmian line and, even if he managed to do so, how could he manage the conquest of the Peloponnese without a fleet? There can be no doubt that they made promises, took Persian gold, but still laid off their bets. The year before Xerxes had looked like an odds-on-favourite, but the same could not be said in the early spring of 479.

The real threat to Mardonius and his commitment to conquer the rest of Greece for Xerxes clearly lay in the Greek fleet, which to a large degree might be equated with the fleet of Athens. He knew well enough that the Athenians and the Spartans were very different types of Greeks – the one brilliant, volatile, and magnificent seamen; the other dour, conservative, and an aristocratic military caste. It was no secret that, even though they had fought together at sea in the previous year, their differences outweighed their Greek consanguinity. 'Divide and rule!', so wise an imperative to all nations with imperial aspirations, was something that Mardonius, son-in-law of Darius, must have learned from his earliest days. And these Greeks were so easy to divide! Since the Athenians lay nearest to hand, since their land was ravaged, and since they were only even now attempting to repair their devastated city, they seemed the easiest target. They had felt the harsh stroke of the Great King and would be unlikely to wish to evacuate Attica once again. They could hardly expect, in any case, to repeat their deceitful success of Salamis. They were therefore clearly the 'soft underbelly' of the Greek axis, to be tempted into withdrawal from the conflict.

The charming, smooth-talking Alexander of Macedon was once again used as a go-between and sent down by Mardonius to propose terms to the Athenians which, on the surface, might have seemed acceptable to a people under such military threat, and who could not, furthermore, be confident that the Peloponnesian land forces would come to their aid. The very fact that Themistocles, the author of Greek victory at sea, had been down in Sparta suggested that he might have been conniving with the Spartans – as many Athenians thought that he had. Mardonius, as a politician well versed in the wiles of the court at Susa, knew how bitter a blow it must have been to Themistocles to find that he no longer had control of the Athenian navy, and that he had been relegated to some almost insignificant place in the Greek command. A bitter man, thrust out of favour, who nevertheless commanded the affections and respect of the 'navy party', might possibly be able to detach the fleet from the control of the hoplite class; the landowners with whom the men at the oar-benches had little or nothing in common.

Alexander faithfully relayed the message which had been given him by Mardonius, and which one can have no doubt came all the way from Xerxes himself: 'I am willing to forget all the injuries that Athens has done me. So, Mardonius, first give the Athenians back their land; and secondly, let them take whatever other territory they wish [a rich inducement], and have self-government. If they are willing to come to terms with me, you are also to rebuild the temples that I burnt.' This was the personal message from the Great King in Susa, but Alexander, taking his lines now from Mardonius, went on to elaborate:

> Why then – I ask you – are you so mad as to take arms against the king? You can never defeat him, and you cannot hold out for ever. You have seen his army, its size, and what it can do; you know, too, how powerful a force I have under me now. Even should you beat us – and, if you have any sense, you cannot hope to do so – another force many times as powerful will come against you. So stop trying to be a match for the king, at the cost of the loss of your country and continual peril of your lives. Come to terms with him instead . . . Make an alliance with us, and so keep your freedom.

Such terms, generous enough on the surface, had yielded fruit in other parts of the Persian Empire, and in any case the Athenians were prepared to deliberate upon them for as long as possible. The reason for this was obvious. 'In Sparta the news of Alexander's visit to try to bring about an alliance between Persia and Athens caused consternation.' No doubt it did. With Athenian seapower allied to Persian military might the Peloponnesians would stand no chance. Their Isthmian line would be bypassed and the steam-roller of Persia would soon be down before the unwalled city. There was also, apparently, an oracle to the effect that 'the Dorians would one day be driven from the Peloponnese by the Persians and Athen-ians'. One might suspect that so curiously explicit an oracle could only have had an Athenian hand behind it and, indeed, even wonder whether the discredited Themistocles could in some way have been involved in its circulation. In any case, the news that the Persians and the Athenians were sitting down in Athens for a long series of talks about forming an alliance caused a panic in the Peloponnese. Sparta swiftly despatched an embassy to Athens.

The Spartans, however, seem to have had good grounds for suspicion that the Athenians were only playing for time, and that they could never in fact reconcile themselves to the idea of being a lient state of Persia. After all, although the Persian terms might appear acceptable to an Aegean island or to a city in Ionia, the Spartans knew the nature of the Athenians, knew their pride in their state, their navy, and their inextinguishable love of freedom. They pointed out Alexander's untrustworthy character and the fact that he was only a ruler because the Persians permitted him to be: he was the lackey of Xerxes. How, they asked, could the Athenians even consider such proposals, which would be a betrayal of all of Greece? These were fine-sounding words which inevitably found an echo in Athenian hearts, but what they had hoped for was a guarantee of the Peloponnesian army. They were not to get it. Indeed, the Spartans even went so far as to reproach the Athenians, pointing out that this war had only started because of Athenian intervention in Ionia, and it now threatened to engulf the whole of Greece. This was true enough, for at the time of the Ionian revolt the Spartans had carefully remained uninvolved. Fence-sitting was part of the Lacedaemonian conservative policy. All that they were prepared to offer the Athenians at this crucial moment was sym-pathy with their hardships through the ruin of their city and the loss of the harvest, and an agreement to provide them with economic aid and 'support for all the women and other non-combatant members of your households, for as long as the war lasts'. This was ominous indeed. The Athenians had thought they had had the Spartans over the proverbial barrel with the veiled intimation that they might accept the Persian proposals but, to their consternation, they now found that the Spartans were not duped. Before Salamis, Themistocles had scared the Spartans badly when he had threatened to withdraw the Athenian fleet and found a new Athens far away in southern Italy, but the Spartans knew now that the Athenians would never leave their beloved city and their land.

There was nothing for it but for the Athenians to make an open rejection of the proposals brought by Alexander:

> We know as well as you do that the Persian strength is many times greater than our own. . . . Nevertheless, such is our love of freedom, that we will defend ourselves in whatever way we can. As for making terms with Persia, it is useless to persuade us; for we shall never consent. And now tell Mardonius, that so long as the sun keeps his present course in the sky, we Athenians will never make peace with Xerxes.

This was fine Churchillian stuff, fully in the vein of '. . . we shall fight in the fields and in the streets, we shall fight in the hills; we shall never surrender'. There can be no doubt that the full speech as reported by Herodotus does represent with some accuracy what was said at the time. The Athenians, like the British in 1940, needed such a rallying call and, with or without allies, they had no option but to brace themselves for the coming struggle.

To the Spartans the Athenians then made a declaration which was clearly designed to shame them if possible into guaranteeing the Greek alliance with the backing of their military might.

> No doubt it was natural that the Lacedaemonians should dread the possibility of our making terms with Persia; none the less it shows a poor estimate of the spirit of Athens. There is not so much gold in the world nor land so fair that we would take it for pay to join the common enemy and bring Greece into subjection.

Aristeides (for it was probably he) went on to say that the Athenians would never forgive nor forget the destruction of their city, the desecration of the Athenian temples, shrines and sacred places, and then he made a dramatic call for Pan-Hellenism: 'Again, there is the Greek nation – the community of blood and language, temples and ritual; our common way of life; if Athens were to betray all this, it would not be well done'.

The implication here is clearly that it 'would not be well done' *either*, if the Peloponnesians betrayed their 'Greekness'. He went on with some distinct element of sarcasm to thank the Spartans for their kindness in offering to look after the Athenian women and non-combatants – 'Nothing could be more generous.' But still the Athenians would carry on, and had no wish to be a burden on their Peloponnesian neighbours. One can almost hear the barb striking home, and see the embarrassment on the faces of the Spartan ambassadors. The sting came in the tail: 'That being our resolve, get your army into the field with the least possible delay; for unless we are much mistaken, it will not be long before the enemy invades Attica – he will do it the instant he gets the news that we refuse his requests. Now, therefore, before he can appear in Attica, it is time for us to meet him in Boeotia.'

The implication was clear. This was from now on to be a hoplite war. The Spartans' courtship of Themistocles and the 'navy party' had back-fired. The landowners, the bronze men, the military, were now in command. The Athenian fleet, unlikely to be challenged again, would be kept as a last resort, possibly to do just what Themistocles had threatened them with before – re-establish Athens elsewhere. Herodotus concludes the eighth book of his *Histories* with a line as succinct as anything ever written by Hemingway, and as laconic as anything that a Spartan might have said: 'Athens had given her answer; and the Spartan envoys left for home.'

SPRING

EARLY IN THE SPRING OF 479 the news came through that the Persian fleet, a large part of which had wintered at Cyme in Ionia, was assembling at Samos. It looked as if a sea-offensive might yet be mounted to combine with the advance of Mardonius' army. It was, however, nothing like the confident armada that had surged through the Aegean the previous year. Samos, with its two great harbours, was an ideal place for assembling a fleet to strike westward across the Aegean, but this was a demoralised and depleted assembly of ships, no more than 300 in all according to Herodotus. It seems that one reason for its presence on the island was to keep an eye on the Ionians as much as anything else. After the reverses at Artemisium and the defeat at Salamis the heart had gone out of the principal constituents of the Persian naval arm, the Egyptians and Phoenicians, who would seem to have returned to their own countries once the army had been transported across the Hellespont, and to have taken no further part in the war. Most of the sailors and oarsmen of the fleet at Samos were probably Ionian Greeks, but to make sure of their trustworthiness they carried Persian marines aboard and were commanded by three Persian admirals, each one, presumably, being in charge of a hundred ships.

There had indeed been an abortive attempt at a coup on the island of Chios, the plot being betrayed by one member of a seven-man junto. The other six managed to escape and made their way to Aegina where the Greek fleet was assembling under the supreme command of yet another Spartan, King Latychidas. They informed him that all Ionia was ripe for revolt, that the Persian fleet was demoralised, and urged him to attack Ionia. Whether this would have been wise or not, the fact was that the Greek fleet which had assembled that year was only a third of its previous size, 110 ships, and was therefore of an essentially defensive nature. Athens was now dominated not only by the hoplite party, but also by the very necessary requirements of land defence. It is clear that her contribution to the Greek fleet was little more than nominal, and she had mobilised 8000 hoplites ready for the attack that must inevitably come from Mardonius in the north. There was another good reason why the Athenians may have decided to keep a large part of their fleet laid up. It was the only card they had to play against the Peloponnesians who, apart from working hard on the defences of the Isthmian wall, showed no signs of sending their army to Attica. If the Spartans and their allies would not come to the help of Athens on land, then the Athenians must look to their own defence and not dissipate their men and energies on the sea.

Late in the spring of that year, after Alexander of Macedon had returned with the Athenian rejection of the Persian proposals, Mardonius began his march south. The spring rains were over and it was time to give these insolent Athenians a second lesson, before moving on to break the resistance of those in the Peloponnese – which largely meant the Spartans – and hand all Greece over to his king and lord, with himself presumably becoming the satrap of the land. The Thessalians, who had long accepted that they were part of the Persian dominion, were naturally pleased to see him gone. It was not only that their leading dynasties were totally committed to the Persian cause, but they must have been eager to see his army eating elsewhere. The attitude at Thebes was different. The Thebans hated the Athenians, and undoubtedly saw themselves, in the event of a Persian victory, as being the natural leaders of the new Grecian kingdom which would be established under Persian control. They did their best to persuade Mardonius to make their city and their country the command headquarters for the campaign and to break up the Greek unity (which had never really existed) by bribing one city and another in the Peloponnese not to support the Spartans. 'Send money to the leading men in the various towns', they said, 'and by doing that you will destroy the unity of the country, after which you will easily be able, with the help of those who take your part, to crush those who still oppose you.' Mardonius was not of their opinion. He wanted to present Xerxes with a fine military victory, to reoccupy Attica, level Athens to the ground, and then, perhaps, make use of the Great King's money to destroy the Peloponnesians. He was a politician, true, but he was above all a soldier and it was as such that he wished to be able to give his lord the rich prize of Greece. He had gone so far as to arrange a chain of beacons through the Aegean islands, so that the news of the second occupation of Athens could be signalled across the sea, whence the Persian couriers would take it swiftly to Xerxes in his palace at Susa.

King Latychidas meanwhile had advanced with his depleted fleet down into the Cyclades, but does not seem to have dared to move farther east than the sacred island of Delos. Similarly, there was no aggressive movement by the Persian admirals on the far side of the Aegean at Samos. At this point in the year, the enemy fleets did no more than glare at each other – and somewhat uneasily at that. The opening moves on the great chessboard of 479 were standard, and even fumbling. Mardonius moved south; the Athenians, receiving no support from the Peloponnesians, withdrew from Athens for a second time; Mardonius reoccupied Athens. One thing which the unimpeded march of the Persians forced upon the Athenians was the reactivation of their fleet which, clearly, they were not going to leave behind to be burned. This now meant that the Greeks were potentially far stronger at sea than the Persians, but it also meant that in their diplomatic battle with their Peloponnesian allies the Athenians had lost a valuable bargaining piece. They no longer held the trump of a fleet 'in being', which they had been able to play against the Peloponnesians' refusal to move beyond their Isthmian wall.

At this desperate moment in the fortunes of the Athenians, withdrawn again to Salamis, while Mardonius prepared to level their partly rebuilt city to the ground, the latter, shrewdly assessing the situation, sent over to Salamis a Greek from the Hellespont area as an envoy. He offered the Athenians yet again the same terms as Xerxes had previously given them: generosity itself, on the surface, since their land was once more occupied and their beloved capital in his hands. There is absolutely no doubt that the iron determination of the previous year had deserted some of the Athenian councillors. One of them, whose name has come down to us in different variants (possibly because the later Athenians were unwilling to commemorate the event), who spoke out in favour of accepting the Persian proposals, was lynched on the spot. This was far from typical of Athenian behaviour – even less so, if one credits the tale, was the subsequent stoning of his wife and children. The envoy, Murychides, who witnessed this alarming scene, was allowed to return unharmed to his master with oral and visual evidence that the Athenians still totally rejected the overtures of the Great King.

Two separate missions in the subsequent weeks were sent off to Sparta, both, in differing degrees, bearing the same message: unless the Spartans were prepared to march north and defend Attica they would very soon find themselves left totally alone. Although the various historians are silent on the subject, one might possibly conclude that the threat made by Themistocles the previous year was never entirely absent from their allies' minds. The people of Athens, and only they, still had enough ships to withdraw a large part of their population from Salamis and Troezen, and found a new city in the rich, comparatively unpopulated lands to the west. Sicily and southern Italy always presented them with an option – 'O my America! my new-found-land.' The Spartans, the other Peloponnesians, even the citizens of mercantile Corinth, did not have sufficient shipping to offer their people a large-scale evacuation. The envoys returned exasperated. The Spartans, who were far more religious (or superstitious) than the Athenians and who could in any case at that moment still afford to indulge in formalities, were celebrating the Hyacinthia; a summertime festival, deriving very probably from the eastern Attis/Adonis rituals. Herodotus comments that 'the people were on holiday and thought it most important to give the God his due'. He adds, which seems far more significant: 'It also happened that the wall they were building across the Isthmus was almost finished and about to have the battlements put on.'

There can be no doubt that there was some hard bargaining, even threatening, at the various meetings which took place. The Spartan Ephors kept quibbling and fobbing the Athenians off with promises to let them have a decision on the following day, and so on. It was not until after the Athenian envoys had given up in disgust, and were on the point of leaving yet again, that the Ephors seem to have rethought the whole situation. One of the principal advocates of responding to the Athenian call and marching north was Chileus, an important citizen of Sparta's neighbour, Tegea, who appears to have commanded considerable influence among the ruling class in that strange state. Having heard from the Ephors that the Athenians were again bringing up the threat of forming an alliance with the Persians under the conditions that Xerxes offered them, he pointed out the grim reality of the situation, saying: 'As I see it, gentlemen, if the Athenians desert us and make an alliance with Persia, then, however strongly the Isthmus is fortified, the postern gates are wide open for the Persian invasion of the Peloponnese. So you had better listen to them before they change their minds and adopt a policy which will ruin Greece.' In this, of course, he was absolutely correct. Without the aid of the Athenian fleet the Isthmian wall would have become as redundant as did that of Maginot centuries later. It would merely be by-passed and the Athenians would land the Persian army wherever they wanted in its rear.

After prevaricating for so long, the Ephors now acted with haste. Almost overnight 5000 Spartiates, out of what was probably a total of 8000, were mobilised and on the march north. With them, according to Herodotus, went 35,000 Helots. These would have been lightly armed troops, but good fighters none the less, as they had already proved at Thermopylae. One reason for taking such a large number of Helots was possibly the fact that, with the bulk of the Spartiate army on its way out of the country, the Ephors did not want to risk any chance of a Helot uprising. In any case the Helots, too, could see that Persian victory would not improve their position but would turn them into total slaves under the Persians and their sympathisers. Pausanias was put in charge of the whole campaign, his cousin King Pheistarchus, the son of Leonidas, being only a boy. Pausanias was himself only in his twenties but he had great strength of character, as he was to prove, and had probably from the very start been one of those who advocated an active policy as against the more conservative Ephors.

The speed of the mobilisation and of the Spartan army's march to the Isthmus was such that, even if the Argives ever had any intention of fulfilling their promise to Mardonius to stop any Spartan move to the north, the Spartans were already passing their frontier. It is difficult to believe, in any case, that, faced by such a weight of men, Argos would have dared to take any action. They did, however, send a runner with a message to warn the Persian commander that 'the fighting force of Lacedaemon is on the march, and that the Argives have been powerless to stop it'. One can only presume that this young Argive bypassed the Isthmian line in a small boat before making his way to Mardonius. All the members of the Spartan league mobilised with almost similar swiftness and marched to join Pausanias at the Isthmus, only Mantinea and Elis were too slow in moving and missed the campaign that was to follow. Mardonius now knew there was no doubt that a large Peloponnesian force combined with the Athenians portended a battle which, even with his numerical superiority, was going to be a hard one. He knew how only 300 Spartiates with a few thousand behind them had held up the full weight of the Great King's army at Thermopylae.

Athens and Attica must again be abandoned and he must fall back on Thebes, where the territory around the Asopus river would afford him the chance to deploy his cavalry in good measure. At the same time, as he knew from the Thebans who had already suggested that he make their city his base, he would have pro-Persian allies whose greatest desire was to see Athens permanently destroyed. Before he left the city he once again sacked as much of it as he could, even though the time-factor prevented his demolition teams from leaving the site as barren as he would have liked. Attica itself, however, was once again ravaged. Mardonius, like any intelligent general, had no intention of leaving food and fodder for an army that was clearly intending to advance against him, and not just hold a defensive position on the Isthmus. For the first time, perhaps, he must have felt more than a twinge of unease. He had failed to divide these two principal Greek states. He knew about the calibre of the Greeks, and in particular the Athenians, at sea; and he knew about the Spartans' prowess on land. The beacons had signalled from island to island across the Aegean the second capture of Athens and of all the Attic land. He was a close blood relation of Xerxes, but that did not count too closely in an autocracy where the title 'King of Kings' literally meant what it said.

28

THE ROAD TO PLATAEA

MARDONIUS HAD ALREADY BEGUN to withdraw into Boeotia
when he received a message that an advance guard of a thousand
Spartans was in Megara. Thinking that he might at least eliminate
this enemy body without much difficulty, he detached part of his
army – probably a fairly large cavalry unit – and sent them down to
the area. The report, as it turned out, was false and some of his men
were cut off and killed by the Megarians. This abortive raid was, in
fact, the farthest to the west that the Persians ever got in the whole
of Xerxes' campaign in Greece. What had started out as the
invasion of western Europe was now turning into a retreat with
only the possibility of a massive victory in a pitched battle to pro-
cure any chance of Xerxes' achieving even a part of his original
dream.

Withdrawing by way of Decelea, the easternmost pass over the
Parnes range, possibly choosing this route because he feared that
an advance guard of Spartans or Athenians might have reached
one or other of the easier routes and be lying in ambush for his
forces, Mardonius was met by local guides. The army stopped for
a night at Tanagra and then made for a village called Scolus which
lay in Theban territory. Herodotus relates that 'in spite of the fact
that the Thebans were on his side he cut down all the trees in the
neighbourhood – not as an act of hostility to Thebes, but simply
for his own military need, for he wished to construct a palisade to
protect his troops and to have somewhere to retreat to in the event
of the battle going against him'. The encampment on the north of
the river-line of the Asopus also commanded the roads leading to
Thebes itself. It possibly extended for about five miles. Mardonius
thus could maintain his friendly contacts and communications
behind him. The Thebans, now aware of the size of the force that
was soon going to break into their territory, and of how far they

were committed to the Persian cause, would probably have been quite willing for the Persians to cut down almost every tree in their area if it would serve to protect them from the wrath of Athens and Sparta. (Incidents such as this, combined with many later wars in Greece, together with the eternal demand for wood for shipbuilding, contributed to that deforestation of the land which has never over all the centuries been successfully reversed.) The area of Mardonius' camp, as carefully calculated by Burn, would probably have accommodated an army of '60–70,000 men, of whom 10,000 might be cavalry'. In any case, even after the addition of several thousands of Boeotians and other Greek allies, it is unlikely that Mardonius had any great superiority in numbers over the allied army that was marching to meet him. There can be little doubt he had come to believe that the Athenians would come over to the Persian cause, and that the Peloponnesians, entrenched behind their Isthmian wall, would never join up and march in a united front against him. He had calculated that, in the seemingly eternal inter-state rivalry and hatred of the Greeks, he could 'Divide and Conquer'. What he, and Xerxes and all the Persian high command, had failed to understand was that these two Greek states – however much they might basically dislike each other – were united against any subjection by an autocratic foreign tyrant.

Evidence of the mistrust felt between the Greek allies, even in this moment of their greatest need for co-operation, is to be found in the famous Oath of Plataea. This was probably administered after the junction of the Athenians under Aristeides, and Pausanias with the Spartiates and other Peloponnesians, at Eleusis. After all the threats and counter-threats that had passed between the principal partners it is not so surprising that something like a sacred oath binding all parties to be true to one another in the hour of battle was considered necessary. There are various versions of the Oath of Plataea, but it is difficult not to sense an Athenian hand behind its construction. The version quoted here is a fourth-century transcription dedicated in Acharnae by one Dion, priest of Ares, the war-god, and of Athena, in her role of war-goddess. The reason one suspects an Athenian behind the Oath's composition is that most of the military requirements itemised would have been familiar, and indeed automatic responses, to a Spartiate after 'his first term at school'.

I will fight to the death, and I will not count my life more precious than freedom. I will not leave my officer, the commander of my Regiment or Company, either alive or dead. I will not withdraw unless my commanders lead me back, and I will do whatsoever the Generals order. I will bury the dead of those who have fought as my allies, on the field, and will not leave one of them unburied. After defeating the barbarians in battle, I will tithe the city of the Thebans; and I will never destroy Athens or Sparta or Plataea or any of the cities which have fought as our allies, nor will I consent to their being starved, nor cut off from running water, whether we be friends or at war.

And if I keep well the oath, as it is written, may my city have

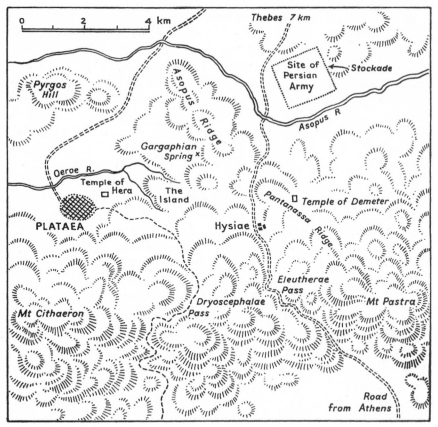

6 PLATAEA

good health; but if not, may it have sickness; and may my land give increase; but if not, may it be barren; and may the women bring forth children like their fathers; but if not, monsters; and may the cattle bring forth after their kind, but if not, monsters.

The whole Greek army now moved out from Eleusis on the road to Thebes. The Athenians had hoped that Mardonius would give battle early, but it was now clear that he intended to make his stand farther north and force the allies to march up to meet him. It was now late July and the farther he could make heavily armoured men sweat over a dusty, burned-out plain the more chance there was of them arriving in an exhausted condition. After putting the plain behind them they had to climb up the slopes of Cithaeron and emerge at the top of the Eleutherae Pass. Ahead of them now lay the steep descent towards the Asopus, on whose northern bank lay Mardonius with his army entrenched behind his palisade. It was indeed good generalship on his part to have forced the allies to come to meet him, while his own men rested, rather than engage them earlier in the plain of Eleusis. The sight might have daunted the Greeks: the harsh way down, the shine of the river, the impressive stockade, the Persian forces deployed, the city of Thebes behind them, and then the great Boeotian plain, with Helicon and Parnassus shining in the far distance.

The Athenians are said earlier to have obtained an oracle from Delphi promising them success if they fought 'in their own land, in the plain of the Eleusinian goddesses Demeter and the Maiden'. When they had been forced to advance into Plataean territory they must have felt some dismay, but the Plataean leader Arimnestus, supposedly inspired in a dream sent by Zeus, solved this problem by persuading his fellow Plataeans to take up their boundary stones on the side facing Attica, thus making a gift of all this Plataean land to Athens. (There is no record as to whether they ever got it back again.) The matter of achieving victory 'in the plain of the Eleusinian goddesses' was another matter altogether. This was solved by the discovery of an old temple of Demeter of Eleusis near Hysiae, at the foot of the Pantanassa ridge. It was an area which would be very favourable for the Greeks to take up their battle stations since the Persians would have little chance of deploying their cavalry. Mardonius watched and waited as the Greeks came down and took up their position in the foothills, hoping by a show of inertia to lure them out into the plain. When they showed that they had no intention of obliging him,

> Mardonius sent his cavalry to attack them in force, under the command of the distinguished Persian officer Masistius . . . who rode a Nisaean horse with a bridle of gold and other splendid trappings. The cavalry advanced to the attack in successive squadrons, and at each assault inflicted heavy losses on the Greeks, taunting them and calling them women. It so happened that the point in the Greek line which was most open and vulnerable to a cavalry charge was held by the Megarians, who found themselves hard pressed by the repeated attacks.

It is possible that the division from Megara was astride the road to Thebes and there were no more than 3000 of them. Pausanias, receiving a call for help, very sensibly despatched not his own heavily armoured hoplites, who would have been of little use in the situation, but the Athenian regiment of archers. As was to be shown in many later wars over the centuries horsemen were particularly vulnerable to nimble men armed with the bow and arrow. Herodotus makes the imputation that Pausanias called for volunteers to back up the men from Megara and that only the Athenians responded. (This is clearly part of his later pro-Athenian bias.) He continues: 'For some time the battle continued, until, during the successive attacks of the Persian squadrons, Masistius' horse, which was in advance of the rest, was shot in the flank. . . .' The horse reared up and Masistius fell to the ground where he lay as helpless as many a medieval knight, for he was wearing under a scarlet tunic a corselet of golden scales. The Athenians rushed upon him, but, despite futile thrusts at his armoured body, it was not until a soldier pierced him through the eye-slit of his helmet that the Persian cavalry leader was killed. The other members of his squadron had not seen him fall, for his horse was hit just at the moment when they were wheeling back before making a further charge. 'It was only when they drew rein again that they missed him – for there was no one to give the commands.' The whole of the Persian cavalry force at once lined up and charged all together, determined upon recovering Masistius' body. It was now the turn of the Athenians to suffer heavy losses and to be forced back. At this point Pausanias and the main body of hoplites came to their support and, confronted by the armoured wall and the bristling hedge of spears, the Persians called off the attack and withdrew. They failed to recover the body of their leader – something that in those days was always considered a grave disgrace, and caused a corresponding loss of morale. Uncertain as to what to do, the cavalry reported back to Mardonius.

> Mardonius and the whole army showed the deepest distress at Masistius' death – a man more highly thought of, both by the king and his subjects, than anyone else in the Persian army except Mardonius himself; they shaved their heads, cut the manes of their horses and mules, and abandoned themselves to such cries of grief that the whole of Boeotia was loud with the noise of them.

The Greeks, naturally enough, were overjoyed at having killed one of Persia's most famous men. (It was somewhat as if the British attempt to capture Rommel in the desert in the Second World War had succeeded.) They had repulsed a heavy attack by Persia's most formidable arm, her horsemen – a great boost to their morale – and now they hoisted the dead Masistius on to a cart and paraded his body through the ranks. 'It was certainly worth looking at, for Masistius was a tall and splendidly handsome man. . . .' Such is war.

Pausanias now decided to re-deploy his forces, coming down from the foothills and moving westwards towards the now-deserted city of Plataea. His object was two-fold: first, he had a good water-supply from springs that flowed into the Asopus; secondly, he had a better position for his hoplites 'in flat country rising here and there in low hills'. The generalship of the Spartan, trained since a boy in the military art, cannot be faulted. There can be little doubt that so experienced a soldier moved most of his troops along the foothills at night, for he would have been foolish indeed to come down into the open plain where the enemy cavalry could have so easily attacked him in daylight hours. He would also have left his right flank exposed. Although the whole army could not possibly have effected the movement during darkness, the hillocks of the Asopus ridge would have largely concealed them in any case. The spring known as Garagaphia (possibly to be equated with what is now known as Rhetsi) would seem to have formed the point for his right wing, where the Spartans, since their leader Pausanias was commander-in-chief, automatically held the post of honour. Next to them came the small contingent from Tegea (about 1500 men), as compared with 10,000 from Lacedaemon of whom 5000 were Spartiates. The right centre was held by the Corinthians with 5000 men and seven smaller states, making a total of over 11,000 men. The left centre, to which Megara made the major contribution of 3000 men, consisted of 7000, and the left wing where 8000 Athenians were stationed was augmented by 600 from little Plataea. The total Greek forces, then, amounted to something like 38,000 men (the figures are taken from Herodotus). Burn notes that in the composition of the battlefront noted enemies such as Corinth and Sicyon were separated from one another by the interposition of another unit (in this case 600 men from Orchomenus in Arcadia). These figures, so far as one can gather, refer only to hoplites, for Herodotus goes on to mention that for every Spartiate there were seven lightly armed Helots, making a Spartan contribution, therefore, of 35,000. Remembering always that, with the large shield on the left arm and the sword or spear in the right hand, the right wing was the attacking wing and, therefore, the Athenians on the left were in the most exposed position. Against them Mardonius opposed an army that would seem to have been somewhat similar in numbers but, if one takes into account the pro-Persian Greeks, a good deal larger.

Between the enemies lay the Asopus river, shallow enough in summertime nowadays but possibly deeper then; in any case a water-barrier to the hoplite, while of little consequence to cavalry. The Persian horsemen, who were also bowmen, had a considerable advantage. They could carry out lightning raids on the Athenians on the left, and did finally manage to deprive them of using the waters of the Asopus. For over a week the Greeks and the Persians faced one another – like boxers waiting for the first false move. Each had different problems. Pausanias was waiting for the arrival of further reserves, while Mardonius was concerned about his commissariat. Although he had friendly (and terrified) Thebes at his back, it was difficult to maintain adequate supplies for so many men. The army, which had largely relied on a great fleet in the previous year, now had no store-ships or grain-vessels. Their ships lay inactive at Samos, demoralised, and blocked by the larger Greek fleet at Delos. The Thebans and the other pro-Persian lands behind Mardonius could not for ever keep coping with his demands. Pausanias, on the other hand, had the resources of the Peloponnese behind him.

It was high midsummer; the 'lion sun' of the Mediterranean beat down; a time when, even under the best of circumstances, men's nerves get frayed and heat-exhaustion can take its toll. It was during this period of waiting that Aristeides discovered a plot among his fellow Athenians to 'subvert the democracy'. As might be expected they were all members of his own class, 'men of leading families'. They met together secretly in a house in Plataea and were clearly prepared to 'sell out' to the Persians, so long as they could have an oligarchic constitution ensured at Athens. The fleet was far away; men like Themistocles were not present; and the democratic navy party might now be defeated in their absence. Out of a large number of suspects Aristeides had eight arrested, the two ringleaders 'contriving' to escape. What Aristeides – to his great credit – did, was to break up a dangerous cabal which, like so many others in the various states of Greece, was prepared to do anything so long as their own class and their own friends could hold the reins of power. The genius of spirit that was later to give Athens her golden fifty years was partly seeded by such idiosyncratic behaviour. One may, perhaps, feel that the disciplined Lacedaemonians (and particularly the Spartiate upper caste) were nobler in many respects than the landowners of Athens.

In this waiting game it was the Persians who were forced to make the opening move. Pausanias, having re-established his troops in a defensible position, could afford to sit and wait. Mardonius was now to find out the truth of the observation of Xerxes' uncle Artabanus that his other great enemy was the land itself. Plutarch says that the priests on both sides agreed on one point – that Pausanias and Mardonius 'would win a victory if they remained on the defensive, but would be defeated if they attacked'. However, after a stalemate lasting over a week, Mardonius, acting on the advice of a Theban named Timagenidas, decided to use his cavalry on a large scale to raid the northern end of the Dryoscephalae Pass.

There can be no doubt that Theban patrols had detected how reinforcements and provisions were regularly reaching the army of Pausanias by this route.

The movement was not without success; a train of five hundred mules bringing food from the Peloponnese for the army was caught, together with the men in charge, just as it was coming down from the hills. The Persian cavalrymen showed no mercy; they killed beasts and men indiscriminately, and drove the remnant, when they were sick of slaughter, back to Mardonius within their own lines.

Two more days went by, and no further action took place. Neither side was willing to begin the general engagement. The Persians provoked the Greek forces to attack by advancing right up to the river, but neither of them ventured actually to cross.

The Persian cavalry, however, seem to have kept up their harassing tactics, making the Greek supply-lines difficult to maintain. Nevertheless it seems that they could not prevent a steady stream of reinforcements getting through to swell the Greek army. At this point the strange two-faced Alexander of Macedon is said to have paid a visit to the Greek lines by night. He brought the information that Mardonius was also having supply problems and that it had even been suggested that the army should withdraw inside the walls at Thebes. Artabazus, apparently, was the advocate of this scheme, but Mardonius had rejected it and was eager for a trial of strength on the field.

Alexander, of course, was as usual sitting on the fence, and Aristeides can have been in little doubt of that. He was hardly likely to trust Alexander on the basis of his record, and he insisted that Pausanias should be informed of this unexpected visit. Aristeides had no intention of being party to any information that was not also immediately divulged to the Spartan commander-in-chief. This was now the night of the eleventh day since the two armies had faced each other across the little Asopus and, if Alexander was to be believed, it was the intention of Mardonius to attack on the following morning. It has sometimes been suggested that Alexander was sent across to spy out the land and to give the Greek leaders deliberate misinformation. This does not seem to square with the events, as the Persians did attack on the next day, although with their cavalry and not their foot-soldiers. One can but guess that Alexander, wily and astute as he was, had sensed a lack of morale among the Persians and, in order to secure his own position if the Greeks did in fact win, gave them the real information. If the Persians won, on the other hand, his secret visit to the Greeks would never be known. Like the dark horse that he was, he disappeared again into the night. Whatever the outcome of events Alexander of Macedon was doing his best to ensure that he was on the winning side.

If one is to believe Herodotus and Plutarch, Pausanias shifted the Spartans from the right wing over to the left, replacing them with the Athenians, who had more experience than the Spartans at fighting against Persians. Mardonius, accordingly, shuffled his pack of cards and moved his best Iranian troops back to face the Spartans. The story, although given by both authorities, seems unlikely. The Athenians were rightly proud of their history at Marathon, but even they would probably have conceded that the finest foot-soldiers in all of Greece were their allies – men who had been trained to fight, and nothing else, since they were boys. In any case, it matters little since, according to this version, both sides then moved their troops back again into their original position. Queer things happen in war, and generals often change their minds, but it seems somewhat unlikely that, at so late a moment, both sides should have embarked upon a major reorganisation of their positions. They had had days staring at one another, trying to assess the situation on the board. But still, even chess-masters with plenty of time on their hands do sometimes embark upon a flurry of movements that surprise the simple onlooker.

It was not in any case to be a day for the infantry. Mardonius decided to hold them back and, instead, to send over wave after wave of cavalry. He probably felt that he had the measure of the defence now and, so long as he kept his men away from the limited company of Athenian archers, they could inflict a great deal of damage on the foot-soldiers. His aim was to get the hoplites down off that ridge, for he knew well enough that, brave though they were, his Iranian infantry were not a match for the heavily armoured Greeks – especially if compelled to advance up a slope. 'The Persian cavalry, being armed with the bow, were not easy to come to grips with; so when they moved forward, they harried all the Greek line with their arrows and javelins. . . .' At the same time a detachment was sent round behind the Greek lines and 'choked up and spoilt the spring of Garagaphia', the Greeks' principal source of water. One finds it difficult to imagine that in so short a time they can have done anything more with stones and rubbish than inconvenience their enemy for a limited time. It is comparatively difficult (or was in those days) to totally block and befoul a spring. In any case, in this first major engagement, there could be no doubt that the position of the Greeks was highly threatened. Unlike Thermopylae, whose narrow pass had precluded the use of horses, the mounted bowmen and horsemen with throwing javelins had a distinct advantage over the hoplite.

A conference of war was held at Pausanias' headquarters on one of the knolls that form the Asopus ridge. The situation was very serious indeed. It was not only that their water supply had been threatened, if not temporarily destroyed, but they were down to one day's ration of food. It seems incredible that Pausanias had let the Persian cavalry cut off their food-supplies to such an extent, and the Spartans were normally considered past-masters at army-supply. They were, however, unused to cavalry tactics, and accustomed to fighting fellow Greeks in situations in the Peloponnese where they always had their own main base behind them. Further-more, Pausanias, like any other Greek general of his time, was not accustomed to handling large numbers of men. The Persians of Xerxes' time were capable of thinking in hundreds of thousands, but to the average Greek city-state general 10,000 was a good-sized army. For them the art of logistics was in its infancy – one reason why Herodotus makes such a play with what he considers to have been the immense and arrogant designs of Xerxes.

There could be no question of withdrawal during those daylight hours, for the cavalry would have cut them to pieces, and any sign of retreat would undoubtedly have brought the Persian army swarming forward across the river. This was clearly what Mardon-ius hoped for, and one cannot help wondering whether Alexander of Macedon (if he was acting for the Persians and not for himself alone) had reported back that the Greeks were short on rations. It is not difficult for an experienced soldier to recognise the look, and the very atmosphere, of hungry troops.

It was generally agreed that they could not hold their current position for another day. The answer for them was to fall back overnight to an area a little east of Plataea which was known as 'the Island' because it lay between two arms of the Oeroe river. The area was far too small to accommodate all the army, but it would form a central base with a left wing spread out towards Plataea, and a right wing extended towards the Garagaphian spring. The plan was sensible enough: by moving westwards the army would be able to cover the descent of their supplies down the Dryoscephalae Pass while they would also have adequate water-supplies. Quite apart from necessity, there was another good reason for this withdrawal to the west. The Persian horsemen had had a good day, and it is possible that Mardonius now felt that he had a demoralised army against him. To withdraw is often – though not always – to show some semblance of defeat. Perhaps, as at Salamis, the Persians might be lured into a major assault?

DECISIVE ROUND

TOWARDS DUSK MARDONIUS WITHDREW his cavalry. The Greeks waited for three hours. They had had a hard day, little food or water, and now they had an overnight march in front of them to take up their new positions. It was hardly surprising that under these circumstances there was a good deal of confusion but certainly not the panic among the allies, who had formed the army's centre, that Herodotus suggests. One has to remember that he was writing some time after the events, that his account was based on Athenian camp-gossip from old men, and that it was related to him at a time when relationships had become embittered between Athens and many of her former allies – notably Corinth and Megara. He even tells an exceedingly improbable story of a Spartan commander, Amompharetus, refusing to obey the orders of Pausanias to withdraw his troops and arguing with his general, thus accounting for the delay in the movement of the Lacedaemonians. From everything that we know about the Spartans, and from the character of Pausanias alone, this is inconceivable.

One thing which is clear is that the Greek centre, which was formed out of contingents from twenty states (certainly a source of confusion), did go astray, and ended up by a temple of Hera outside the walls of Plataea. Rather than risk any further mistakes in the dark they gathered together there and waited for the dawn. At first light Pausanias, seeing what had happened, ordered the Athenians, who were on Pyrgos hill, to march down towards the Spartans. At the same time, he moved his own troops southward, leaving behind one battalion under the supposedly almost mutinous battalion commander to serve as rearguard. No sooner had the latter rejoined the main body under Pausanias – marching in disciplined and regular order – than the first of the Persian cavalry attacks began.

It was at this point that Mardonius made his fatal error. Seeing the ridges opposite him, which had formerly been occupied by the Greek troops, had been deserted overnight he came to the conclusion that, after the hammering they had taken the previous day, the Greeks were in full flight. Although Pausanias' plan had gone awry owing to the troops forming his centre not having got themselves into the correct position, his main object had succeeded. By leaving the withdrawal of the best troops, the Athenians, and his Lacedaemonian and Tegean force until dawn, he had ensured that Mardonius would actually see him withdrawing and reach the conclusion that he did. Mardonius is said to have summoned three brothers from Thessaly, who were among the Greeks in his camp, and to have mocked them with the words: 'Well, gentlemen, what will you say, now that you see that place deserted? You, who are neighbours of the Lacedaemonians, used to tell me that they were grand fighters, and never ran away!' Mardonius had fallen for the lure just as some of Xerxes' crack troops had done at Thermopylae. As Green points out: 'The trick was a speciality of the Spartans. . . .' What Pausanias was doing, only on a very large scale, was the same ruse as Leonidas had used. He was pretending to flee in order to draw the enemy within fighting distance; then wheeling about and presenting them with the bronze shields and the bristling 'hedgehog' wall.

'. . . Mardonius gave the order to advance. His men crossed the Asopus and followed at the double in the track of the Greek forces, who, it was supposed, were in full flight.' Actually, it was the Spartans and Tegeans only that Mardonius was after, for the Athenians, who had marched by a different route across the level ground, were hidden from sight by the intervening hills.

When the officers of the other divisions of Mardonius' army saw the Persian contingent in hot pursuit, they immediately ordered the standards to be raised, and all the troops under their command joined in the chase as fast as their legs would carry them. Without any attempt to maintain formation they swept forward, yelling and shouting, never doubting that they would make short work of the fugitives.

There seems little doubt (though many eminent scholars dispute it) that the famous battle of Plataea ended up as a soldiers' battle rather than one directed by the opposing generals – hardly surprising in days when communications were limited to runners or, at the best, horsemen. Pausanias had laid out what seems on the surface a neat entrapping strategy into which the Persians had blundered. In fact, the commanding positions of the Persian cavalry – the 'Knights' in the harsh game – more or less counterbalanced the careful withdrawal play of their opponents. There was only one way in which the 'Poor Bloody Infantry' could work things out and that was by the superiority of their arms, discipline, and morale. In this case, as always, the attacked were fighting for their homelands, crofts, wives and children. The invaders were far from home, and had been so for well over a year. Except for the pro-Persian Greeks, the hard core of the army that had come out of the East was long sick and disillusioned with the fate that had led them so far, and over so long a time, out of their familiar lands. In the wise words of old Artabanus, when he had counselled Xerxes against the whole expedition from the very beginning: 'I venture a prophecy: the day will come when many a man left at home will hear the news that Mardonius has brought disaster upon Persia and that his body lies a prey to dogs and birds somewhere in the country of the Athenians or the Spartans – if not upon the road thither.'

Pausanias was now confronted by the main weight of the Persian cavalry and, formidable though the Spartan shield-line was, what he needed was archers. He sent an urgent message for the Athenians to close up on him, which Aristeides was in the process of doing when the Athenians themselves were hit by the cavalry of the pro-Persian Greeks, followed hard on their heels by the Boeotian hoplites. The preliminaries of Plataea then resolved themselves into two separate battles. Pausanias and the Spartans on the right wing against the Persians under Mardonius, and the Athenians to the left of him against the Thessalians and Boeotians. Meanwhile Artabazus with the Persian centre had had to struggle up the Asopus ridge and was late upon the scene. One suspects, perhaps, that he did not hurry his troops overmuch. He had long been against the whole concept of the Persians remaining in Greece, and certainly against this pitched battle which Mardonius had decided upon. It was Artabazus, it must be remembered, who had been in favour of withdrawing to Thebes and of allowing the Greeks time to quarrel amongst themselves, at the same time expediting their divisions by the generous usage of bribes. Looking down from his position on the ridge, Artabazus could see the two battles taking place below him and, while no doubt he was debating whether to cut down through the middle of them, he would have seen the large body of Greeks from Plataea, who should have formed the Greek centre, coming hard and fast to help their comrades. They divided into two main columns, one going to the aid of the Athenians and the other cutting round behind to lend strength to the left wing of the Spartans.

The hardest hit were the Greeks who formed the left-centre, for they crossed open ground in order to join up with the Athenians and were not to escape the attentions of the Theban cavalry. There were about 7000 of them in all, the main body formed of Megarians, the rest being small contingents, both Peloponnesian and non-Peloponnesian. Even if their discipline had been better than it probably was, their action, though brave, was somewhat foolhardy in open country. The Theban cavalry fell upon them and cut them to pieces, killing some six hundred and driving them back.

Herodotus, writing at a time when Megara and Athens were at loggerheads, makes the snide remark that 'they perished ingloriously'. Far from it, their action had served to draw off the Theban cavalry – thus bringing relief to the Athenians, who could now proceed with a straightforward hoplite battle against the Boeotian infantry. Meanwhile on the right wing, harassed by the cavalry and by Mardonius' infantry, who would not come to grips with those armoured men but 'made a fence of their wicker shields and poured in showers of arrows', the Spartans and Tegeans waited with the dogged discipline of superb soldiers. Before giving the orders for his men to advance, Pausanias, as was customary, was taking the omens. Inspection of the hearts and lights of the sacrificial animals failed to produce a satisfactory augury. It was necessary to go on then with further sacrifices before the general could order his men to advance. Even sheltered as they were behind their great shields, their armour and their helmets, 'many men fell in this time'. Among them was Callicrates, accounted 'the handsomest and tallest man in the Greek army', who was hit by an arrow that pierced his lungs. After the battle was over, Arimnestus of Plataea visited him as he lay dying and tried to console him, saying that his death was not in

vain and that he had died for Hellas. Callicrates' response was that
he did not mind dying for his country, but that he had not had a
chance to strike a blow or 'do anything worthy of himself'.

Some commentators have suggested that the continuance of the
unfavourable omens may have been deliberate on Pausanias' part;
that he was waiting until the Persian rearguard came up behind the
men who now confronted him and would thus prevent the front
ranks from being able to turn in flight - when at last the Spartan
charge came. This seems very likely: the Spartans, as has been seen,
were religious to a degree, but generals are also pragmatic. Then at
last 'Pausanias turned his eyes to the temple of Hera outside Plataea
and called upon the goddess for her aid, praying her not to allow
the Greeks to be robbed of their hope of victory. While the words
were still upon his lips the Tegeans sprang forward to the attack. . .'
A moment later – and not a moment too soon – the omens were
favourable. The Lacedaemonian bronze wall moved forward
against the Persian line, and the latter, who had had the pleasure of
killing their foe from a safe distance, now knew what it was like to
face the most formidable warriors in the world. As Plutarch puts it,
'. . . suddenly there came over the whole phalanx the look of
some ferocious beast, as it wheels at bay, stiffens its bristles and
turns to defend itself, so that the barbarians could no longer doubt
that they were faced with men who would fight to the death'.

Herodotus takes up the account of that never-to-be-forgotten
day when the power of Persia and the dream of Xerxes were
extinguished on the field of Plataea.

> First there was a struggle at the barricade of shields; then, the
> barricade down, there was a bitter and protracted fight, hand to
> hand, close by the temple of Demeter, for the Persians would lay
> hold of the Spartan spears and break them; in courage and
> strength they were as good as their adversaries, but they were
> deficient in armour, untrained and greatly inferior in skill.

This tribute to the courage of the Iranians is well deserved, but it
could not be said that these crack troops were untrained. Certainly,
no other soldiers were as skilled as the Spartans in warfare, but it
was the technological difference between the two cultures that
made the victory at Plataea possible, just as it had helped in the

stand of Leonidas and his handful of men at Thermopylae. Those long-dead Greek bronze-smiths and armourers, who had evolved the techniques that gave the warriors of Homeric times their weapons and protection, played their part on that day.

Herodotus relates how the Persians,

. . . sometimes singly, and sometimes in groups of ten men – perhaps fewer, perhaps more – fell upon the Spartan line and were cut down. They pressed hardest at the point where Mardonius fought in person – riding his white charger, and surrounded by his thousand Persian troops, the flower of the army. While Mardonius was alive, they continued to resist and to defend themselves, and struck down many of the Lacedaemonians; but after his death, and the destruction of his personal guard – the finest of the Persian troops – the remainder yielded to the Lacedaemonians and took to flight. The chief cause of their discomfiture was their lack of armour, fighting without it against heavily armoured infantry.

The bronze soldiers of Sparta had conquered. No one – not even the finest warriors out of the whole Eastern world – could defeat men who had been raised since childhood to fight to the end. 'Thus the prophecy of the oracle was fulfilled, and Mardonius rendered satisfaction to the Spartans for the killing of Leonidas; and thus, too, Pausanias, son of Cleombrotus and grandson of Anazandrides, won the most splendid victory which history records.'

Mardonius himself was killed by a distinguished Spartiate, named Arimnestus, not with spear or sword according to Plutarch, but by a stone which broke his skull. As soon as the news came that the Persian right wing had collapsed and was in full flight, the Boeotians on the left realised that their position was hopeless and took to their heels, their retreat being covered by the Theban cavalry. As for the wily Artabazus, in command of the Persian centre which had never been engaged at all, he withdrew with all possible speed and headed back north, 'not to the barricade, or to Thebes, but direct to Phocis, in his desire to reach the Hellespont with the least possible delay'. He and the troops with him, apart from a few casualties in brushes with the Thracians on the way, were all ferried safely across to Asia by boats from Byzantium. Astonishingly enough, perhaps, Xerxes did not have him executed for his apparent desertion – and Mardonius was the Great King's brother-in-law – nor apparently censure him. This suggests a pragmatism in the king's nature which is hardly apparent in Herodotus' original portrait of an Oriental despot.

All the other Persians at first withdrew behind the stockade. Here they put up a fierce resistance, defying Pausanias and his Spartans, who were unable to get to grips with them. The arrival of the Athenians and the rest of the Greek army changed the balance, and the absence of Artabazus and his men probably meant that the defenders could not man all the defences. Finally the Athenians effected a breach and the Greeks, headed by the gallant men from little Tegea, stormed in, and an appalling slaughter took place. With their leaders dead or gone, the morale of the Persian army collapsed completely and the Greeks butchered them like cattle. The battle of Plataea was over. The vast shadow of the Great King, King of Kings, was lifted from Greece for ever. When the full extent of the defeat finally reached Susa one may imagine that Xerxes' wise old uncle, Artabanus, was careful and circumspect enough to remain very silent.

The extent of the Persian and the Greek losses in the campaign and in the final battle has provoked many an argument among scholars. Certainly Herodotus grossly underestimates the number of Greek dead, as well as equally overestimating the number of Persian and pro-Persian Greeks who were killed. Most scholars seem to settle for the figure given by Plutarch of 1360 Athenian, Spartan and allied Greeks killed – this very probably being the figure for hoplites only. There were Helots, for instance, among the Lacedaemonians, and there can be no doubt they were in the thick of the action along with the Spartiates, but there is no record of their casualties, although Plutarch relates that they had their own burial-mound on the field of battle. As for the Persian losses there seems to be more or less general agreement, *pace* Herodotus, that they lost somewhere in the region of 10,000 men at Plataea. One of the reasons that Xerxes did not execute or disgrace Artabazus for his rapid withdrawal of the Persian centre was that he retired to Asia with the best part of an army corps, possibly some 40,000 men. After the disaster of Plataea, had he attempted to fight a rear-guard action through country which, though nominally pro-

Persian, would probably have risen up against him, the losses would have been infinitely worse – or even total.

The Greeks encamped on the battlefield, burying their dead as well as garnering the spoils of war. These were considerable, for Persian armies did not travel light like the Greeks, who were relatively poor in any case, but with gold and silver vessels, silken tents, women, and slaves. All these had to be apportioned out, and Pausanias seems to have used his authority with considerable skill for, if he had not, one can be sure that later Athenian historians would have accused the Lacedaemonians of taking more than their fair share. Looting was forbidden on pain of death, and Helots were despatched all over the area to gather together the innumerable – and to them almost incomprehensible – valuables that had been left behind by the fleeing army. Of course, in the first hours of triumph, quite a lot of obviously precious things, like gold cups or ornaments, must have disappeared into many a private 'kit-bag' – but this has happened in every war. One cannot help suspecting that there must have been a good deal of cheating on the side, but it seems more than likely that had the commander-in-chief been an Athenian or a Corinthian there would have been very much more. The Spartiate class, at that time, corrupt though they were to become at a later date, were still so strictly indoctrinated with the iron laws of Lycurgus that they saw in wealth and golden objects the very things that caused corruption and softness amongst men and nations. To take one instance of correct and chivalric behaviour, Pausanias refused to allow the body of Mardonius to be desecrated – as that of Leonidas had been – but had it quietly and secretly buried at night. The Greek mistress of one of the dead Persian commanders, having carefully dressed herself up in her best clothes, and accompanied by her handmaids, fell at the feet of Pausanias, imploring mercy. Although, as his life was to show, Pausanias was very attracted to women, he had her sent back under escort to Aegina. He could not send her to her native island of Cos, because this was still under Persian domination. The colour of all later accounts of the whole of Xerxes' invasion was to show the Athenians in the best of all possible lights, while denying to their allies any true evaluation of their particular contribution to the defeat of Persia. It is rather as if some future historian, searching through the records of the Second World War in our century, should only come up with the accounts of one of the victorious allies.

Despite a somewhat futile attempt to besiege Thebes and exact that tithe promised in the Oath of Plataea, the allies soon realised that, with the summer coming to an end, this would prove almost impossible. The exact date of the Battle of Plataea is difficult to ascertain, for calendars in those days varied widely between city and city, but it would seem to have been in mid-August of 479. To have proceeded to tithe not only Thebes, but all the other northern Greek states which had sided with the Persians, would have proved quite beyond the capabilities of the Greek allied forces. In any case, all had work to do in their native states. It was time for ploughing, while the Athenians, in addition, had yet again to start rebuilding their city. It is melancholy to record that only a very short time after this victory, which had temporarily united so many of the city-states of Greece, dissension between them all too soon began. Their brilliance, which still funds the whole of what is left of Western civilisation, stemmed from their anarchic individualism.

For the brief moment, though, in the elation of such a victory and in the mutual realisation of the danger from which they had escaped, they set up many memorials in honour of the event: a bronze Poseidon at the Isthmus of Corinth, for instance, and a Zeus at Olympia. Most famous of all these monuments was dedicated to Apollo at Delphi: a bronze pillar formed of three entwined serpents supporting a tripod of gold. It is hardly surprising that the golden tripod vanished long ago in one of the interminable, internecine Greek wars, but the column still survives. The visitor to modern Istanbul can see it in the dusty, tourist-occupied Hippodrome. Few recognise it for what it really is: a memorial to those ancient Greeks who, so many centuries ago, ensured that the patterns of freedom and individual liberty should survive in the West.

SELECT BIBLIOGRAPHY

Aeschylus, *The Persians*, trans. H. W. Smyth, Loeb Classics (London, 1922).

Bengston, H., *The Greeks and the Persians* (London, 1968).

Bradford, E., *Mediterranean* (London, 1971).

Burn, A. R., *Persia and the Greeks* (London, 1962).

—, *Greece and the Eastern Mediterranean* (Berlin, 1977).

Cambridge Ancient History, vol. IV, *The Persian Empire and the West* (London, 1926).

Diodorus Siculus, *Works*, trans. C. H. Oldfellow (London, 1946).

Frye, R. N., *The Heritage of Persia* (London, 1962).

Green, P., *The Year of Salamis* (London, 1970).

Grundy, G. B., *The Great Persian War* (London, 1901).

Hammond, N. G. L., *Studies in Greek History* (London, 1973).

Herodotus, *The Histories*, trans. A. de Selincourt (London, 1976).

Hignett, C., *Xerxes' Invasion of Greece* (London, 1963).

Jones, A. H. M., *Sparta* (Oxford, 1967).

Morrison, J. S. and Williams, R. T., *Greek Oared Ships* (London, 1968).

Plutarch, *The Rise and Fall of Athens*, trans. I. Scott-Kilvert (London, 1976).

Powell, J. E., *The History of Herodotus* (London, 1939).

Snodgrass, A. M., *Arms and Armour of the Greeks* (London, 1967).

Toynbee, A., *Hellenism* (London, 1959).

INDEX